A gift for:

From:

INSPIRED *faith*

365 Days a Year

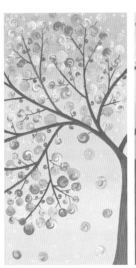

Daily Motivation in God's Word

THOMAS NELSON
Since 1798

NASHVILLE   DALLAS   MEXICO CITY   RIO DE JANEIRO

Published in Nashville, Tennessee, by Thomas Nelson. Thomas Nelson is a registered trademark of Thomas Nelson, Inc.

Originally published by Simple Truths LLC
1952 McDowell Road, Suite 300
Naperville, IL 60563
Toll Free: 800.900.3427
www.simpletruths.com

This edition published under license from Simple Truths exclusively for Thomas Nelson, Inc.

Thomas Nelson, Inc., titles may be purchased in bulk for educational, business, fund-raising, or sales promotional use. For information, please e-mail SpecialMarkets@ThomasNelson.com.

Unless otherwise noted, Scripture quotations are taken from the Holy Bible, New International Version®, NIV®. Copyright © 1973, 1978, 1984 by Biblica, Inc™. Used by permission of Zondervan. All rights reserved worldwide. www.zondervan.com.

Other Scripture quotations are from the following sources:

The New King James Version (NKJV). © 1979, 1980, 1982, 1992, 2002 Thomas Nelson, Inc. Used by permission. All rights reserved. The English Standard Version (ESV). © 2001 by Crossway Bibles, a division of Good News Publishers. The King James Version of the Bible (KJV). The New American Standard Bible (NASB) © 1960, 1962, 1963, 1971, 1972, 1973, 1975, and 1977 by the Lockman Foundation. Used by permission. The Holy Bible, New Living Translation (NLT) © 1996. Used by permission of Tyndale House Publishers, Inc. Wheaton, IL. All rights reserved.

ISBN: 978-1-4003-2032-5

Printed in China

12 13 14 15 16 WAI 6 5 4 3 2 1

What a Difference a Day Makes

*A*n apple a day keeps the doctor away.

The power of a daily habit is woven throughout our common-sense prescriptions for a better life. I don't know if an apple a day really keeps the doctor away, though I'm pretty certain that eating ten apples in one day is missing the point of the proverb. Some medicine does its work all at once, in one dose. But most of the important things in life—a marriage, raising children, a career, a reputation—require daily attention.

No wonder the power of our daily habits is woven throughout God's Word.

- God's mercies are new every single day (Lamentations 3:23).
- God's strength is provided for us each day to meet the challenges of that particular day (Deuteronomy 3:25).
- We are advised to put each of our days in proper order (Psalm 90:12).
- Jesus calls us to follow Him daily (Luke 9:23).

If we were to list all the verses that talk about the importance of a single day and our daily activities, that list alone would fill up this book. That's why spending time with God *each day*—in His Word, in prayer, in reflection of His love and plans for you—will

make a tremendous positive difference in your life and spirit. Day by day you will be transformed.

This 365-day devotional is divided into motivational topics for each day of the week:

- SUNDAY: First Priorities
- MONDAY: Power to Persevere
- TUESDAY: Praise for Our Great God
- WEDNESDAY: Leading with Grace
- THURSDAY: A Prayerful Heart
- FRIDAY: Serving Others
- SATURDAY: Peace and Encouragement

Our prayer is that these Bible verses, short devotions, and prayer starters will be a special part of your time with God each day, and every day of the year.

A Ready Vessel

Seek the Lord while he may be found;
call on him while he is near. (Isaiah 55:6)

Faith asks us neither to destroy nor to exalt human desire but to gather it
into an even greater desire: the thirst for God. (author unknown)

A Classic Devotion from A. W. Tozer

*P*ick at random a score of great saints whose lives and testimonies are widely known. Let them be Bible characters or well-known Christians of post-biblical times. You will be struck instantly with the fact that the saints were not alike. Sometimes the dissimilarities were so great as to be positively glaring. The differences are as wide as human life itself—differences of race, nationality, education, temperament, habit and personal qualities. Yet they all walked, each in his day, upon a high road of spiritual living far above the common way.

I venture to suggest that the one vital quality which they had in common was *spiritual receptivity*. Something in them was open to heaven, something which urged them Godward. I shall say simply that they had spiritual awareness and that they went on to cultivate it until it became the biggest thing in their lives.[1]

Lord, I ask that You would help me be open to You. Help me to hear Your voice and do Your will. Amen.

A Beloved Bride

And so we know and rely on the love God has for us. (1 John 4:16)

We are His beloved. Let us but feel that He has set His love upon us,
that He is watching us from those heavens with tender interest, that
He is working out the mystery of our lives with solicitude and fondness.
(A. B. Simpson)

*E*vangelist and philanthropist George Müller once said that not once in his marriage did he pass his wife or see her enter a room without love filling his heart. He always saw her as a gift from God, and his love intensified each time they were near each other.

The kind of love between Müller and his wife is perhaps rare, but still stands as a marker, a reminder, of what God intends between husband and wife.

What's most amazing is that the Bible refers to Christ's church as His bride. He loves us more tenderly, deeply, and devotedly than the best husband on earth could ever cherish his beloved.

Life suddenly becomes more wonderful when we live in the knowledge that we are as precious to God as a beloved bride.

Thank You, Lord, for Your love for me, Your child. Help me
allow Your love to fill my life with joy, and help me spread
that joy everywhere I go. Amen.

Hope for a New Year

Praise be to the God and Father of our Lord Jesus Christ! In his great mercy he has given us new birth into a living hope through the resurrection of Jesus Christ from the dead. (1 Peter 1:3)

The beautiful thing about this adventure called faith is that we can count on Him never to lead us astray. (Charles Swindoll)

We begin the New Year with resolutions only to leave them by the wayside by February. Unfulfilled promises and commitments leave us with feelings of guilt and failure for not living up to our own expectations. One obvious solution is to not try at all. It's probably wiser to frame our resolutions as goals, not promises.

But the real question is where we place our confidence. Is it in our own strength? Our own efforts? Start by accepting God's unconditional love. Allow Him to work through you. You might end up accomplishing more than you initially set out to do!

Your outlook for the year will be much brighter if you begin by asking God first for direction, then for strength to accomplish the tasks He sets before you. Jesus called Himself our Good Shepherd. When we follow Him, we find green pastures and an abundance of joy.

Lord, give me wisdom as I write out goals for this year.
Show me what You would have me accomplish. And thank
You for Your ever-present love and strength. Amen.

The Unlovables

Therefore, as God's chosen people, holy and dearly loved, clothe yourselves with compassion, kindness, humility, gentleness and patience. Bear with each other and forgive whatever grievances you may have against one another. Forgive as the Lord forgave you.
(Colossians 3:12–13)

Love means to love that which is unlovable; or it is no virtue at all.
(G. K. Chesterton)

Every living creature has been blessed by God with a way to protect itself. When a sand particle gets inside the oyster's shell, for example, that tiny abrasive becomes life-threatening to the oyster and its soft, porous tissue. But the oyster responds by secreting a substance that creates a pearl from the grain of sand.

What would happen if we, like the oyster, didn't try to discard the abrasive and unlovable people in our lives—even when we feel threatened—but rather welcomed them as opportunities for God's love to create something beautiful inside us?

Those bothersome people might need you to help them experience God's new life. Likewise, you might need them to develop your patience and godly love. So don't automatically expel difficult people from your life; ask God to help you turn an annoyance into a pearl.

Lord, I want to allow You to work in my life through any circumstances, even the unpleasant ones. Teach me to love with Your love. Amen.

All Spiritual Blessings

Praise be to the God and Father of our Lord Jesus Christ, who has blessed us in the heavenly realms with every spiritual blessing in Christ. (Ephesians 1:3)

Those blessings are sweetest that are won with prayers and worn with thanks. (Thomas Goodwin)

A Classic Devotion from R. A. Torrey

*J*esus Christ, by His atoning death and by His resurrection and ascension to the right hand of the Father, has obtained for every believer in Him every possible spiritual blessing. There is no spiritual blessing that any believer enjoys that may not be yours. It belongs to you now; Christ purchased it by His atoning death, and God has provided it in Him. It is there for you; but it is your part to claim it, to put out your hand and take it. God's appointed way of claiming blessings, or putting out your hand and taking hold of the blessings that are procured for you by the atoning death of Jesus Christ, is by prayer. Prayer is the hand that takes to ourselves the blessings that God has already provided in His Son.[2]

Lord, thank You for Your abundant blessings—including the ones I have yet to experience. Teach me to ask You for what I need. Amen.

The Miracle

God is our refuge and strength,
an ever-present help in trouble. (Psalm 46:1)

When God is involved, anything can happen. (Charles Swindoll)

*H*erman Ostry's barn floor was under twenty-nine inches of water after a flood. He needed a miracle—and fast—to salvage his barn and be ready for winter. He needed to move his entire seventeen-thousand-pound barn to a new foundation more than 143 feet away. His son, Mike, devised a latticework of steel tubing. He nailed, bolted, and welded the lattice on the inside and outside of the barn, with hundreds of handles attached.

After one practice lift, 344 volunteers slowly walked the barn up a slight incline, each supporting less than fifty pounds. In just three minutes, the barn was on its new foundation. And Herman had his miracle.

If you're holding out for a miracle today, don't be surprised if the one God sends you comes at the hands of your friends and neighbors. We can always count on Him to come through, but He very often uses those nearest to us to see us through a difficult time.

Father, even though I sometimes feel as though I'm hoping against hope, I know You will come through for me. Help me to see Your hand at work. Amen.

The Author of Peace

Lord, you establish peace for us;
all that we have accomplished you have done for us. (Isaiah 26:12)

How completely satisfying to turn from our limitations to a God who has none. Eternal years lie in His heart. For Him time does not pass, it remains; and those who are in Christ share with Him all the riches of limitless time and endless years. God never hurries. There are no deadlines against which He must work. Only to know this is to quiet our spirit and relax our nerves. (A. W. Tozer)

In a study on "peace of mind" performed by Duke University, several factors were found to contribute greatly to emotional and mental stability. Among common-sense indicators like avoiding self-pity and accepting challenges as a part of life, researchers identified other factors of peace of mind, including the ability to forgive and avoid living in the past, and a belief in something larger than oneself. Not surprisingly, these findings support God's recipe for personal peace: accept His will, believe in His love for you and His plan for you, forgive and receive forgiveness, and look forward to the future.

No matter what circumstances or habits are waging war on your inner peace right now, God can give you the grace to live in peace in His presence.

Dear God, I need to trust You more to experience Your peace. I do affirm my absolute faith in You. Amen.

New Beginnings

Forget the former things;
do not dwell on the past.
See, I am doing a new thing!
Now it springs up; do you not perceive it?
I am making a way in the desert
and streams in the wasteland. (Isaiah 43:18–19)

Always bear in mind that your own resolution to succeed is more
important than any one thing. (Abraham Lincoln)

God promised that He will transform us when we become part of His family. He will do a new thing in us and He will continue to bring forth change that will be for our good and His highest.

If God can make rivers spring forth in the desert, He can be trusted to cover the messes we made in our past—and supply everything we need for a bright new future. That's the kind of God He is. He is the One who is able to take broken, worn-out, failed, dusty experiences—and plant a beautiful garden.

If we want to experience all that He has for us, we must begin with the simple belief that He loves us and wants to do something special in us—no matter what has transpired up to this very moment.

Ready for a fresh start? A new start? Turn to God. He is faithful to guide you to a brand-new beginning!

Thank You, God, for Your love that draws me back to You
when I've made a mess of my life and for showing me Your
power to produce flowing rivers in the desert of life. Amen.

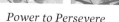

The Still, Small Voice

But I have stilled and quieted my soul;
like a weaned child with its mother,
like a weaned child is my soul within me. (Psalm 131:2)

Are you weak? Weary? Confused? Troubled? Pressured? How is your
relationship with God? Is it held in its place of priority? I believe the greater
the pressure, the greater your need for time alone with Him. (Kay Arthur)

A Classic Devotion from A. B. Simpson

God said, "Be still, and know that I am God." Then came the conflict of thoughts for tomorrow, and its duties and cares; but God said, "Be still." As I listened, it became to me the voice of prayer, the voice of wisdom, the voice of duty, and I did not need to think so hard, or pray so hard, or trust so hard; but that "still small voice" of the Holy Spirit in my heart was God's prayer in my secret soul, was God's answer to all my questions, was God's life and strength for soul and body, and became the substance of all knowledge, and all prayer and all blessing. . . .

It is thus that our spirit drinks in the life of our risen Lord, and we go forth to life's conflicts and duties like a flower that has drunk . . . cool and crystal drops of dew. But as dew never falls on a stormy night, so the dews of His grace never come to the restless soul.[3]

Dear Lord, teach me to quiet my soul so that I can hear
Your still, small voice. Thank You for the peace of Your
presence. Amen.

Peace Within

Be anxious for nothing, but in everything by prayer and supplication, with thanksgiving, let your requests be made known to God.
(Philippians 4:6 NKJV)

Where there is peace, God is. (George Herbert)

A Classic Devotion from T. M. Anderson

*P*aul would have us understand that Christ imparts a measure of His own peace to our worshipping hearts when we make everything pertaining to life a matter of prayer. We can readily comprehend the possibilities of prayer when we perceive that mortal man can obtain a measure of the peace which the God of Peace possesses in His divine nature. It is not necessary for the children of God to enter heaven in order to enjoy the priceless possession of peace. Christ wills to give the heavenly heritage of His Peace to all the sons of God. He revealed this truth when He said in John 14:27, "Peace I leave with you; My peace I give to you; not as the world gives do I give to you. Do not let your heart be troubled, nor let it be fearful."[4]

Lord, thank You for the gift of peace. Teach me to be still
before You and lay my worries at Your feet. Amen.

Rejoice in the Success of Others

Rejoice with those who rejoice; mourn with those who mourn.
(Romans 12:15)

If God accepts me as I am, then I had better do the same.
(Hugh Montefiore)

*W*e live in a competitive world in which it is difficult for many people to find joy in the success of others. How do you feel when a friend gets a promotion? When someone else in the company wins the award? When a classmate gets the top score on a test? When a sibling gets an incredible return on an investment? Do you feel instant joy or pangs of resentment and jealousy?

We are often much better at comforting people in their times of sorrow than sincerely celebrating their moments of triumph.

The answer is simple but difficult: we must first realize that our own success is measured in the eyes of God—not in comparison to others. When that sinks into our hearts and minds, it is so much easier to sincerely rejoice in the success of others.

Thank You, heavenly Father, for defining success in
my life. Thank You for blessing me and for blessing
those around me. Amen.

Ask for What You Need

"What do you want me to do for you?" Jesus asked him.
(Mark 10:51)

Children do not find it difficult or complicated to talk to their parents, nor do they feel embarrassed to bring the simplest need to their attention. Neither should we hesitate to bring the simplest requests confidently to the Father. (Richard J. Foster)

A Classic Devotion from Andrew Murray

*O*ur prayers must be a distinct expression of definite need, not a vague appeal to His mercy or an indefinite cry for blessing. It isn't that His loving heart does not understand or is not ready to hear our cry. Rather, Jesus desires such definite prayer for our own sakes because it teaches us to know our own needs better. Time, thought, and self-scrutiny are required to find out what our greatest need really is.

Our desires are put to the test to see whether they are honest and real and are according to God's Word. We also consider whether we really believe we will receive the things we ask. Such reflective prayer helps us to wait for the special answer and to mark it when it comes.[5]

Dear Father, You know my needs at this time in my life.
Help me to fully bring them to You and please teach me to
pray, Holy Spirit. Amen.

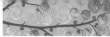

Love Is a Verb

Dear children, let us not love with words or tongue but with actions and in truth. (1 John 3:18)

You learn to love by loving. (Francis de Sales)

*I*f love is a mere emotion, then our love for spouses, children, even God, is dependent on how we feel about them at a given moment. But feelings are fickle and can be up or down based on factors as simple and mundane as the amount of sleep we've had or whether or not we exercised.

No wonder people fall in and out of love so much. They are treating love as an emotion or feeling rather than what it really is, an active verb.

God demonstrated His love for us by sending His Son to redeem us. That's no mere act of emotion; it is an act that lives out love. Ultimately, we too love God and those around us when we actively demonstrate it.

Have you shown others you love them today?

Dear God, I marvel at how much You love me and at how You came to redeem me. Help me to love as You do, with actions as well as words. Amen.

Be Glad in the Lord

Therefore, since we are receiving a kingdom that cannot be shaken, let us be thankful, and so worship God acceptably with reverence and awe. (Hebrews 12:28)

Thou who has given me so much, give me one more thing: a grateful heart. (George Herbert)

A Classic Devotion from Dietrich Bonhoeffer

We prevent God from giving us the great spiritual gifts He has in store for us, because we do not give thanks for daily gifts. We think we dare not be satisfied with the small measure of spiritual knowledge, experience, and love that has been given to us, and that we must constantly be looking forward eagerly for the highest good. Then we deplore the fact that we lack the deep certainty, the strong faith, and the rich experience that God has given to others, and we consider this lament to be pious. We pray for the big things and forget to give thanks for the ordinary, small (and yet really not small) gifts. How can God entrust great things to one who will not thankfully receive from Him the little things?[6]

Lord, today I choose to notice all the things You do for me—for Your spiritual blessings as well as temporal ones.
Amen.

The Great Race

*Commit to the L*ord *whatever you do,*
and your plans will succeed. (Proverbs 16:3)

God has a great race for you to run. Under His care, you'll go where
you've never been and serve in ways you've never dreamed. But you
have to release your burdens. (Max Lucado)

Life has often been compared to a race, and it is often a test of our will, our endurance, and our resilience in the same way a physical race is.

What's the secret of making it to the finish line? Is it determination? Is it trying harder? Is it mustering every ounce of courage we can find? Is it asking great people to help us? Those things all sound great, but we'll never make it to the finish line on our own efforts—even if others help us. In this way the Christian race is different from a marathon or sprint.

The Christian life has always been and will always be about trusting God and relying on His power and help, not just to bring us salvation but to help us take each step of our life journeys. That victorious finish will not come by trying harder—but by trusting Him more!

Dear God, I know I can't win the race of life on my own.
I need Your help and guidance every step of the way.
Thank You for being there for me! Amen.

Watch Your Faith

*[Abraham] did not waver through unbelief regarding the promise
of God, but was strengthened in his faith and gave glory to God.*
(Romans 4:20)

*The true, living faith, which the Holy Spirit instills into the heart,
simply cannot be idle.* (Martin Luther)

A Classic Devotion from C. H. Spurgeon

*C*hristian, take good care of thy faith; for recollect faith is
the only way whereby thou canst obtain blessings. If we
want blessings from God, nothing can fetch them down but faith.
Prayer cannot draw down answers from God's throne except it be
the earnest prayer of the man who believes. Faith is the angelic
messenger between the soul and the Lord Jesus in glory. Let that
angel be withdrawn, we can neither send up prayer, nor receive
the answers. Faith is the telegraphic wire which links earth and
heaven—on which God's messages of love fly so fast, that before
we call He answers, and while we are yet speaking He hears us.
O, then, Christian, watch well thy faith; for with it thou canst win
all things, however poor thou art, but without it thou canst obtain
nothing.[7]

Lord, teach me to grow in my faith. Amen.

Friendship and Fear

The LORD confides in those who fear him;
he makes his covenant known to them. (Psalm 25:14)

A proper fear of God is that indefinable mixture of reverence and
pleasure, joy and awe. . . . It is a love for God which is so great that
we would be ashamed to do anything which would displease or
grieve Him, and makes us happiest when we are doing
what pleases Him. (Sinclair B. Ferguson)

*F*riendship and fear don't naturally go together. And yet our relationship with God is characterized by both familiarity and formality, closeness and reverence.

Friendship with God is a miraculous gift. In the Old Testament, only a few were said to enjoy friendship with God; in the New Testament, Jesus tells His disciples, "I have called you friends" (John 15:15). The necessary attitude for anyone who wants to be friends with God is to "fear" Him. This doesn't mean we regard Him as someone who might unpredictably harm us. But it does mean recognizing how much we need Him, how we would be lost without Him, and that He is the center of all life and deserves our respect.

When we fear God, we enjoy His company and guidance through prayer and His Word. And that is truly a friendship to celebrate.

Dear God, thank You for reaching out to me. Please
cultivate in my heart a healthy fear of You and help me to
walk in Your ways. Amen.

The Mark of a Hero

The LORD is my strength and my shield;
my heart trusts in him, and I am helped.
My heart leaps for joy
and I will give thanks to him in song. (Psalm 28:7)

We should not be concerned about working for God until we have
learned the meaning and delight of worshiping Him. (A. W. Tozer)

What makes a hero a hero? Great deeds are usually what sets a hero apart from others. But what makes one eligible to be a hero before the great deeds are accomplished? A biblical hero is always characterized by great faith and a sense of joy. Not joy in circumstances but joy that is focused on God.

- Mary's heart leaped with joy toward God at the foretelling of the birth of Jesus (Luke 1:46–55).
- The apostle Paul rejoiced in God even when facing certain death (Philippians 4:4).
- David could not contain his joy in God and danced through the streets (2 Samuel 6:14–15).

The list goes on and on. Where can you see opportunities to find joy in God today?

Heavenly Father, You are my source of joy in life;
I rejoice in You. Amen.

Your Little Secret

"When you give to the needy, do not let your left hand know what your right hand is doing, so that your giving may be in secret. Then your Father, who sees what is done in secret, will reward you."
(Matthew 6:3–4)

If you serve others for the reward of gaining their admiration and gratitude, then your reward will be fleeting and ultimately dissatisfying. If you serve others for the reward of bringing pleasure to your Father God's heart as you work side by side with him, then you will gain eternal rewards. (author unknown)

*T*he art of self-promotion is alive and well. We have photographers, publicists, and brand specialists to shape a wonderful impression of the good things we do. We blog and Tweet and update Facebook with our every act of kindness.

There are causes, organizations, needs, and ministries that need to be promoted so that some people will be inspired to participate in and help with worthy acts of service. But all of us need to check our own hearts and motives for why we do what we do. Is it for the praise and admiration of others, or is it out of love for people and the desire to honor God? Some acts of service need to be a well-kept secret between you and God.

Lord, I want to love others and honor You in my
words and deeds. Amen.

Say Thanks

*I thank God . . . as night and day I constantly remember
you in my prayers.* (2 Timothy 1:3)

Silent gratitude isn't much use to anyone. (G. B. Stern)

*E*veryone wants to feel appreciated. How do you feel when it seems your contributions at home, at work, or in a church or civic group are taken for granted? Just as important, how well do you say thank you to those who make a difference in your life? Colleagues? Friends? Family members? Mentors?

Paul began and ended all his New Testament letters by expressing his gratitude for the colaborers who helped him spread the gospel of Jesus Christ. One letter, Philemon, is a very practical epistle written to a church leader. He says to Philemon, "I always thank my God as I remember you in my prayers, because I hear about your faith in the Lord Jesus and your love for all the saints" (vv. 4–5). Paul knew to express appreciation to his fellow workers meaningfully and often.

To whom can you say thanks today? And how would your thank-you be most effective? Do you need to write a long letter, purchase a meaningful gift, or make a special visit? Ask God to give you a spirit of gratitude—and the ability to express it well.

Lord, so many people have contributed to my life and
success over the years. Please show me who deserves my
thanks and help me bless them with my gratitude. Amen.

The God of All Comfort

*[He] comforts us in all our troubles, so that we can comfort those in
any trouble with the comfort we ourselves have received from God.*
(2 Corinthians 1:4)

*In Christ the heart of the Father is revealed, the higher comfort there
cannot be than to rest in the Father's heart.* (Andrew Murray)

*T*oo much comfort can be a problem. Too much convenience,
too little discipline can cause us to grow complacent, in-
effective, unready for challenges that come our way. But there's a
different, more necessary type of comfort—the kind of loving care
that makes life not only bearable but joyful. And the Bible tells
us that God offers us that kind of comfort in abundance. Paul
calls God the "Father of compassion and the God of all comfort"
(2 Corinthians 1:3), and David says of the Good Shepherd, "your rod
and your staff, they comfort me" (Psalm 23:4).

It's not that God is cushiony and coddling. It's that He has
entered our world and taken on our pain. Even if He doesn't take
away our hard times, He promises to stay beside us, loving us
every step of the way.

And that is a very comforting thought.

Lord, thank You for the comfort of knowing You. Help me
experience Your loving care today. Amen.

Live Smart

Teach us to number our days aright,
that we may gain a heart of wisdom. (Psalm 90:12)

As we trust God to give us wisdom for today's decisions, He will lead
us a step at a time into what He wants us to be doing in the future.
(Theodore Epp)

Some troubles come though we have done nothing to deserve them. An illness. An accident. A betrayal. An act of evil.

But other troubles run our way because we call for them through carelessness, questionable decisions, and sin.

In Psalm 90, David catalogs how hard life can be, how many woes befall us. He would know. He experienced troubles that were not of his own making, but he also experienced heartache and woe that he brought on himself. No wonder he tells us to live, order, and walk our days in righteousness (v. 12). We are wise to heed the words of one who knows.

Are there thoughts or deeds in your life that are inviting trouble?

Oh God, help me to walk with wisdom and righteousness
every day of my life. Amen.

Pressing On

I do not consider myself yet to have taken hold of it. But one thing I do: Forgetting what is behind and straining toward what is ahead, I press on toward the goal to win the prize for which God has called me heavenward in Christ Jesus. (Philippians 3:13–14)

Never be afraid to trust an unknown future to a known God.
(Corrie ten Boom)

God is all-knowing and able to direct our steps so that we can press forward confidently—even when the future is uncertain. He encourages us to handle whatever challenges are before us with the knowledge that He is always with His children and we truly can trust Him to show us how to accomplish the tasks of each day. Since we are assured of His constant presence and help every day throughout the year, we should embrace the New Year—and each day—with a spirit of perseverance and confidence in our heavenly Father.

And be assured, you don't even have to be reading this at the beginning of the year to experience a quiet confidence about what the future holds for you.

Father, I want to begin this year—and each day of the
year—by seeking Your guidance. Show me the plans You
have for my life. Amen.

A God Who Forgives

Have mercy on me, O God, according to your unfailing love;
according to your great compassion blot out my transgressions.
Wash away all my iniquity and cleanse me from my sin. (Psalm 51:1–2)

Our Savior kneels down and gazes upon the darkest acts of our lives.
But rather than recoil in horror, he reaches out in kindness and says, "I
can clean that if you want." And from the basin of his grace, he scoops a
palm full of mercy and washes our sin. (Max Lucado)

A granddaughter timidly approached her grandmother to ask forgiveness for something she had done wrong. The two hugged and cried and prayed together. Then the granddaughter promised her grandmother she would never act that way again.

Her grandmother forgave her and told her how much she appreciated her heart and her intentions. But then she added that she might not be able to keep her promise, because as long as we live on earth, we will struggle with sin. Then she told her the story of King David and how he had to repent from sin numerous times—even though he was known as a man after God's heart.

Jesus saves us from our sins. He wants us not to sin. But if we do, we are to confess, repent, and ask for forgiveness, and He says that He is faithful to forgive us.

Father, thank You for Your love that always welcomes me
back home and helps me find the right path. May my life be
pleasing to You today. Amen.

Game Day

For physical training is of some value, but godliness has value for all things, holding promise for both the present life and the life to come. (1 Timothy 4:8)

True willpower and courage are not on the battlefield, but in everyday conquests over our inertia, laziness, and boredom. (D. L. Moody)

*A*thletes love to compete. Nothing beats game day: a brisk fall evening of football, a hot summer day of baseball, a basketball or volleyball game in a packed field house where the winds of winter are forgotten. Game days are what you work for, what you live for as an athlete.

Now, practice is a different matter for many of these same athletes. Practice? That's tough! What enormous, beefy football lineman wants to run sprints on a sizzling August day? What soccer player wants to do sit-ups and planks in December until his or her muscles are quivering? And yet training provides the strength, speed, and agility for a successful game day.

Life is filled with challenges. Some are life's training ground in which to build our strength and character so we can face whatever comes our way. Other challenges are the game days of life, when all our training and knowledge is put to the test. Are you ready for game day?

Dear God, thank You for all the challenges of life that help me grow stronger in spirit and faith. I pray that I will always be ready for whatever life throws my way. Amen.

Always Enough

Taking the five loaves and the two fish and looking up to heaven, he gave thanks and broke the loaves. Then he gave them to the disciples, and the disciples gave them to the people. They all ate and were satisfied, and the disciples picked up twelve basketfuls of broken pieces that were left over. (Matthew 14:19–20)

The will of God will never take us where the grace of God cannot sustain us.
(Billy Graham)

*I*n the nineteenth century, evangelist George Müller founded many homes for children throughout England to care for kids orphaned by war. With so many mouths to feed, he daily prayed for provision for the children. One particular day, when supplies were especially low, Müller prayed, "You are the God who knows our every need. I know we will have enough food today." Not long after he prayed, his wife came in and announced, "A man I'd never seen before came to the back door and gave me this food. He said, 'I know you're trying to feed some orphans. God bless you for it. This is to help you in that good work.'"

"Praise God!" said Müller. "Today I will tell the story of how Jesus fed the five thousand."

Maybe you're feeling a little low on resources today, unsure of how to help those around you. Remember that for every great need, there is a great God.

Father, thank You for always providing for me. Help me
share from my abundance. Amen.

Be Fruitful

*Our people must learn to devote themselves to doing what is good,
in order that they may provide for daily necessities and not live
unproductive lives.* (Titus 3:14)

An idle life and a holy heart are a contradiction. (Thomas Brooks)

*O*ne of Paul's faithful coworkers in his missionary travels throughout the Roman Empire was Titus. Paul left Titus on the island of Crete to encourage believers and establish order in the churches there (Titus 1:5). He instructed Titus by telling him that salvation is not a matter of works but God's kindness: "But when the kindness and love of God our Savior appeared, he saved us, not because of righteous things we had done, but because of his mercy" (3:4–5).

But in verse 14 he used an image from farming. Fruitfulness does not happen unless seeds of good works and acts of love are planted: "Our people must learn to devote themselves to doing what is good, in order that they may provide for daily necessities and not live unproductive lives."

Fall is coming and your fruitfulness will be in measure with the seeds of love and obedience you've planted. What seeds will you plant today?

God, teach me to live well, bearing fruit of faithfulness
to You. Amen.

Peace and Encouragement

The Prayer of Saint Francis

Delight yourself in the Lord *and he will give you the desires of your heart.* (Psalm 37:4)

Prayer is not intended to change God's purpose, nor is it to move Him to form fresh purposes. God has decreed that certain events shall come to pass through the means He has appointed for their accomplishment. (Arthur W. Pink)

A Classic Devotion from Saint Francis of Assisi

A Prayer for Peace, Growth, and Recovery

Lord, make me an instrument of your peace.
Where there is hatred, let me sow love;
Where there is injury, pardon;
Where there is doubt, faith;
Where there is despair, hope;
Where there is darkness, light;
Where there is sadness, joy.
O Divine Master, grant that I may not so much seek to be
   consoled as to console;
To be understood as to understand;
To be loved as to love.
For it is in giving that we receive.
It is in pardoning that we are pardoned.
It is in dying that we are born to eternal life.

Your heart, O Lord, is open to Your children. Help me
to be willing to learn from You. Amen.

Out of Love

"Therefore go and make disciples of all nations, baptizing them in the name of the Father and of the Son and of the Holy Spirit, and teaching them to obey everything I have commanded you. And surely I am with you always, to the very end of the age." (Matthew 28:19–20)

Missionary zeal does not grow out of intellectual beliefs, nor out of theological arguments, but out of love. (Roland Allen)

*I*t was a huge pop hit in the 1960s sung by Jackie DeShannon, and was a huge hit again in the 1970s as sung by Dionne Warwick. The Hal David lyrics asserted, "What the world needs now is love, sweet love—no, not just for some, but for everyone." Even if you weren't born yet when the song was a hit in either decade, chances are you know the tune and at least some of the words.

Sentimental and sappy? Maybe. Okay, probably. But perhaps the song was such a hit because it expressed a powerful truth.

We do live in a lost and hurting world. People run to addictions and entertainment to numb their pain. But the heartfelt cry of every human heart is to be loved.

How is God's love shared? Simple. From the heart, words, and service of His people. And what makes that happen is "love, sweet love."

Lord, please give me a heart that longs to reach others
with Your love. Amen.

All Things!

And we know that in all things God works for the good of those who love him, who have been called according to his purpose. (Romans 8:28)

I am mended by my sickness, enriched by my poverty, and strengthened by my weakness. (Abraham Wright)

*O*ur culture craves comfort, the avoidance of pain, easy projects, nothing but success, leisure time, entertainment, fun hobbies, and anything else that can fit under the umbrella of "smooth sailing."

When things don't go right—a slip on ice, a conflict with a loved one, a demanding and troublesome boss, a leaky roof, car trouble, financial setbacks—there is a prevailing attitude of surprised anger and resentment, a strong sense that life is unfair and cruel.

Paul, a survivor of every sort of calamity, challenges this mind-set. Not only are difficulties inevitable, but they become opportunities to grow—and even become catalysts for great things to happen. Are you convinced that all things work together for good in your life?

Accept discipline. Ask God to help you get the most out of the difficulties you encounter. You might feel pain for a moment, but the long-term rewards will be great.

Heavenly Father, I don't understand why bad things happen, and I especially don't understand how You can use them for good in my life, but You do. Thank You! Amen.

A New Heart

I will give you a new heart and put a new spirit in you; I will remove from you your heart of stone and give you a heart of flesh. (Ezekiel 36:26)

God became man to turn creatures into sons: not simply to produce better men of the old kind but to produce a new kind of man. (C. S. Lewis)

Near death, a man received word that a new heart was available. A young man had been killed in a motorcycle accident. The older man had his transplant surgery that same week.

With the surgery came a new life for him. He was suddenly healthier than he had been in years. He regained energy that had been drained. He was joyful and excited about life. And he understood the sacrifice that was made so that he could truly live again.

He said, "As a Christian, this tragic and joyous experience made me more fully understand that God gave His only Son so that I could have new life, not just here on earth but for eternity. I am grateful to God for the gift of life and the sacrifice that brought this to me."

God gives us new beginnings, but His very best gift of life is the one we will experience throughout eternity.

Father, thank You for the new life You have
given me in Christ. Amen.

False Interpretation

*But false prophets also arose among the people, just as there will also
be false teachers among you, who will secretly introduce destructive
heresies, even denying the Master who bought them, bringing
upon themselves swift destruction.* (2 Peter 2:1 ESV)

*A false interpretation of Scripture causes that the gospel of the Lord
becomes the gospel of man, or, which is worse, of the devil.* (Saint Jerome)

Though Martin Luther made the proclamation of "sola scriptura" as the only authority for the Christian's life, part of the phrase has been commonly ignored. He actually said, "Scripture rightly divided," which simply means "interpreted correctly."

One of the most important reasons to read God's Word and know it ourselves is that it protects us from false prophets. In every age of the church there have been men and women who use the Bible for their own purposes, not to build God's kingdom.

We don't need to live in a posture of skepticism and over-analyze every word from a Bible teacher's lips. But we do need to know God's Word well enough to know when someone has an agenda that is not God's.

Lord, protect us from false prophets and false teachings.
Help me be true to You and Your Word. Amen.

We Must Pray

Devote yourselves to prayer, being watchful and thankful.
(Colossians 4:2)

*Pray often, for prayer is a shield to the soul, a sacrifice to God,
and a scourge for Satan.* (John Bunyan)

A Classic Devotion from E. M. Bounds

No insistence in the Scriptures is more pressing than that we must pray. No exhortation is more often reiterated, none is more hearty, none is more solemn and stirring, than to pray. No principle is more strongly and broadly declared than that which urges us to pray. There is no duty to which we are more strongly obliged than that of praying. There is no command more imperative and insistent than that of praying. Are you praying in everything without ceasing (1 Thessalonians 5:17)? Are you praying in your prayer closet, hidden from the eyes of others? Are you praying always and everywhere? These are personal, pertinent, and all-important questions for every soul.

God's Word shows us, through many examples, that God intervenes in this world in answer to prayer. How clear it is, when the Bible is consulted, that the almighty God is brought directly into the things of this world by the prayers of His people.[8]

Lord, I know that I can't do Your will without praying.
Draw me close to You today. Amen.

Joyfully Working

Blessed is the man who fears the LORD,
who finds great delight in his commands.
(Psalm 112:1)

Joy, not grit, is the hallmark of holy obedience. We need to
be light-hearted in what we do to avoid taking ourselves too
seriously. It is a cheerful revolt against self and pride. Or work
is jubilant, carefree, merry. Utter abandonment to God is done
freely and with celebration. (Richard J. Foster)

The motivational adage tells us: if you enjoy what you do for a living, you'll never work a day in your life. There is a parallel in the Christian life: if you find joy in God and doing the things that bring God joy, your service to Him will never feel like drudgery or an unwelcome burden.

We worry a lot about taking time for ourselves so that we don't burn out and become weary in doing good. But perhaps it is a sense of self-preoccupation that saps us of energy, while the act of giving and serving reenergizes us.

Does service energize you and bring you joy? If not, turn your attention to the heart of God and what brings Him joy. You will find God's joy to be contagious!

Dear God, show me the things I can do that will
bring joy to You. Amen.

The Best Motivation

"Whoever has my commands and obeys them, he is the one who loves me. He who loves me will be loved by my Father, and I too will love him and show myself to him." (John 14:21)

Obedience deepens our intimacy with Jesus. If we want to know the Father, we must not only love Him, but also obey Him. (John Wimber)

As a parent, would you prefer that your child pick up his room because he knows he will be punished if he doesn't, or because he wants to please you? As a husband, would you prefer your wife to show you affection because she is afraid you will be in a bad mood, or because she is in love with you? As a manager, do you want your assistant to do good work because he doesn't want a bad review in his personnel file, or because he enjoys what he does?

In all these examples from everyday life, we prefer that people respond to us out of love, not fear. In the same way our heavenly Father desires that we follow His will not because we are terrified of judgment—or because we want to earn His love—but because we love Him wholeheartedly.

Obedience to God is always a good thing, no matter what the motivation, but it is better for Him—and for you—when it is expressed out of a deep, enduring love.

Lord, thank You for Your goodness to me. Please deepen my love for You and make me ready and willing to serve You. Amen.

A Loving Family

Dear friends, since God so loved us, we also ought to love one another. (1 John 4:11)

Let your love grow as God wants it to grow. Seek goodness in others.
Love more persons more. Love them more impersonally, more
unselfishly, without thought of return. The return, never fear, will
take care of itself. (Henry Drummond)

*H*ave you ever noticed that we tend to be at our very best—charming, kind, considerate—with casual acquaintances and even complete strangers? And that we act our absolute worst—rude, impatient, moody, ungrateful—with those who are closest to us, our family?

The good news is that it doesn't have to be that way! In fact, there are two simple steps that will cure the majority of family conflicts—and make any family stronger.

The first step is cultivating a spirit of gratitude. When was the last time you felt thankful for the people living in your home—and said thank you? The second step is demonstrating your love. How can you show those in your home that you truly love them? The apostle James said that faith without works is dead (James 2:17); in the same way love, without actions is empty.

Relationships are among the best of God's gifts. We can be good stewards of those gifts by practicing love toward those closest to us.

Heavenly Father, thank You for my family. Help me to
express the love I truly have for them. Amen.

Our Lot in Life

The boundary lines have fallen for me in pleasant places;
surely I have a delightful inheritance. (Psalm 16:6)

How completely satisfying to turn from our limitations to a God
who has none. God never hurries. There are no deadlines against
which He must work. Only to know this is to quiet our spirits and
relax our nerves. (A. W. Tozer)

*A*t nineteen months old, Helen Keller was stricken with a rare infection that caused her to lose both her sight and her hearing. The road ahead was long and difficult. She had to blaze new trails in living life with disabilities. Yet she was able to express her gratitude to God by saying, "I thank God for my handicaps, for, through them, I have found myself, my work, and my God."

Our lot in life may not be what we would have picked for ourselves. Some days we might wish we could do away with this flaw or that difficulty—a physical problem, a complicated background, a troublesome quirk or tendency. But what we so often forget is that God has a plan and purpose for each of us. He knows what is best and can use even the worst of our problems for good. View yourself and your life prayerfully and gratefully. If you keep yourself open to God's plan, you will see His great purposes fulfilled.

God, I know that You have a plan, and I thank You for it in advance. Help me to cooperate with You. Amen.

Rejoice

Sing and make music in your heart to the Lord. (Ephesians 5:19)

When we bless God for mercies, we usually prolong them. When we bless God for miseries, we usually end them. Praise is the honey of life which a devout heart extracts from every bloom of providence and grace. (C. H. Spurgeon)

Some days find us more eager to rejoice than others. Some days, something big and wonderful happens in our lives, and joyful feelings flow freely. Other days are difficult, and still other days are simply ordinary—nothing to write home about.

But Paul admonishes us to rejoice always (Philippians 4:4). And whether we realize it or not, we have good reason to. We have the promise of God's love and salvation and His grace to pull us through any circumstance. We also have the promise of His Spirit working within us to make us more like Him and more able to live joyful, productive lives.

When we know God and walk closely with Him, every day can be extraordinary. So rejoice throughout the day!

God, Your presence is the best thing in my life.
Today I want to pray prayers of rejoicing and thanks
throughout the day. Amen.

Joy for Eternity

Then I saw a new heaven and a new earth, for the first heaven and the first earth had passed away, and there was no longer any sea.
(Revelation 21:1)

The enjoyment of God is the only happiness with which our souls can be satisfied. To go to heaven, fully to enjoy God, is infinitely better than the most pleasant accommodations here. Fathers and mothers, husbands, wives, or children, or the company of earthly friends, are but shadows, but God is the substance. These are but scattered beams, but God is the sun. These are but streams. But God is the ocean. (Jonathan Edwards)

It's been said that those who let their minds dwell on heaven are of no earthly good. But is it possible that the opposite is true? The history of the Christian church is filled with examples of how those who thought most of heaven did the most good here on earth.

The realization that this present life is not all there is does give one a perspective that every moment here on earth counts. It challenges us to walk closely with God so as not to miss an eternity in heaven with Him—and to put our hands to the task of bringing friends, family members, and others along with us.

Are you making your life count in eternity? And are you inviting others to enjoy the presence of God for eternity with you?

> Lord, thank You for the gift of eternal life and for inviting me to spend eternity with You. I pray that my loved ones will join me in heaven. Amen.

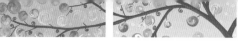

Nothing to Fear

I sought the L\ORD, and he answered me;
he delivered me from all my fears.
Those who look to him are radiant;
their faces are never covered with shame.
(Psalm 34:4–5)

God walks with us. He scoops us up in His arms or simply sits with
us in silent strength until we cannot avoid the awesome recognition
that yes, even now, He is here. (Gloria Gaither)

*A*little boy had been admitted to the hospital. When his parents briefly left him in the room alone for the first time, his nurse, who knew that he was alone, called his name over the intercom to ask him how he was doing. This was long before the wireless age, and electronic gadgetry was new to him. The wide-eyed child sat up in his bed and responded, "Is that You, Lord?!"

Even when we feel all alone and afraid, we can know that God is speaking to us, wanting to know how we're doing, sometimes in mysterious ways. All that's required is the simple belief that God is always near and desires to speak to our hearts.

Lord, thank You for Your nearness. Thank You for hearing
my prayers. Give me an open heart to hear You and see
Your hand in my life. Amen.

Overcoming Distortion

*His letters contain some things that are hard to understand, which
ignorant and unstable people distort, as they do the other Scriptures,
to their own destruction.* (2 Peter 3:16)

*We should not interpret Scripture in the light of our experiences,
but we should examine our experiences in the light of the teaching of
Scripture.* (Martyn Lloyd-Jones)

*I*n the first ten chapters of Acts, the leading man, the hero of the
faith, is Peter. But in chapter 11, it is Paul who becomes the leading figure. This makes sense on the basis of 1:8, where we find the
outline of the book—and the marching orders for the early believers—to share the gospel in Jerusalem, Samaria, and the ends of the
earth. Paul, the great missionary, is the one who took Jesus to the
Roman Empire—the ends of the earth.

Peter was acquainted with Paul's writings and admits they can
be tough to understand. But his warning about our responsibility in
handling God's Word is crystal clear. We are to be careful in how we
interpret and teach the words of the Bible. Those who are careless
or, worse, deliberately distort God's Word will be held accountable.

Be bold in sharing God's Word with others—but always with
respect and reverence.

God, I never want to go astray in reading Your Word—or
cause anyone else to do so either. I pray for wisdom and a
spirit of reverence as I spend time with Your Word. Amen.

The Benefits of Obedience

I lift up my hands to your commands,
which I love,
and I meditate on your decrees.
(Psalm 119:48)

God's commands are designed to guide you to life's very best. You
will not obey Him, if you do not believe Him and trust Him. You
cannot believe Him if you do not love Him. You cannot love Him
unless you know Him. (Henry Blackaby)

We all know there are negative consequences to disobeying God, but do we ever stop to consider all the blessings and rewards that come to us through obedience? Have we made obedience a drudgery that steals the fun from life, rather than affirming how much sweeter and better it makes life? There are more rewards and blessings from obedience than can be listed on a single page, but consider the following as you look up the corresponding Bible verses.

- Obedience gives us a clean conscience: Psalm 19:13.
- Obedience keeps us from danger: Psalm 119:109.
- Obedience brings material blessings: Deuteronomy 11:13–15.
- Obedience prolongs life: Deuteronomy 11:9.
- Obedience is a blessing to our family: Psalm 112:1–3.
- Obedience brings joy: Psalm 119:33–35.

Lord God, thank You for enriching my life as I
walk in Your ways. Amen.

What Matters Most

Jesus replied: "'Love the Lord your God with all your heart and with all your soul and with all your mind.' This is the first and greatest commandment. And the second is like it: 'Love your neighbor as yourself.'" (Matthew 22:37–39)

Let your religion be less of a theory and more of a love affair.
(G. K. Chesterton)

Some people claim to love God but have a strong aversion to "religion." But we are called to be part of the body of Christ, so an isolated faith isn't part of God's plan. However, the desire to keep things simple isn't so bad. When the religious leaders of His day asked Jesus what matters most, He was able to summarize the Ten Commandments and the entire body of religious law into two simple commands:

- Love God with all your heart.
- Love your neighbor as yourself.

What more is there? It doesn't get any simpler than that. But don't mistake *simple* for *easy*. Jesus Himself showed us the true cost of loving God and others!

Dear God, I do love You with all my heart. Help me to love
my neighbors as You love them. Amen.

The Right Armor

But since we belong to the day, let us be self-controlled, putting on faith and love as a breastplate, and the hope of salvation as a helmet.
(1 Thessalonians 5:8)

God hath in Himself all power to defend you, all wisdom to direct you, all mercy to pardon you, all grace to enrich you, all righteousness to clothe you, all goodness to supply you, and all happiness to crown you. (Thomas Brooks)

God sees us in our need, saves us from our sins, and puts us on the right path. Our life changes for the better. We are thankful. But sometimes we get proud. And we begin to feel self-sufficient. And we forget that God is the One who turned our lives around in the first place. We make a mess of things. But God sees us, hears our call for help, redeems us, and puts us on solid ground again. And oftentimes, again.

Rather than live in a cycle of defeat, wouldn't it be better to remember—to never forget—that God is the source of our salvation and strength?

Are you facing life with your own sufficiency? Or are you wearing His armor?

Lord, I acknowledge my need for You. You are my strength
and salvation. Help me to walk humbly with You. Amen.

Rumbling Sounds

I will both lie down in peace, and sleep;
For You alone, O Lord, make me dwell in safety.
(Psalm 4:8 NKJV)

'Tis lasting calm, 'tis heavenly rest:
Come, Spirit of the Living God,
And in our spirits shed abroad
The peace that makes the troubled blest. (John Brownlie)

*E*ven though we teach our children that thunder will not hurt them, the thunder of a violent storm does frighten them, especially during the night. Many a parent has woken in the middle of a stormy night to find a child squirming into the middle of the bed. Sure, it's a bit of an inconvenience; a little sleep is lost. But there's an unmistakable joy in comforting a child, reassuring him or her that everything will be all right.

As our heavenly Father, God finds the same joy in comforting us. He loves it when we need Him. He wants to reassure us that He will always provide for us and protect us. And He delights to hear our prayers.

Lord, thank You for being such a perfect, loving parent.
Thank You for Your love and comfort. Amen.

Every Jot and Tittle

Every word of God is flawless;
he is a shield to those who take refuge in him.
Do not add to his words,
or he will rebuke you and prove you a liar.
(Proverbs 30:5–6)

We must allow the Word of God to confront us, to disturb our
security, to undermine our complacency and to overthrow our
patterns of thought and behavior. (John Stott)

A Classic Devotion from John Wesley

*I*f, then, we have spoken the word of God, the genuine unmixed word of God, and that only; if we have put no unnatural interpretation upon it, but have taken the known phrases in their common, obvious sense—and when they were less known, explained scripture by scripture; if we have spoken the whole word, as occasion offered, though rather the parts which seemed most proper to give a check to some fashionable vice, or to encourage the practice of some unfashionable virtue; and if we have done this plainly and boldly . . . then, believe ye our works, if not our words; or rather, believe them both together. Here is all a Preacher can do; all the evidence that he either can or need give of his good intentions.[9]

Lord, help me share Your Word with others in a way
that leads them to You. Amen.

A Joyless Faith

"But I tell you: Love your enemies and pray for those who persecute you, that you may be sons of your Father in heaven."
(Matthew 5:44–45)

Nothing graces the Christian soul as much as mercy.
(Saint Ambrose)

Is someone making your life miserable? If so, what is your response to that person? Do you complain to others about that person's unfairness? Or do you pray for him or her?

One of the ways to lose the joy of salvation is to focus on the faults of someone who feels like an enemy. But we can maintain and restore joy by loving the unlovable person through intercessory prayer. Don't just ask God to make that person start treating you better; ask God to change him or her on the inside—and to use you to minister in that person's life. That's not an easy prayer to pray. But the reward for truly loving as Christ loves is amazing. It may not be a physical or monetary reward, but what greater gift can we receive than the gift of joy?

Lord, I lay aside my legitimate complaints and frustrations right now in order to bless and pray for those who act against me. Thank You for allowing me to experience You more fully in my life as I intercede for others. Amen.

Valentine's Day

How great is the love the Father has lavished on us, that we should be called children of God! And that is what we are! The reason the world does not know us is that it did not know him. (1 John 3:1)

You can give without loving, but you cannot love without giving.
(Amy Carmichael)

*P*lush teddy bears, extravagant flower arrangements, rich velvety chocolates—the signs of Valentine's Day are inescapable in the middle of February. Some think that this particular holiday is not for Christians, that it's a completely secular and commercial occasion. But if God is love—and we know that He is—and if love is a beautiful sign of His work in the world, then maybe we should put even more emphasis on a holiday set apart for celebrating love.

Of course, the love proclaimed on Valentine's Day can stray far from the pure love of God—it can be tawdry, cheap, and conditional. But if you get creative and ask for help from God, you just might find ways to share His unrelenting love with those around you.

Lord, help me to be salt and light in my world, sharing
Your love with others. Amen.

The Right Motivation

But God demonstrates his own love for us in this: While we were still sinners, Christ died for us. (Romans 5:8)

Get yourself into the presence of the loving Father. Just place yourself before Him, and look up into His face; think of His love, His wonderful, tender love. (Andrew Murray)

Following Marie's doctor's advice, the couple purchased a treadmill. For several days she walked faithfully. Before long, however, she quit. When her husband confronted her, she unfurled a list of excuses. "It's boring" was the first. Her husband purchased a television and mounted it on the wall above the treadmill. "It's too hot," Marie further complained. Her husband purchased a fan on a stand and placed it near the exercise equipment. "My feet are hurting," she moaned. Together, they went shopping and bought her a pair of walking shoes.

Marie finally understood her husband's deep concern for her— he only wanted her to be healthy. She decided to walk faithfully and quit using lame excuses. The time on the treadmill passed quickly when she thought about how much her husband loved her.

Somehow it's easier to persevere when we're doing so for someone we love. Whatever God has asked you to do, remember that He loves you. Reflecting on His abundant love will make the task at hand lighter and easier.

Lord, I know that You love me. Help me to see Your love in each circumstance of my life. Amen.

First Priorities

A Courageous Hope

Be of good courage,
And He shall strengthen your heart,
All you who hope in the Lord.
(Psalm 31:24 NKJV)

We can walk without fear, full of hope and courage and strength to
do His will, waiting for the endless good which He is always giving as
fast as He can get us able to take it in. (George MacDonald)

*W*hat keeps us from attempting—let alone accomplishing—great things? Nothing other than fear! No wonder the phrase "fear not" is found more than a hundred times throughout the Bible. The opposite of fear is courage. But how do you get courage if you're afraid?

The psalmist tells us that there is something we can do to build our courage: hope in the Lord (Psalm 31:24). There's no other starting point. It's the only thing that enabled David to face Goliath (1 Samuel 17:1–51); Gideon to lead a small, ragtag army against the mighty Midianites (Judges 6:1–7:25); Joshua to cross the Jordan River and later conquer Jericho (Joshua 3:1–17); Peter to walk on water (Matthew 14:22–29). And it's the only thing that enables you and me to face any giants and challenges that come our way.

Is your hope in God?

Oh Lord, I do put my hope in You this day. Give me the
courage and strengthen my heart so I can do something
great for You. Amen.

Why Me?

He causes his sun to rise on the evil and the good, and sends rain on the righteous and the unrighteous. (Matthew 5:45)

Stand still and refuse to retreat. Look at it as God looks at it and draw upon His power to hold up under the blast. (Charles Swindoll)

I love God. I serve God. I help out at church. I'm nice to my neighbors. I volunteer in my community. I don't use bad language. I never kick the dog. I'm not greedy; I don't ask for much.

So why me? My car is making funny sounds; my interest rate went up so my mortgage payment is higher; no raises or bonuses at work; my kid needs braces; the doctor wants to run some tests; I think my mom is showing signs of Alzheimer's.

You get the idea. Life doesn't always seem fair. It would seem fair if bad things happened to bad people and good things to good people. But life comes fast. It is both wonderful and difficult—for all of us.

So does it matter that we are loving and serving God? Absolutely! Ultimately, there is a day of judgment. Those who live for God will receive an eternal reward and those who ignore God will then be ignored by God. Rain in someone's life is never a sign of God's disapproval. In fact, the storms of life become wonderful days when we display God's presence within us!

Lord, give me grace under pressure. Thank You for reassurance during difficult days. And thank You that they don't last. Amen.

Praise for Our Great God

When a Storm Isn't Really a Storm

*Praise the L*ord*, O my soul,*
and forget not all his benefits.
(Psalm 103:2)

God does not give us everything we want, but He does fulfill His
promises. (Dietrich Bonhoeffer)

Not all the things that we think are problems are really problems.

We live in a prosperous time when even the "poor" are often wealthier than those who are considered wealthy in another culture. We've become so accustomed to having so much that what once felt like a special blessing now feels like a necessity. Again, this does not apply to all areas of discontent, and it does not mean that demands for fairness are selfish and indulgent. But many of us need to do a reality check on what we think we need to be happy.

How about you? Are you more demanding than giving? Have you turned blessings into necessities? Have you moaned and complained over things that really aren't that big of a deal in the grand scheme of life? Maybe the trouble is not God's goodness but our ability to receive the gifts He gives us.

Dear God, help me to cry for justice and fairness on the
same things that burden Your heart. And help me to take
in stride the petty annoyances of life! Amen.

Pursuing Peace

*The kingdom of God is not eating and drinking, but righteousness
and peace and joy in the Holy Spirit. For he who serves Christ in
these things is acceptable to God and approved by men. Therefore let
us pursue the things which make for peace and the things by which
one may edify another.* (Romans 14:17–19 NKJV)

*One day we must come to see that peace is not merely a distant
goal we seek, but that it is a means by which we arrive at that
goal. We must pursue peaceful ends through peaceful means.*
(Martin Luther King Jr.)

*W*hat does a peacemaker look like?

- Not self-absorbed and insistent on one's own way
- Generous and happy to share
- Doesn't hold grudges
- Not envious of others' success and blessings
- Doesn't criticize harshly
- More focused on solutions than problems
- Self-confident—doesn't get feelings hurt easily
- Sees the big picture of life, not petty quarrels

When others see you—and when you look in the mirror—do
you see a peacemaker?

Lord, help me to bring peace into all my relationships and
all areas of my own life. Amen.

Listen Up!

*Give me understanding, and I will keep your law and obey it
with all my heart.* (Psalm 119:34)

*When God works in us, the will, being changed and sweetly breathed
up by the Spirit of God, desires and acts, not from compulsion, but
responsively.* (Martin Luther)

*T*he idea of obedience has fallen on hard times in our culture. Some don't believe that obedience, in the traditional sense of following a set of moral guidelines, is even possible. Others think that obedience is only for those who are not strong or smart enough to order their own lives.

Is there a better, healthier way of looking at obedience? The English word is derived from the Latin *obaudire*, which means "to listen well." At the heart of obedience in the Bible is relationship. Obedience is based on the deepest level of communication where the other person is heard and understood. For Christians, this means that obedience cannot be reduced to a simple list of dos and don'ts, but is tantamount to an act of worship. We look closely at God and listen closely for His voice so that we are engaged in conversation and communion with God.

Obedience. Listening intently. Understanding the heart of another. When looked at that way, how obedient are you to God?

Lord, teach me to listen to Your voice and follow You in
loving obedience. Amen.

We Get What We Give

"Give, and it will be given to you. A good measure, pressed down, shaken together and running over, will be poured into your lap. For with the measure you use, it will be measured to you." (Luke 6:38)

As base a thing as money often is, yet it can be transmuted into everlasting treasure. It can be converted into food for the hungry and clothing for the poor. Any temporal possession can be turned into everlasting wealth. Whatever is given to Christ is immediately touched with immortality. (A. W. Tozer)

There's a principle in life that seems oxymoronic at first glance: we get what we give. But a second look shows the wisdom of the principle. When we bless others, we are blessed; when we love, we are loved; when we give—even in the midst of our own needs—we greatly receive. It's possible to give beyond our resources and find ourselves burned out and broke. But over time, if we're willing to give, we'll receive a lot more in return.

Gratitude unlocks the doors of generosity. Even if you're in need, gratitude helps you give to others sacrificially, just like the poor widow Jesus praised (Mark 12:41–44). Do your own soul a favor by sharing generously from the abundance of your life. You'll be grateful you did!

Father, show me where I can give today and help me to do so out of gratitude. Amen.

Peace and Encouragement

The Armor of God

*For our struggle is not against flesh and blood, but against the
rulers, against the authorities, against the powers of this dark
world and against the spiritual forces of evil in the heavenly realms.*
(Ephesians 6:12)

*There are two equal and opposite errors into which our race can fall
about the devils. One is to disbelieve in their existence. The other is
to believe, and to feel an excessive and unhealthy interest in them.
They themselves are equally pleased by both errors.* (C. S. Lewis)

*A*mong people of faith, there is some variation in doctrine
about spiritual warfare. Some see demons in everything;
others have more or less eliminated a personal devil from the equa-
tion of their spiritual practice. While we can go astray by devoting
too much thought and care to Satan, the Bible does tell us that we
must be on our guard against spiritual attacks.

Fortunately, we are never in the battle alone. God always arms
us with His strength and enables us to defeat temptation and
assaults on our Christian walk. In Ephesians 6, Paul tells us to take
up the armor of God, including the shield of faith and the sword of
the Spirit. We can deflect the attacks that would wound our souls
by diligently nurturing our faith in God.

God, help me to be vigilant and protective of my spiritual
life. Guard me from the attacks of the devil today. Amen.

The Secret of Life

The mystery that has been kept hidden for ages and generations, but is now disclosed to the saints. To them God has chosen to make known among the Gentiles the glorious riches of this mystery, which is Christ in you, the hope of glory. (Colossians 1:26–27)

Follow hard after Him, and He will never fail you. (C. H. Spurgeon)

Mysteries and lost codes have never been more popular than in today's entertainment culture. Prophecies, cryptic clues, secret societies, dangerous searches, untapped divine power, buried treasures—all are common components of a thrilling blockbuster or best-selling novel.

The world the apostle Paul preached to was similar. There was a fascination with mysteries that unlocked godlike power and riches for humans inquisitive and skillful enough to solve difficult and arcane riddles.

Paul wasn't a man to keep a powerful secret for just a few select individuals, hidden and protected from the masses. Instead he revealed the identity of the mystery that had eluded humans for generations: Jesus. The mystery solved is Jesus inside your life.

Have you experienced the glory and power of God inside you? You don't even have to search for God. He will find you!

God, I am so grateful to discover the answer for all
life's riddles: Jesus Christ. Amen.

A Delayed Hope

These were all commended for their faith, yet none of them received what had been promised. God had planned something better for us so that only together with us would they be made perfect. (Hebrews 11:39–40)

It takes some of us a lifetime to learn that Christ, our Good Shepherd, knows exactly what He is doing with us. He understands us perfectly. (Phillip Keller)

When you were a child or teen, did you ever hope for something with seemingly all of your heart—but it never came to pass? A particular toy? A part in the musical? A certain someone to be your boyfriend or girlfriend?

Even when it comes to temporal desires, Solomon says, "Hope deferred makes the heart sick, but a longing fulfilled is a tree of life" (Proverbs 13:12). How are we supposed to handle the grown-up disappointment of having noble and spiritually motivated hopes delayed and deferred?

In Hebrews 11 we find a hall of fame of faith. Some received what they were promised, while others didn't—at least not here on earth. And therein lies the secret of maintaining a positive and optimistic sense of hope and expectation when things don't appear to be working out. It's the realization that in eternity, all hope is realized.

Lord, I affirm a positive sense of expectation that You will
do all that You promised in my life! Amen.

Blessed Is the One Who Reads

Blessed is the one who reads the words of this prophecy, and blessed are those who hear it and take to heart what is written in it, because the time is near. (Revelation 1:3)

Down through the centuries in times of trouble and trial God has brought courage to the hearts of those who love Him. The Bible is filled with assurances of God's help and comfort in every kind of trouble which might cause fears to arise in the human heart. (Billy Graham)

*P*eter and John were with Jesus shortly before His return to His Father's right side. In their poignant conversation, Jesus foretold Peter's violent death as a martyr and John's long life (see John 21:18–24). All the other apostles died at the hands of those who persecuted the Christian faith, but John died of old age as an exile on the island of Patmos. It was there that he received a vision that came directly from God, which is known as the book of Revelation, the final entry in the New Testament.

This is not just a book a prophecy, but a hard look at how believers—now and then—live in the present. In John's preface he provides a word of wisdom all people of faith are wise to heed: "Blessed is the one who reads the words of this prophecy, and blessed are those who hear it and take to heart what is written in it, because the time is near" (1:3).

Lord, thank You for the blessings that follow when I read Your Word. Today I choose to make reading Scripture a priority in my life. Amen.

God's Gift of Rest

By the seventh day God had finished the work he had been doing; so on the seventh day he rested from all his work. (Genesis 2:2)

Jesus knows we must come apart and rest a while, or else we may just plain come apart. (Vance Havner)

According to Genesis 2:2, even God rested after creating the universe. And unlike God, we get tired. When our bodies and brains are tired, they don't function like they were created to and need renewal. But just as much as physical rest, we need to recharge our spirits as well. We need to take a moment at the end of the day to simply breathe slowly and say a short prayer in order to take care of our souls.

Few men lived as intense a life as King David. Kingdom builder and warrior, he faced strife and danger—some of it self-induced—his entire adult life. As an emotional man who was subject to the same laws of fatigue and exhaustion as the rest of us, is it any wonder David described the blessed man as one who meditates on God in the morning and at night (Psalm 1:2)?

Sometimes we run the risk of burning ourselves out even in serving God. Don't wait until the point of exhaustion to take time to slow down, thank God, and ask Him for His help and grace.

Dear Lord, I need Your refreshing, renewing grace
to keep me going. Amen.

A Call to Prayer

Every day they continued to meet together in the temple courts.
They broke bread in their homes and ate together with glad and
sincere hearts, praising God and enjoying the favor of all the
people. And the Lord added to their number daily those who
were being saved. (Acts 2:46–47)

I had rather stand against the cannons of the wicked than against
the prayers of the righteous. (Thomas Lye)

*I*n September 1857, Jeremiah Lanphier, a city minister, began a
weekly noon prayer meeting in New York that by October had
grown into a daily prayer meeting attended by hundreds of busi-
nessmen. By March of the next year, newspapers carried front-page
reports that over six thousand were attending daily prayer meetings in downtown New York and Pittsburgh, and similar meetings
were being held in Washington at five different times to accommodate the crowds. By May 1859, fifty thousand New Yorkers had
reported accepting Christ through these meetings.

It might be hard to envision a similar resurgence of faith in
our own time. But the biggest movements often begin with the
smallest steps of prayer. What would happen if you began meeting
with just a few friends to pray? Why not try it and see?

Lord, I'm amazed at what You do in response to the
prayers of Your people. Today I bring the concerns of my
community before You, and I ask for Your guidance as I
seek out friends to pray with. Amen.

Hospitality

*Do not forget to entertain strangers, for by so doing some people
have entertained angels without knowing it.* (Hebrews 13:2)

When there is room in the heart, there is room in the house.
(Danish proverb)

*W*hen was the last time you visited someone and felt truly
welcome and comfortable? What made you feel that way?
In all likelihood, it wasn't just fancy sheets or top-shelf meals. It
was the effort your friend put into making you feel at home.

Throughout Scripture, an act of hospitality became the scene
for a holy moment. Abraham served a meal for three strangers
who turned out to be from God, delivering His prophecy about
Abraham and Sarah's future (Genesis 18:1–15). The widow at
Zarephath made a cake of bread for Elijah out of the very last
of her flour and oil, and miraculously she never ran out of food
(1 Kings 17:7–24). Peter's mother served Jesus and the disciples
after He healed her from a fever (Matthew 8:14–15).

In our modern day, hospitality can turn into something no
less holy. God blesses us for receiving others into our homes. And
when we take the time to demonstrate care for someone else, we
realize that we are merely returning the love God gives to us.

God, thank You for the people You've given me to love.
Be with me as I plan to show them hospitality this week.
Amen.

Losing to Gain

"The man who loves his life will lose it, while the man who hates his life in this world will keep it for eternal life." (John 12:25)

He is no fool to give what he cannot keep to gain what he cannot lose. (James Elliott)

*A*s he gained speed going down a hill, the young boy racing along on his bike saw a sharp turn just ahead. But the speed was exhilarating, so he paused a second—and then another and another—reluctant to apply the brakes. He hit the curb at full speed. When he hit it, he lost control and found himself flying off the bike. Both he and the bicycle were a bit mangled, but he survived. The boy learned the simple truth that sometimes we must give up something we enjoy in order to get something better—or simply to survive. That is true in the physical world, but even more so in the spiritual realm.

Jesus said, "Whoever wants to save his life will lose it, but whoever loses his life for me and for the gospel will save it" (Mark 8:35). Giving something up in obedience to God might sting a little. But in the end, it's the only course for keeping our bikes on the road and living our best possible lives.

Lord, please nurture my character and give me enough discipline to surrender to You. Amen.

Christ Is All

Christ is all, and is in all. (Colossians 3:11)

We Recognize No Sovereign but God, and no King but Jesus! (John Adams and John Hancock)

A Classic Devotion from C. H. Spurgeon

Christ must be all, as your principal object in life—your chief good. Your great aim must be to glorify Christ on the earth, in the hope and expectation of enjoying Him for ever above. The true Christian will say, "I know that I am bound to be diligent in business; but I want to work for eternity as well as for time. I need something besides earthly riches; I want an inheritance not made with hands, a mansion not built by man, a possession in the skies."

If you can say that Christ is your all, then your treasure will never be gone; for He will never leave you, nor forsake you. Not only in this world, but also in that which is to come, you shall be happy and blessed, for you shall be crowned with glory, and made to sit with Christ on His throne for ever.[10]

> Help me, Lord, to do everything for You, and thank You for the joy and fulfillment of following closely after You. Amen.

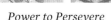

A Healing Word

This is my comfort in my affliction: for thy word hath quickened me.
(Psalm 119:50 KJV)

Nothing ranks higher for mental discipline than a planned and systematic study of God's Word, from whence life's parameters and values are planted in the mind. (Ravi Zacharias)

*M*ental illness is a difficult thing for any individual or family to deal with. With it comes a host of issues—painful emotions, financial difficulties due to medical bills and missed work, alienation from loved ones, and a harsh and persistent stigma, to name just a few. But even though it might seem a simplistic solution, many people dealing with mental illness have found great value in memorizing Scripture. They find that God does speak to them through His Word and that comforting words from Scripture—verses that speak of God's faithfulness and love in particular—help to calm their thinking processes, making them better able to deal with what life throws at them.

The truth is that the Bible offers all of us hope, and memorizing Bible passages can give us strength for all our day-to-day difficulties. When we mull over the truths of God's Word, we are better equipped for life.

Lord, thank You for the comfort of Your Word. Direct me
to truths in the Bible that will help me to love You better.
Amen.

Praise for Our Great God

The Lions' Den

God has said, "Never will I leave you; never will I forsake you."
(Hebrews 13:5)

Do not let Satan deceive you into being afraid of God's plans for your life. (R. A. Torrey)

When you follow God's call on your life, you might find yourself in some unfamiliar places. A seedy part of town. Onstage, speaking in front of a large group. A completely different country. You might get a little scared. And that's okay. What's important to remember is that God is always with you.

Remember Daniel in the lions' den? He was kept overnight in a sealed pit with hungry lions, but when morning came, he shouted from the bottom, "My God sent his angel, and he shut the mouths of the lions. They have not hurt me, because I was found innocent in his sight" (Daniel 6:22). You probably won't be thrown into a literal pit of lions, but you might find yourself under pressure as you serve God. Whatever happens—whether God delivers you miraculously or simply gives you strength to cope—know that He is near you, pleased with you, helping you, turning a lions' den into a sanctuary of praise.

Lord, sometimes I get scared. I feel unable to meet the challenges in front of me. Help me remember that You are working in and through me. Amen.

Overcome Grumbling with Gratitude

The LORD said to Moses, "How long will these people treat me with contempt? How long will they refuse to believe in me, in spite of all the miraculous signs I have performed among them?" (Numbers 14:11)

The careless soul receives the Father's gifts as if it were a way things had of dropping into his hand. Yet he is ever complaining, as if someone were accountable for the problems which meet him at every turn. (George MacDonald)

"That's not fair!" seems to be written into our DNA. Almost every child has loudly lodged this protest with the proper authorities, usually Mom or Dad. What's not fair? A sibling got a larger brownie. A friend got a new bike. Other kids' parents let them watch a movie forbidden to them.

After being delivered safely from captivity and given free food each morning on their journey, the Hebrew children began a pattern of grumbling, to the point that some said slavery was better than eating manna every day (Numbers 11:4–6). Apparently few things bother God as much as ungrateful grumblers. And had it not been for Moses' intercession, He would have been done with them.

There is a huge price tag on grumbling for you and everyone around you. The antidote is always gratitude.

Lord, I know that You provide so richly for me. Help me never to take Your goodness for granted. Amen.

A Prayerful Heart

Be Specific

This is the confidence we have in approaching God: that if we ask anything according to his will, he hears us. And if we know that he hears us—whatever we ask—we know that we have what we asked of him. (1 John 5:14–15)

Don't pray when you feel like it. Have an appointment with the Lord and keep it. A man is powerful on his knees. (Corrie ten Boom)

A Classic Devotion from C. H. Spurgeon

*T*here is no need for us to go beating about the bush, and not telling the Lord distinctly what it is that we crave at His hands. . . . I believe in business prayers. I mean prayers in which you take to God one of the many promises which He has given us in His Word, and expect it to be fulfilled as certainly as we look for the money to be given us when we go to the bank to cash a check. We should not think of going there, lolling over the counter chattering with the clerks on every conceivable subject except the one thing for which we had gone to the bank. . . . We needed; but we should lay before the clerk the promise to pay the bearer a certain sum, tell him in what form we wish to take the amount, count the cash after him, and then go on our way to attend to other business. That is just an illustration of the method in which we should draw supplies from the Bank of Heaven.[11]

God, thank You for the assurance that You hear my
prayers. I lay my needs before You today. Amen.

The Truce of 1914

Glory to God in the highest,
and on earth peace to men on whom his favor rests. (Luke 2:14)

To cherish peace and goodwill, to be plenteous in mercy, is to have
the real spirit of Christmas. (Calvin Coolidge)

It happened in the midst of the fiercest fighting of World War I. The story most remembered was that a German soldier began singing "Stille Nacht" and his solo soon became a chorus as he was joined by English voices singing "Silent Night." A British regiment serenaded the Germans with "The First Noel" and the Germans sang back to them "O Tannenbaum."

Men from both armies laid down their weapons and crept cautiously and then quickly into no-man's-land to share food, cigars, drinks, and even play a game of soccer together.

Funny how a song about the Savior's birth became a rallying point for peace—right in the middle of a war. But that's exactly why Christ was born: to bring "peace on earth."

Does your attitude proclaim that you are a person of peace and goodwill? Is there a person with whom you need to call a truce and be reconciled? Not just for a day but from this point forward?

Lord, thank You for coming to bring us peace. I pray that
You would fill my heart and make me a peacemaker. Amen.

His Joy and Our Joy

"I am coming to you now, but I say these things while I am still in the world, so that they may have the full measure of my joy within them." (John 17:13)

Joy is a net of love by which you can catch souls. (Mother Teresa)

A Classic Devotion from Oswald Chambers

*W*hat was the joy that Jesus had? It is an insult to use the word *happiness* in connection with Jesus Christ. The joy of Jesus was the absolute self-surrender and self-sacrifice of Himself to His Father, the joy of doing that which the Father sent Him to do. Jesus prayed that our joy might go on fulfilling itself until it was the same joy as His. Have I allowed Jesus Christ to introduce His joy to me?

The full flood of my life is not in bodily health, not in external happenings, not in seeing God's work succeed, but in the perfect understanding of God, and in the communion with Him that Jesus Himself had. Be rightly related to God, find your joy there, and out of you will flow rivers of living water. Be a centre for Jesus Christ to pour living water through. The life that is rightly related to God is as natural as breathing wherever it goes. The lives that have been of most blessing to you are those who were unconscious of it.[12]

Lord, please fill me with Your joy, and pour it into the
lives of others through me. Amen.

Too Busy to Worry

Set your minds on things above, not on earthly things. (Colossians 3:2)

It is of no use to say to men, "Let not your heart be troubled," unless you finish the verse and say, "Believe in God, believe also in Christ."
(Alexander Maclaren)

*T*he act of hope is so much more enjoyable than the act of worrying. And yet it's often so much easier to mull over our worries than to think about the hope God offers us.

An anonymous quote declares, "Blessed is the person who is too busy to worry in the daytime, and too sleepy to worry at night." Maybe if we busy our minds with meditating on the goodness of God and how we can serve Him, we'll have less mental energy to worry.

Reading the Psalms, making a list of God's works in our own lives, singing along to a favorite worship song, serving others as a volunteer—there are all kinds of ways to spend our time that cultivate faith in God's promises and keep us from brooding over what may or may not happen.

God, thank You for Your faithfulness. Help me set
my mind on You today. Amen.

God at Work

It is God who works in you to will and to act according to his good purpose. (Philippians 2:13)

The Lord doesn't promise to give us something to take so we can handle our weary moments. He promises us himself. That is all. And that is enough. (Charles Swindoll)

A father and his young son returned home after a trip to the grocery store. The son loved being with his dad and wanted to help him finish the chore. In fact, he wanted to carry the largest bag—which was much too heavy for him—inside. The father had a simple solution. He put the bag in his son's arms and then picked him up and carried both inside.

What a lovely picture of how our heavenly Father works within us. He loves our willingness to take on any assignment. But He knows what we can and cannot do in our strength. When the load is too heavy, the assignment too big, He honors our willing spirit by lifting us up and allowing us to do His work. He empowers us to accomplish more than we can in our own strength.

Do all you can—but realize it is God's power working through you that makes the difference.

Dear God, I can accomplish great things with You
working in and through me. Amen.

The Free Obedience of Christ

"The reason my Father loves me is that I lay down my life—only to take it up again. No one takes it from me, but I lay it down of my own accord." (John 10:17–18)

Obey God one step at a time, then the next step will come into view.
(Catherine Marshall)

A Classic Devotion from Robert Murray M'Cheyne

*T*here is nothing more certain than that no man can lay down his life for another. Two things that made it right in Christ to lay down His life: He is the Lord of all and the Father gave Him a commandment to lay it down. "I have power to lay it down, and I have power to take it again. This commandment have I received of my Father." He was not forced to lay His life down though men bound Him, but He laid down His life Himself. At Nazareth, they tried to cast Him over the hill on which the city was built, but He passed through the midst of them and escaped. He could have done this to the very end. When He saw them at a distance, coming down the hill with their torches, He could have fled; but He would not. The Father said, "Go into the world, and lay down your life for sinners." . . . It is true, it pleased the Lord to bruise Him, but He put Himself into the hands of divine justice.[13]

Jesus, thank You for the living example of how You lay down Your life for me. Help me to do so for others out of obedience to Your commands. Amen.

Bless My Family

But as for me and my household, we will serve the L*ord*. (Joshua 24:15)

Consider family religion not merely as a duty imposed by authority, but as your greatest privilege granted by divine grace. (Samuel Davies)

*O*ne of the greatest blessings you can give to your family is a heritage of prayer. That means your children and spouse know that you have a committed prayer life that includes them and that there are times when the whole family gathers together for prayer. Of course it's great to pray together before a meal. But in our fast-paced, media-saturated, activity-filled culture, it is difficult to get a whole family together for a meal in the first place. So you'll have to be deliberate and intentional if you want to make it a reality.

What's required is a commitment on your part to see it happen. That means first of all that you believe family prayer is important. Second, it means you won't be turned aside by distractions and obstacles. Third, it means you will have a plan. How about posting a new verse around the house each day? Before everyone gets out the door in the morning or goes to bed in the evening, you could read the verse together and say a short prayer based on it. Ask others—even young children—to pray aloud as well.

Prayer is both a personal blessing and a family blessing.

Father, I am part of Your family and enjoy all the blessings
that come from You being my Abba—Daddy. I ask for
guidance to create a climate of prayer in my family. Amen.

Joyfully Asking

*Delight yourself in the L*ORD
and he will give you the desires of your heart. (Psalm 37:4)

*They who love God with all their hearts, find that His ways are ways
of pleasantness, and all His paths are peace. Such joys, such brimful
delights, such overflowing blessednesses, do the saints discover in
their Lord.* (C. H. Spurgeon)

*I*f you're a parent, you're familiar with the innate desire to give
gifts to your children, things that will make them happy. In
fact, you may even have to check your impulse to spoil them. As
our heavenly Father, God too enjoys giving His children gifts. In
Matthew 7:11, Jesus says, "If you, then, though you are evil, know
how to give good gifts to your children, how much more will your
Father in heaven give good gifts to those who ask him!"

Of course not every prayer will be answered the way we expect
or want. God won't give us what is not in our ultimate best interest, and He won't give us what would distract us from Him. But
He does desire that we live joyfully. And that knowledge should
inspire us to pray boldly—and to rejoice that we have such a wonderful God.

Lord, please work in my heart so that I delight in You. And
thank You for the gifts You give. Amen.

A Heavy Load, Not a Burden

"Come to me, all you who are weary and burdened, and I will give you rest." (Matthew 11:28)

No one is useless in this world who lightens the burden of it for anyone else. (Charles Dickens)

After the loss of her husband, a young widow received a call from a friend who said, "I have no idea what you are feeling now, but I want you to know that even though I don't understand, I am here for you. If all I can do is listen to you cry, or even cry with you, that is what I will do." Together they cried as the woman talked about her dear husband and how much she missed him. Then they laughed and talked about the good memories they both had of him.

You might pass by or sit beside people every day—in your office, in your home, in your church—who are crushed to the core and would love to have someone just listen to them or cry with them. What a great way to lift the burdens that weigh down those around us: to be a friend who reaches out and listens.

Father, You are the burden bearer. Thank You for inviting me to cast my cares upon You. Help me to ease the burden for someone else today, God. Amen.

In the Fiery Furnace

When you walk through the fire, you will not be scorched,
Nor will the flame burn you. (Isaiah 43:2 NASB)

Faith does not operate in the realm of the possible. There is no
glory for God in that which is humanly possible. Faith begins
where man's power ends. (George Müller)

In the biblical story of Shadrach, Meshach, and Abednego, three young men abducted into Babylon during King Nebuchadnezzar's reign, we literally see grace under fire. The three young men refused to bow to any idol or serve any god other than the God of their fathers. When the king decreed that anyone who would not bow to an idol would be thrown into a furnace, Shadrach, Meshach, and Abednego stayed true to their principles. Then the king had them bound and dragged into a fiery furnace. Miraculously, the three emerged from the furnace not only unscathed but without even the smell of smoke on them.

They believed that God would rescue them from the flames. But just as important, they determined that even if He did not, they would not bow down to an idol. They had faith in God and faithfulness to Him. One tends to feed the other. Maybe you aren't facing a fiery furnace today, but you probably have your own tests of faith. If you cultivate faithfulness like Shadrach, Meshach, and Abednego's, your faith will grow. And you just might witness the impossible.

Lord, please give me such faith and confidence in You that
I will always exhibit faith under fire. Amen.

Today Is Your Day

*Then they would put their trust in God
and would not forget his deeds
but would keep his commands.*
(Psalm 78:7)

*Living in the present means squarely accepting and responding to it
as God's moment for you now while it is called "today" rather than
wishing it were yesterday or tomorrow.* (Evelyn Underhill)

A Classic Devotion from Alexander Maclaren

*M*emory and hope are meant to fit us for work in the flying moment. Both should impel us to the keeping of the commandments of God; for both yield motives which should incline us thereto. A past full of blessing demands the sacrifice of loving hearts and of earnest hands. A future so fair, so far, so certain, so sovereign, and a hope that grasps it, and brings some of its sweet fragrance into the else scentless air of the poor present, ought to impel to service, vigorous and continual. Both should yield motives which make such service a delight.[14]

Heavenly Father, I thank You for my countless blessings.
Because of all You have done for me, give me a heart to
serve others in Your name. Amen.

God's Strength

That is why, for Christ's sake, I delight in weaknesses, in insults, in hardships, in persecutions, in difficulties. For when I am weak, then I am strong. (2 Corinthians 12:10)

Feed on Christ, and then go and live your life, and it is Christ in you that lives your life, that helps the poor, that tells the truth, that fights the battle, and that wins the crown. (Phillips Brooks)

It's true that God is mighty, that He can do anything. And yet, Scripture also tells us that God often uses humble means of exercising His power. In 2 Corinthians 4:7, Paul tells us that God can use imperfect people to do His will: "We have this treasure in earthen vessels, that the excellence of the power may be of God and not of us" (NKJV). And Jesus taught us that if we want to be great, we must serve. Philippians 2:7 tells us that Jesus Himself "made Himself of no reputation, taking the form of a bondservant, and coming in the likeness of men" (NKJV).

So if you're feeling not-so-powerful or unsure of what contributions you can make, take heart. God in you is more powerful than you could ever be on your own, and He has prepared great things for you to do.

Dear Lord, thank You for working in and through me.
Thank You for Your will for me. Help me accomplish all that
You want me to do. Amen.

Praise for Our Great God

All My Songs Are Wonderful

I praise you because I am fearfully and wonderfully made;
your works are wonderful,
I know that full well.
(Psalm 139:14)

From all eternity you and I have been in the mind of God. God's love for
us is utterly reliable and has no conditions whatsoever. (Cyril Brooks)

Irving Berlin has been one of America's best-loved composers, with more than one thousand songs in his catalog. In addition to the familiar favorites "God Bless America," "Anything You Can Do I Can Do Better," and "Easter Parade," he wrote "I'm Dreaming of a White Christmas," the world's all-time best-selling musical score.

In an interview when he was in his nineties, Berlin was asked, "Is there any question that you've never been asked but that you would like to be asked?"

"Well, yes, there is one," he replied. "'What do you think of the many songs you've written that didn't become hits?' My reply would be that I still think they are wonderful."

God too has an unshakable delight in the things—and people—He has made. Whether or not they're a "hit" in the eyes of others, He thinks each of His children is wonderful!

Lord, it boggles my mind that You made me and delight in me. I pray that this knowledge would sink deep into my heart. Amen.

Keep in Step

Since we live by the Spirit, let us keep in step with the Spirit.
(Galatians 5:25)

God is God. Because He is God, He is worthy of my trust and obedience. I will find rest nowhere but in His holy will, a will that is unspeakably beyond my largest notions of what He is up to.
(Elisabeth Elliot)

What goes into living the Christian life? Many traditions of the faith have answered that question differently, but three common answers are faith, trust, and obedience.

Faith is a belief in the reality of God, the goodness and love of God, and the relationship God desires to have with us. "Now faith is being sure of what we hope for and certain of what we do not see" (Hebrews 11:1). Trust is an ongoing expression of faith; it is placing our confidence in God and depending on Him every step of the way. It is our basis for assurance that God is with us in all circumstances of life. "Though he slay me, yet will I hope in him" (Job 13:15).

Obedience is when we acknowledge that Jesus is not only our Savior but our Lord. It is the full expression of faith, where we trust God so much we submit to His commands, His ways, His will. "But if we walk in the light, as he is in the light . . . the blood of Jesus, his Son, purifies us from all sin" (1 John 1:7).

Lord, I want to keep in step with the Spirit. Give me the faith and trust to obey Your commands and will in all my steps. Amen.

Things That Corrupt

*Be self-controlled and alert. Your enemy the devil prowls around like
a roaring lion looking for someone to devour.* (1 Peter 5:8)

Keep your thoughts right, for as you think, so are you.
(Henry H. Buckley)

A Classic Devotion from Richard Baxter

*B*e thoroughly acquainted with your temptations and the
things that may corrupt you—and watch against them all
day long. You should watch especially the most dangerous of the
things that corrupt, and those temptations that either your company or business will unavoidably lay before you.

Watch against the master sins of unbelief: hypocrisy, selfishness, pride, flesh pleasing, and the excessive love of earthly
things. Take care against being drawn into earthly mindedness
and excessive cares, or covetous designs for rising in the world,
under the pretence of diligence in your calling.

At first these things will be very difficult, while sin has any
strength in you, but once you have grasped a continual awareness
of the poisonous danger of any one of these sins, your heart will
readily and easily avoid them.[15]

Lord, temptations surround me all day. Give me strength
to direct my attention to You and Your Word in order to
avoid temptation. Amen.

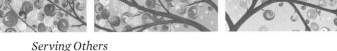

New Shoes

As a father has compassion on his children,
so the Lord has compassion on those who fear him. (Psalm 103:13)

God's goodness is the root of all goodness; and our goodness, if we
have any, springs out of His goodness. (William Tyndale)

In New York City during the Depression years, a little boy of ten was standing before a shoe store, barefoot, peering through the window and shivering with cold. A lady approached the boy and said, "My little fellow, why are you looking so earnestly in that window?"

"I was asking God to give me a pair of shoes," was his answer.

The lady took the boy by the hand and went into the store. After washing and drying his feet, she tucked them into a pair of socks and bought him a pair of shoes. As she turned to go, the incredulous boy caught her by the hand, and looking up at her with tears in his eyes, he asked, "Are you God's wife?"

No question, life is hard. But sometimes we lose sight of the truth that God is good, that it is in His nature to give. We can experience His goodness by thanking Him for it and by reflecting His giving nature to others.

God, You have made my life so good. Help me to bring
some of Your goodness into the lives of others. Amen.

The Secret to True Wealth

*But may the righteous be glad
and rejoice before God;
may they be happy and joyful.*
(Psalm 68:3)

You say, "If I had a little more, I should be very satisfied." You make a mistake. If you are not content with what you have, you would not be satisfied if it were doubled. (C. H. Spurgeon)

A man lives in a mansion in a zip code known for wealth, his garage filled with expensive automobiles. And yet he lives in poverty, for he is miserable—a word that shares its origin with the word *miser*. Never satisfied, nothing seems to make him happy.

Contrast him with the man who works hard every day and barely makes ends meet, despite living in a small, tidy home in a neighborhood that has seen better days and driving a car that is anything but flashy. But he is wealthy. Life is good. He wishes some business decisions had turned out better, but he has a roof over his head and his family is fed and happy.

How can the man with so much be poor and the man with so little be rich? The difference is simple. One man is grateful for nothing. The other sees blessings everywhere. What is the secret to wealth that can never be taken away? Gratitude.

God, help me to see the wealth around me. Help me find my satisfaction in Your love and provision, not in earthly wealth. Amen.

Keep Going

The LORD our God said to us at Horeb, "You have stayed long enough at this mountain. Break camp and advance into the hill country of the Amorites." (Deuteronomy 1:6–7)

Keep adding, keep walking, keep advancing; do not stop, do not turn back, do not turn from the straight road. (Saint Augustine)

A Classic Devotion from A. W. Tozer

*W*hen our Lord said, "One of you will betray Me," thank God those disciples had enough spirituality that nobody said, "Lord, is it he?" Instead, every one of them said, "Lord, is it I?" . . . Self-righteousness is terrible among God's people. If we feel that we are what we ought to be, then we will remain what we are. We will not look for any change or improvement in our lives. This will quite naturally lead us to judge everyone by what we are. This is the judgment of which we must be careful. To judge others by ourselves is to create havoc in the local assembly.

I hear the voice of Jesus saying to us, "You have stayed long enough where you are. Break camp and advance into the hill country." This would be a new spiritual experience that God has for us.[16]

Lord, I don't want to stay where I am. Give me the courage and humility to see myself clearly, and thank You for Your unconditional love. Amen.

A Bold Move

Let us run with perseverance the race marked out for us. (Hebrews 12:1)

Why wilt thou defer thy good purpose from day to day? Arise, and begin in this very instant, and say, "Now is the time to be doing; now is the time to be striving; now is the fit time to amend myself." Unless thou dost earnestly force thyself, thou shalt never get the victory over sin. (Thomas à Kempis)

The easiest step and the hardest step is the first step.

What's keeping you from getting started? Why are you wallowing in a self-destructive attitude or habit that deep down you want to be rid of?

- Someone you won't forgive
- A temptation you run toward rather than away from
- An area of your life that is weak and needs strengthening
- A sin from your past that needs restitution

Is it laziness? Is it procrastination? Is it stubborn pride? Is it a sense of defeat before you even start?

Today is your day. It won't be easy. But you can succeed, with God's help. Take the first step.

Lord, I've lived with defeat too long. Please help me make the move, the first step toward recovery and new life. Amen.

Pass It On

*These commandments that I give you today are to be upon your
hearts. Impress them on your children. Talk about them when you sit
at home and when you walk along the road, when you lie down and
when you get up.* (Deuteronomy 6:6–7)

*Your top-priority job as a parent, then, is to be an evangelist in your
home. You need to teach your children the law of God; teach them the
gospel of divine grace; show them their need for a Savior; and point them
to Jesus Christ as the only One who can save them.* (John MacArthur)

King David knew the importance of God's Word for his personal life. He said, "I have hidden your word in my heart that I might not sin against you" (Psalm 119:11). But he was also committed to passing on a love and reverence for God's Word to the next generation. According to his son Solomon, David said to him, "My son, pay attention to what I say; listen closely to my words. Do not let them out of your sight, keep them within your heart; for they are life to those who find them and health to a man's whole body" (Proverbs 4:20–22).

Do you share God's Word with your children? If they are still in the home, do you take them to church and Bible class? Do you ever sit down and read aloud from a Bible storybook or a Bible passage? One of the greatest privileges and responsibilities of parenting is to pass on our faith to the next generation.

Father, help me to share with children a love for Your Word
that will guide their steps all of their days. Amen.

One Man's Faith

*Do not let this Book of the Law depart from your mouth; meditate on
it day and night, so that you may be careful to do everything written
in it. Then you will be prosperous and successful.* (Joshua 1:8)

*When led of the Spirit, the child of God must be as ready to wait as to
go, as prepared to be silent as to speak.* (Lewis Sperry Chafer)

*I*n Exodus 14 we read that God commanded the children of
Israel to turn on their journey toward the south, which would
cause Pharaoh to think that they had lost their way in confusion
and would be easy to overtake. As Pharaoh gathered his army of
many men and rushed to catch up with the newly freed slaves, the
Israelites grew fearful. But Moses obeyed God and stretched his
hand over the sea, and it parted for the Israelites to cross to safety.

It's a familiar story, one with many life applications. It tells us
of God's might in our weakness and His provision for His people.
It also shows how a generation of people can be affected by one
person's obedience to God. How can you help steer your generation into a bright future?

Lord, I want to be obedient to You in all things, to gain
blessings not just for myself but for others. Show me how I
can faithfully follow You today. Amen.

When You Have No Words

We do not know what we ought to pray for, but the Spirit himself intercedes for us with groans that words cannot express. (Romans 8:26)

For the Holy Spirit is prayer's great Helper. We are incapable of ourselves to translate our real needs into prayer. The Holy Spirit does this for us. (author unknown)

There's good news when we just don't seem to have the words to pray. First, we are told that Jesus Christ is at the right side of God, interceding for us. It's always great to have someone put in a good word for us, but think about it: right now, Jesus is doing just that for us. For you. What better reference could we have? Second, the Holy Spirit helps us as well. Paul tells us, "He who searches our hearts knows the mind of the Spirit, because the Spirit intercedes for the saints in accordance with God's will" (Romans 8:27).

Is there a problem in your life for which you can no longer come up with words to pray? Do you feel a heaviness of heart and just can't muster the words to express what you're feeling? Maybe it's okay to just sit quietly and depend on the Holy Spirit to do your praying for you, to tell the Father what you can't quite say yourself.

God, You know my heart and thoughts before I can
even form the words in my mind. Thank You for
listening to the deepest parts of my life, even when I
can't get the words out. Amen.

A Debt of Gratitude

*How can we thank God enough for you in return for all the joy we have
in the presence of our God because of you?* (1 Thessalonians 3:9)

*There is as much greatness of mind in acknowledging a
good turn, as in doing it.* (Seneca)

Years ago a wealthy English family was entertaining friends
at their home. As the children swam, one ventured into the
deep water and began to drown. The gardener heard the other
children screaming, jumped into the water, and saved the child.
That youngster was none other than Winston Churchill. Deeply
grateful to the gardener, when the Churchills learned that he
wished his son to go to medical school, they vowed to pay his way.

Years later when Sir Winston was prime minister, he became
ill with pneumonia. The best physician the king could find
was called to the bedside of the ailing leader. His name was Sir
Alexander Fleming, the developer of penicillin—and the son of
that gardener who long ago saved his life. Churchill later said,
"Rarely has a man owed his life twice to the same person."

Gratitude is a wonder. It not only improves our attitudes but
also has a way of bringing rewards later down the line. Never miss
an opportunity to give thanks.

Father, I want to show thanks to the people in my life who
help me. Please nurture my relationships. Amen.

A Prayer for Peace

The mind controlled by the Spirit is life and peace. (Romans 8:6)

First keep the peace within yourself, then you can also bring peace to others. (Thomas à Kempis)

A Classic Devotion from Reinhold Niebuhr

God grant me the serenity
to accept the things I cannot change;
courage to change the things I can;
and wisdom to know the difference.
Living one day at a time;
enjoying one moment at a time;
accepting hardships as the pathway to peace;
taking, as He did, this sinful world
as it is, not as I would have it;
trusting that He will make all things right
if I surrender to His Will;
that I may be reasonably happy in this life
and supremely happy with Him
forever in the next.
Amen.

Lord, I want to live in Your presence at all times, finding my peace in You. Teach me to live the way You want me to. Amen.

True Happiness

Is not the L$_{ORD}$ your God with you? And has he not granted you rest
on every side? . . . Now devote your heart and soul to seeking the
L$_{ORD}$ your God. (1 Chronicles 22:18–19)

A life of obedience is not a life of following a list of dos and don'ts, but
it is allowing God to be original in our lives. (Vonette Z. Bright)

A Classic Devotion from J. C. Ryle

*I*t may be you are struggling hard for the rewards of this world. Perhaps you are straining every nerve to obtain money, or place, or power, or pleasure. If that be your case, take care. You are sowing a crop of bitter disappointment.

Thousands have trodden the path you are pursuing, and have awoke too late to find it end in misery and eternal ruin. They have fought hard for wealth, and honour, and office, and promotion, and turned their backs on God, and Christ, and heaven, and the world to come. And what has their end been? Often, far too often, they have found out that their whole life has been a grand mistake.

For your own happiness' sake resolve this day to join the Lord's side. Shake off your past carelessness and unbelief. Come out from the ways of a thoughtless, unreasoning world. Take up the cross, and become a good soldier of Christ. Fight the good fight of faith, that you may be happy as well as safe.[17]

Lord, give me strength and wisdom to turn to You in all
things and make You my only goal. Amen.

A Peek at What We Hope For

But the needy will not always be forgotten,
nor the hope of the afflicted ever perish.
(Psalm 9:18)

The best we can hope for in this life is a knothole peek at the shining
realities ahead. Yet a glimpse is enough. It's enough to convince our
hearts that whatever sufferings and sorrows currently assail us
aren't worthy of comparison to that which waits over the horizon.
(Joni Eareckson Tada)

Joni Eareckson Tada is one who understands the real meaning of hope when everything looks hopeless. She was an active young woman on a swimming trip with her sister and friends when she was injured diving into water she didn't know was shallow. The injury to her spinal column left her paralyzed and wheelchair bound for life.

Her story of tragedy and hope as described in her book, simply titled *Joni*, has helped hundreds of thousands to look upward for a glimpse of hope that is to come. Her story has inspired many to look for that "knothole peek" of hope that we find in the living Christ, no matter how challenging our circumstances. He does not allow suffering without hope.

Lord, thank You for sustaining me even in the most difficult
and painful circumstances. Teach me to look to You for
hope for the future. Amen.

A Loving Touch

Filled with compassion, Jesus reached out his hand and touched the man. (Mark 1:41)

Our God is not made of stone. His heart is the most sensitive and tender of all. No act goes unnoticed, no matter how insignificant or small. (Richard J. Foster)

For many of us, God is more an idea, a principle, a concept, a distant thought than He is a Person. A real, live, feeling Person. No wonder we forget that God loves us not in principle—but with feeling! Think back to childhood, to climbing up on your father's lap and experiencing the strength and warmth of his arms. Even if that wasn't your exact experience, you get the picture. How lovely to know that our heavenly Father cares that much.

There are many stories throughout the Gospels about people being touched by the Lord: Jesus feeding the five thousand and calming the storm; Jesus healing a boy who was paralyzed; Jesus raising Jairus's daughter from her deathbed; and Jesus healing the blind man are just a few. And He continues to touch His children and make a difference in their lives today.

Lord Jesus, thank You for being available to me and for loving me in so many practical ways. I love You. Amen.

Led by the Spirit

Paul and his companions traveled throughout the region of Phrygia and Galatia, having been kept by the Holy Spirit from preaching the word in the province of Asia. (Acts 16:6)

The teacher of teachers gives his guidance noiselessly. I have never heard him speak, and yet I know that he is within me. (Saint Thérèse of Lisieux)

*D*on't know where God wants you to serve? Just ask Him to show you and then keep your eyes open to the opportunities all around you. Many will come as a complete surprise:

- A missed flight connection puts you in a seat next to someone dealing with spiritual issues.
- A wrong turn takes you by an outreach center you had never heard of.
- A waitress opens up and shares some difficulties she is experiencing.
- A conflict with a neighbor becomes the open door for a new relationship.

Paul had plans to minister in Bithynia. God had plans for him to minister in Macedonia—and introduce the good news to a whole new continent (Acts 16:6–10). He was led by the Spirit. And the same Spirit of God will lead you too.

God, thank You for giving Your Spirit to guide and direct my steps and work. Amen.

A Prayerful Heart

Right Motives

When you ask, you do not receive, because you ask with wrong motives,
that you may spend what you get on your pleasures. (James 4:3)

Prayer does not change God; it changes me. (C. S. Lewis)

No other biblical writer is more pragmatic and in-your-face than James. In his letter, he puts great emphasis on faith in action. Does this mean he was a legalist who didn't believe in salvation as a gift? Was he calling for us to base our relationship with God on our good works? Not at all. He simply believed that the person who has experienced God's grace will show it in his or her daily walk.

On the topic of prayer, James extols the power of prayer—"The prayer of a righteous man is powerful and effective" (5:16)—but he also challenges us to check our motives. Is your prayer focused on an easy life or on doing great things for God? Never stop taking your needs before God, but do pause and check your heart from time to time.

God, make my prayer life a powerful force to do great
things for You and the building of Your kingdom. Amen.

Beautiful Music to Share

Let your light shine before men, that they may see your good deeds and praise your Father in heaven. (Matthew 5:16)

If we want to keep our faith, we must share it. (Billy Graham)

Concert violinist Fritz Kreisler earned a fortune with his concerts and compositions, but he generously gave most of it away. So when he discovered an exquisite violin on one of his trips, he wasn't able to buy it. Later, having raised enough money to meet the asking price, he returned to the seller. But to his great dismay, it had been sold to a collector. Kreisler made his way to the new owner's home and offered to buy the violin, but the collector would not sell it.

"Could I play the instrument once more before it is consigned to silence?" Kreisler asked. Permission was granted, and the great virtuoso filled the room with such moving music that the collector exclaimed, "I have no right to keep that to myself. It's yours, Mr. Kreisler. Take it into the world, and let people hear it."

We are to take the gospel, the Word of God, to the masses and not lock it away in silence. Sharing the good news and proclaiming the truths of the Bible is the work not only of overseas missionaries but also of every believer.

Lord, it amazes me that You have entrusted me with sharing the gospel message with the world. Give me diligence to follow Your calling. Amen.

The Future Is Bright

No eye has seen,
no ear has heard,
no mind has conceived
what God has prepared for those who love him.
(1 Corinthians 2:9)

The future is as bright as the promises of God. (Adoniram Judson)

No one knows the future. Oh, some economists are better than others at predicting tomorrow's economic conditions; some technology experts are better at predicting what tools we will be using in the days to come; some sociologists are better at predicting societal changes and shifts that are ahead. But no one knows the future.

Except God. He knows the plans He has for you, some of which are greater and more exciting than you can imagine.

Yes, we should plan appropriately for the future. But we aren't to think about the future with fear and anxiety.

What lies ahead? You already know the answer. With an open and obedient heart, you can expect great works and great moments that God has planned specially, just for you!

Dear God, thank You for Your promise of a bright,
meaningful, and surprising future. Amen.

Worst-Case Scenario

So he said to them, "Why are you afraid, O you of little faith?"
After he got up, he rebuked the winds and the sea, and there was a
great calm. (Matthew 8:26 ESV)

The saints in heaven are happier but no more secure than are true
believers here in this world. (Loraine Boettner)

*M*any of Jesus' disciples were fishermen, and they knew from experience that the Sea of Galilee was notorious for its sudden storms. The squall recorded in Matthew 8:23–27 was especially furious. As the high winds whipped the sea into vicious waves, the disciples grew frightened and frantic.

While all this was happening, Jesus was sleeping calmly in the back of the boat. The disciples woke Him because they were certain they were about to drown! Jesus was calm and told the storm to be still. And it obeyed Him. He then looked at His disciples and asked why they had such little faith!

What did Jesus know that they didn't know? Ultimately, He understood the true worst-case scenario in life is death without an eternity with God. He also knew that His work on the cross would deliver us from that worst-case scenario. No wonder He was at peace. And that's exactly how we can experience peace in the midst of storms.

Lord, I pray that the knowledge of Your eternal love and
protection will so pervade my heart that I can walk through
life's storms with confidence in You. Amen.

A Beautiful Perseverance

So we fix our eyes not on what is seen, but on what is unseen.
For what is seen is temporary, but what is unseen is eternal.
(2 Corinthians 4:18)

By perseverance the snail reached the ark. (C. H. Spurgeon)

A woman planted a rare rosebush, fussed over it, fertilized it, watered it, and was incredibly disappointed when she saw no reward of her labors. The rose bush simply wouldn't grow.

Then one day she visited her neighbor and discovered that shoots from this bush had pushed through to the other side of the fence and were blooming in splendid beauty there. She thought of some recent disappointments in her prayer life and realized that faith in God is much like her rose bush. You can't always see the results of what God is doing in your life, but if you have patience and perseverance, you will discover that He was creating something beautiful all along.

Hope requires perseverance. The rewards found inside us and that await us in heaven are worth any struggles we face here on earth.

God, thank You for giving me so much to look forward to.
Please strengthen my spirit and help me persevere. Amen.

On Top of the World

Every good and perfect gift is from above, coming down from the Father of the heavenly lights, who does not change like shifting shadows. (James 1:17)

His command is the sure guarantee that He will give what He desires us to possess. (Andrew Murray)

*T*he highest peak in the country of Wales is affectionately called "the Top of the World." On a visit one summer, the wind blew and the clouds billowed, and all around as far as the eye could see were white spots—sheep dotting every pasture all the way to the lowest valley below. It was a breathtaking sight. No one on earth could create such a scene, not even the best set designer in all of Hollywood. Nothing compares to the intensity and exhilaration we feel when we are actually on top of a mountain.

We will experience mountaintop highs in life—and we will walk through some deep valleys as well. We can't always experience life on top of the world, but the mountaintop moments God grants us—spiritually and through the splendor of His world—will give us reminders of His love when we walk the inevitable valleys.

Take time to remember some of those special moments God has brought into your life and be ready to face anything with optimism, hope, and confidence!

Father, help me to lean on You whether I'm on top of the world or walking through a valley. Amen.

A Sure Foundation

"Therefore everyone who hears these words of Mine and acts on them, may be compared to a wise man who built his house on the rock." (Matthew 7:24 NASB)

When you have read the Bible, you will know it is the word of God, because you will have found it the key to your own heart, your own happiness and your duty. (Woodrow Wilson)

When the late Queen Victoria was asked the secret of England's greatness, she took down a copy of the Scriptures, and pointing to the Bible, she said, "That Book explains the power of Great Britain." Daniel Webster once affirmed, "If we abide by the principles taught in the Bible, our country will go on prospering and to prosper." These great leaders truly believed that the only sure foundation of a nation's belief and practice was God's Word.

There are plenty of wise books on history's shelf, some of which offer unintentional wisdom and examples of what not to do. But the wisdom of the Bible teaches us not only how to order our earthly lives for maximum gains but also how to align our hearts and spirit with the almighty God. And that's wisdom of eternal value.

The words of God are truly a firm foundation for nations—and for our lives.

Thank You, God for the solid foundation of Your Word. Help me to know it well enough to build my life upon it. Amen.

Listen with Your Legs

Whether you turn to the right or to the left, your ears will hear a voice behind you, saying, "This is the way; walk in it." (Isaiah 30:21)

In many ways, the attitude of obedience is much more vital than the act, because if the attitude is right, the act will naturally follow.
(John MacArthur)

Four-year-old Beverly was playing with her toys. Her mother, who was folding laundry across the room, noticed that Beverly's shirt was dirty and needed to be changed. She told Beverly to take it off and bring it to her so that she could wash it.

After telling her twice with no response, her mother finally gave her the full three-name call: "Beverly Elizabeth Provost, did you hear me?" Beverly answered, "Yes, Mama. My ears did, but my legs didn't."

Sometimes we don't hear God's directions because we're simply too busy; we're not listening with our whole being. What is God calling you to do today? Are you ready to listen with your legs as well as your ears?

Dear God, help me to be still and listen to You so that I know what You want me to do. Amen.

Thankful Service

He touched her hand and the fever left her, and she got up and began to wait on him. (Matthew 8:15)

We should spend as much time in thanking God for His benefits as we do asking Him for them. (Saint Vincent de Paul)

A Classic Devotion from John Henry Jowett

*M*ay we not with advantage accept the suggestion which is contained in these words? The fever-stricken woman was healed by the Saviour; and then, when she was delivered from her fever, "She arose and ministered unto Him." She had been lifted out of sickness into sanity, out of aches and pains into peace, out of feverishness into comfort, out of unrest into a healthy calm, and now she uses her restored strength to minister to her Saviour. It is ever the way of the healed and invincible life. We shall best preserve our health by serving our Lord. As to what that service shall be, He has given us a broad and spacious conception in His own Word. "I was an hungred, and ye gave Me meat." "Lord, when saw we Thee an hungred?" When did we minister unto Thee? "Inasmuch as ye did it unto one of the least of these, ye did it unto Me."[18]

Lord, You have done so much for me. I want to serve You each day out of gratitude. Amen.

Listening Hard for God

"Call to me and I will answer you and tell you great and unsearchable things you do not know." (Jeremiah 33:3)

Surrender your mind to the Lord at the beginning of each day.
(Warren Wiersbe)

A Classic Devotion from G. P. Pardington

*W*aiting upon God is necessary in order to see Him, to have a vision of Him. The time element in vision is essential. Our hearts are like a sensitive photographer's plate; and in order to have God revealed there, we must sit at His feet a long time. The troubled surface of a lake will not reflect an object.

Our lives must be quiet and restful if we would see God. There is power in the sight of some things to affect one's life. A quiet sunset will bring peace to a troubled heart. Thus the vision of God always transforms human life.[19]

Lord, teach me to be still before You and listen
for Your voice. Amen.

Hold Yourself Accountable

*Great peace have they who love your law,
and nothing can make them stumble.*
(Psalm 119:165)

*Do with your hearts as you do with your watches, wind them up
every morning by prayer, and at night examine whether your hearts
have gone true all that day, whether the wheels of your affections
have moved swiftly towards heaven. Oh, call yourselves to account!
Keep your reckonings even, for that is the way to keep your peace.*
(Thomas Watson)

When you think of experiencing peace in your life, you probably don't think of words like *discipline* and *accountability*. But think again. When you lack discipline in your life, when you don't hold yourself accountable, what results? Usually chaos and problems. In other words, the opposite characteristics of peace.

If you want to experience peace in all its forms, it always begins with God's grace. But on that foundation, God has laid out a framework of plans and decisions within which we can live according to His will. They always require effort in the form of discipline and accountability. But what sounds like it could be a burden becomes a source of great satisfaction and reward.

Heavenly Father, help me to walk in Your will and ways
each step of my life. Amen.

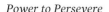

A Joy No One Can Steal

"Now is your time of grief, but I will see you again and you will rejoice, and no one will take away your joy." (John 16:22)

God made you. He knows how you operate best. And He knows what makes you happy. The happiness He gives doesn't stop when the party's over. It lasts because it comes from deep within. (John MacArthur)

Even with the most expensive and sophisticated security system in the world, you can never make your home fail-safe from burglars. But there is something you have that can't be stolen from you. You don't even have to hide it but can keep it right out in the open. It's your joy in Christ.

Oh, there are some who will try to rob it from you by using hurtful words or slighting you in some other way. But they do not have the power to seize it. You can decide to let them take it—but that's your choice, not their cunning.

There are some people who are so committed to killing joy wherever it is found that we might be wiser just to steer clear of them. But even in circumstances where there is no escape from the thief who wants to rob joy so that gloom can take root, you can still keep your joy by simply putting your eyes on the author and giver of joy, Jesus Christ.

Dear God, Your gift of joy makes life wonderful. Help me experience it and share it, no matter who would try to bring depression and gloom to my life and world. Amen.

The Promise of Peace

If it is possible, as much as depends on you, live peaceably with all men. (Romans 12:18 NKJV)

Anger is an acid that can do more harm to the vessel in which it stands than to anything on which it is poured. (author unknown)

Jesus' own life was anything but peaceful. He was born in a stable after Mary and Joseph's arduous journey. His family was forced to flee to Egypt when he was an infant because a madman was murdering baby boys. His father died. He became the most celebrated teacher of His country, drawing the wrath of the religious and political establishment. Ultimately, He died on the cross.

But Jesus brought peace: between God and man, peace between estranged family members, and even peace between enemies.

Why don't we see more evidence of it? As long as humans have the freedom to live for or against God, we will not see peace in full bloom. But the seed is planted. Sprigs and shoots can be seen in the most unlikely places. It is the promise of what is to fully be!

God of peace, thank You for sending the Prince of Peace to bring hope and promise to the world. Amen.

The Right Path

*Trust in the Lord with all your heart
and lean not on your own understanding.*
(Proverbs 3:5)

*Trust the past to God's mercy, the present to God's love, and the
future to God's providence.* (Saint Augustine)

We rightfully teach our children—and attempt to live our own lives—by the credos of responsibility, self-control, and mature self-reliance. And yes, being responsible is a very good thing. But when our attitude reaches the point where we trust more in ourselves than in God, twin temptations suddenly confront us, both leading to spiritual shipwreck.

One temptation is pride, an unhealthy arrogance that slips (or roars) into our thinking when things are going great in our lives. We become convinced that we are in control of our own world. The second temptation, despair, works itself into our hearts when we face the inevitable difficulties and setbacks of life that are outside of our control.

Daily trusting in God—acknowledging that He is the one source of all good gifts and success and the only safe refuge when life is difficult—steers us from these twin dangers. When we trust Him, He directs our steps in the most fulfilling paths for our lives.

God, I know that You are in control. Help me trust in You
day by day, moment by moment. Amen.

The Wrong Kind of Pride

When pride comes, then comes disgrace,
but with humility comes wisdom.
(Proverbs 11:2)

If you are humble, nothing will touch you, neither praise nor
disgrace, because you know what you are. (Mother Teresa)

The sin of pride can be hard to define. Arrogance can be part of it, yes; but it's possible to have both pride and poor self-image at work in one's life at the same time. God doesn't want us to lack self-respect either. Maybe it's best simply to be ever aware that all of us are vulnerable to vain pride and that it can find us at any time, anywhere.

Pride says, "I can do what I want," "I'm better than others," and "I'm looking out for number one." Above all, pride says, "I don't need God or anyone—I can make it on my own." But of course we do need God. And when we resist surrendering to Him, depending on Him, we experience damage to our souls.

Fortunately, we can resist our pride by simply praying and asking God to heal us from a prideful attitude and help us think rightly about ourselves, God, and others. When that happens, we can rest content in God's will and at peace with ourselves and those around us.

Lord, please heal me of a vain pride and set me in right
relationship with You. Amen.

Heeding God's Call

"The harvest is plentiful, but the workers are few. Ask the Lord of the harvest, therefore, to send out workers into his harvest field. Go! I am sending you out like lambs among wolves." (Luke 10:2–3)

God always gives us strength enough, and sense enough, for everything He wants us to do. (John Ruskin)

A Classic Devotion from William Booth

A young Christian once came to me, and told me that for some time she had been giving the Lord her profession and prayers and money, but now she wanted to give Him her life. She wanted to go right into the fight. In other words, she wanted to go to His assistance in the sea. As when a man from the shore, seeing another struggling in the water, takes off those outer garments that would hinder his efforts and leaps to the rescue, so will you who still linger on the bank, thinking and singing and praying about the poor perishing souls, rush to the rescue of this multitude of dying men and women.

Does the surging sea look dark and dangerous? Unquestionably it is so. He who beckons you from the sea however, knows what it will mean, and knowing, He still calls to you and bids to you to come. You must do it! You cannot hold back.[20]

Lord, I ask You to show me my path and strengthen my resolve to serve You with my whole being. Amen.

Patiently Waiting

Guide me in your truth and teach me,
for you are God my Savior,
and my hope is in you all day long.
(Psalm 25:5)

How we spend our days is, of course, how we spend our lives. (Annie Dillard)

Waiting is difficult—crawling behind a car that is going well below the speed limit in a no-passing zone, tapping your foot in line at the coffee shop, anxiously waiting for the mailman so you can get your hands on that check that was promised weeks ago, and, of course, trying to keep a great attitude in church on the very Sunday that you planned to meet friends for lunch at 12:30 and your pastor decides to go overtime. Maybe the toughest waiting is when we ask God for direction on an important life decision.

No, waiting is not easy, but God tells us to wait patiently for Him: His choices, His answers, His news, His guidance, His perfect spouse for us, His desire for our vocation, His love, and yes, even His coming again. Waiting patiently means trusting that God knows what is best for us because we are His children. When we acknowledge Him in all our decisions, we truly begin to walk in wisdom.

Dear God, help me to overcome the temptation of impatience. Help me to trust You with the choices and decisions of my life because You know what is best. Amen.

First Things First

"Seek first his kingdom and his righteousness, and all these things will be given to you as well." (Matthew 6:33)

When you put God first, you are establishing order for everything else in your life. (Andrea Garney)

A Classic Devotion from Oswald Chambers

*I*mmediately we look at these words of Jesus, we find them the most revolutionary statement human ears ever listened to. "Seek ye first the kingdom of God." We argue in exactly the opposite way, even the most spiritually-minded of us—"But I must live; I must make so much money; I must be clothed; I must be fed." The great concern of our lives is not the kingdom of God, but how we are to fit ourselves to live. Jesus reverses the order: Get rightly related to God first, maintain that as the great care of your life, and never put the concern of your care on the other things.

Jesus is not saying that the man who takes thought for nothing is blessed—that man is a fool. Jesus taught that a disciple has to make his relationship to God the dominating concentration of his life, and to be carefully careless about everything else in comparison to that. It is one of the severest disciplines of the Christian life to allow the Holy Spirit to bring us into harmony with the teaching of Jesus in these verses.[21]

Lord, I want to reorder my thoughts today and preoccupy myself with knowing and following You. Amen.

To the End

God is not unjust; he will not forget your work and the love you have shown him as you have helped his people and continue to help them. We want each of you to show this same diligence to the very end, in order to make your hope sure. (Hebrews 6:10–11)

Consider the postage stamp: its usefulness consists in the ability to stick to one thing till it gets there. (Josh Billings)

*Y*ou haven't run a marathon until you cross the finish line 26.2 miles from the start. You haven't really read a new novel until you turn the last page. You aren't actually married until you exchange vows and the minister declares you husband and wife.

Throughout the Bible, one of the key themes is finishing strong. Paul ran the race of life to win—even though it meant martyrdom. He was not alone. Of the original apostles, only John died of natural causes. But even he was exiled because of his faith.

Are you as good at finishing as you are at starting? Not every endeavor we start requires our follow-through. Some things don't matter that much. But faith is not one of them.

We may never face physical persecution for our Lord's sake, but each one of us has been called to walk with God, not just for a season, but for all our days. Look to God for hope and strength on your spiritual journey.

Lord, help me to stand firm till the end. Please give me strength to stand up for You until the end of my days. Amen.

Pass It On

Teach me to do your will,
for you are my God;
may your good Spirit
lead me on level ground.
(Psalm 143:10)

If we have the true love of God in our hearts, we will show
it in our lives. (D. L. Moody)

A Classic Devotion from A. B. Simpson

Give out the blessing that you have, start larger plans for service and blessing, and you will soon find that the Holy Ghost is before you, and He will present you with blessings for service, and give you all that He can trust you to give away to others. . . .

There is no music so heavenly as an Aeolian harp, and the Aeolian harp is nothing but a set of musical chords arranged in harmony, and then left to be touched by the unseen fingers of the wandering winds. And as the breath of heaven floats over the chords, it is said that notes almost Divine float out upon the air, as if a choir of angels were wandering around and touching the strings.

And so it is possible to keep our hearts so open to the touch of the Holy Spirit that He can play upon them at will, as we quietly wait in the pathway of His service.[22]

Lord, I want to be used by You to bless others. Help me
attune myself to Your song today. Amen.

Joy Multiplied

But thanks be to God, who always leads us in triumphal procession in Christ and through us spreads everywhere the fragrance of the knowledge of him. (2 Corinthians 2:14)

It is no use walking anywhere to preach unless we preach as we walk.
(Saint Francis of Assisi)

A Classic Devotion from F. B. Meyer

*O*urs must be the joy of the Lord. It begins with the assurance of forgiveness and acceptance in the Beloved. It is nourished in trial and tribulation, which veil outward sources of consolation, and lead us to rejoice in God through our Lord Jesus. It is independent of circumstances, so that its possessors can sing in the stocks. It lives not in the gifts of God, but in God Himself. It is the fruit of the Spirit, who begets in us love, joy, peace, long-suffering. Get the Lord Himself to fill your soul, and joy will be as natural as the murmur of a brook to its flow.

And such joy will always reveal itself to others. You will desire to send portions to those for whom nothing is prepared. Your joy will be contagious; it will shed its kindly light on sad and weary hearts.[23]

Father in heaven, help me to show a joy that is irresistible and contagious to those around me. Thank You for placing that joy in my heart. Amen.

A Good Listener

The eyes of the LORD are on the righteous
and his ears are attentive to their cry.
(Psalm 34:15)

All who call on God in true faith, earnestly from the heart, will
certainly be heard and will receive what they have asked and desired.
(Martin Luther)

A seventh-grade teacher asked her students what action by their peers upset them most. One girl said that she hated to be talking to someone and have them walk away as if she was not there. Adults have learned at least to appear more polite and don't just walk off in midsentence. But we all know it doesn't feel good when someone subtly or obviously tunes us out. The feeling that someone is listening is encouraging; feeling ignored brings a distinct sting.

When we pray, God never turns away before we're finished. He is always watching out for us. We always have His attention. Since we know God listens to us, our prayer lives are enriched when we learn to be still and listen to Him.

Lord, thank You for Your ever-present attention
and care. Help me to direct my attention to You
throughout the day. Amen.

The Ant and the Dove

Make sure that nobody pays back wrong for wrong, but always try to be kind to each other and to everyone else. (1 Thessalonians 5:15)

Be thankful for the smallest blessing, and you will deserve to receive greater. Value the least gifts no less than the greatest and simple graces as especial favors. If you remember the dignity of the Giver, no gift will seem small or mean, for nothing can be valueless that is given by the Most High God. (Thomas à Kempis)

*I*n one of Aesop's Fables, an ant went to the bank of a river to drink, fell into the stream, and found itself on the brink of drowning. A dove sitting on a tree overhanging the water plucked a leaf and let it fall into the stream close to the drowning ant. The ant climbed onto it and floated in safety to the bank. Shortly afterward, a bird catcher came and stood under the tree and began laying a trap for the dove. The ant, seeing his intent, seized the opportunity to sting him in the foot. In pain, the bird catcher threw down the trap, and the noise alerted the dove to fly away.

It is wonderful to be blessed by random acts of kindness. It's even more wonderful when we can return the favor. Who has helped you get by? Is there a way you can show them your gratitude?

Lord, thank You for the people who have helped me in life.
Show me how I can be a blessing to others today. Amen.

Praise for God's Goodness

But you are a chosen people, a royal priesthood, a holy nation, a people belonging to God, that you may declare the praises of him who called you out of darkness into his wonderful light. (1 Peter 2:9)

Jesus loves us with fidelity, purity, constancy, and passion, no matter how imperfect we are. (Stormie Omartian)

A Classic Devotion from Adam Clarke

*A*s there is no end to the merits of Christ incarnated and crucified; no bounds to the mercy and love of God; no hindrance to the almighty energy and sanctifying influence of the Holy Spirit; no limits to the improvability of the human condition; so there can be no bounds to the saving influence which God will dispense to the heart of every genuine believer.

We may ask and receive, and our joy shall be full! Well may we bless and praise God, "who has called us into such a state of salvation"; a state in which we may be thus saved; and, by the grace of that state continue in the same to the end of our lives.[24]

God, thank You for Your boundless love and grace. Help me to experience the fullness of You today. Amen.

First Priorities

Peace in My Heart

Let us draw near to God with a sincere heart in full assurance of faith,
having our hearts sprinkled to cleanse us from a guilty conscience and
having our bodies washed with pure water. (Hebrews 10:22)

God will not lightly or easily lose His people. He has provided well for us:
blood to wash us in; a Priest to pray for us, that we may be made to persevere;
and, in case we foully fall, an Advocate to plead our cause. (John Bunyan)

*Y*ou can do everything right and still not feel at peace in your heart about your relationship with God. Eighteenth-century theological giant John Wesley came to America as a missionary, ministered to prisoners, and later preached throughout the English countryside in open-air revival services. He read his Bible and prayed every day. But despite all those efforts, he still felt insecure and unsure of his salvation.

If Wesley had a troubled heart, what hope is there for us? He discovered that peace and assurance of our relationship with God can come only from God, not our efforts. After listening to the works of Martin Luther, Wesley remarked, "While he was describing the change which God works in the heart through faith in Christ, I felt my heart strangely warmed. I felt I did trust in Christ, Christ alone for salvation; and an assurance was given me that He had taken away my sins, even mine, and saved me from the law of sin and death." Turn to Christ alone, and your heart too can be "strangely warmed."

Lord, I need peace and assurance of Your presence. Help
me to trust in You and not my own efforts. Amen.

Peace in the Storm

Oh, that I had the wings of a dove!
I would fly away and be at rest . . .
I would hurry to my place of shelter,
far from the tempest and storm.
(Psalm 55:6, 8)

It is said that in some countries trees will grow, but will bear no fruit
because there is no winter there. (John Bunyan)

Years ago several artists were asked to illustrate the calm in a storm. One that stood out depicted a raging storm at sea near some jagged, mountainous rocks. Nestled in one of the rocks' crevasses was a bird resting peacefully, seemingly unaware of the storm's lashes from the tossing sea or the wind that caused the water to spray high above.

God wants us to know the same kind of peace: when the storms of life assail us, we can calmly watch as the crashing waters break and the wind blows spray all around us. He wants us to experience a perfect peace—His peace—trusting that the storm will move on by and that we will be safe in the arms of Jesus.

Dear Lord, I want to experience perfect peace in the middle
of life's storms. Be my shelter and refuge, Father. Amen.

Praise for Our Great God

His Faithfulness

*God, who has called you into fellowship with his Son Jesus Christ
our Lord, is faithful.* (1 Corinthians 1:9)

*The promises of God which are made through Christ relate to the
pardon of sin to the penitent; the sanctification of His people; support
in temptation and trial; guidance in perplexity; peace in death, and
eternal glory beyond the grave. All of these are made through a
Redeemer, and none of these shall fail.* (Albert Barnes)

*E*ven if people haven't kept their promises to you, even if no one else in the world is faithful and true, even if you feel let down by others, there is One who is faithful and true to His Word.

God has never turned away anyone who has asked Him for forgiveness. God has never left the side of any of His followers—even if they were untrue to Him. God will never withhold the hope of glory and heaven from one who seeks Him.

What greater promises can we receive? What else do we truly need? No wonder the hymnist Thomas O. Chisholm declared, "Great is thy faithfulness!"

Father, thank You for Your continuous presence, for Your
commitment to me as Your child. Help me live in the
light of Your love. Amen.

Tough Love

My son, do not despise the LORD's discipline / and do not resent his rebuke, / because the LORD disciplines those he loves, / as a father the son he delights in. (Proverbs 3:11–12)

God had one Son without sin, but not a single child without the rod.
(C. H. Spurgeon)

*D*iscipline is a somewhat lost concept in our culture. Those of us who are a little older can remember a parent—or even a teacher—getting out the "board of education" when we got in trouble. It was far from pleasant, but it certainly got the point across.

Solomon, the wisest man who ever lived, told his son not to be resentful over discipline received from God because it is actually a sign of love. Perhaps Solomon was reflecting on whether a firmer hand of parental discipline would have benefited him in his own life!

Discipline yourself—or leave it to someone else to do it for you. Even if a boss, parent, spouse, friend, or customer won't step up and hold us accountable for our decisions, the good news is we have a heavenly Father who cares too much about us to just ignore things we do wrong. That's His tough love.

Have you experienced God's chastening? Did you respond with resentment or with an open heart?

Dear God, I don't like to experience discipline in my life and I too easily get resentful. Help me to learn what You have to teach me in moments of correction. Amen.

Restored Peace

Restore to me the joy of your salvation
and grant me a willing spirit, to sustain me.
(Psalm 51:12)

Our Savior kneels down and gazes upon the darkest acts of our lives.
But rather than recoil in horror, he reaches out in kindness and says,
"I can clean that if you want." And from the basin of his grace, he
scoops a palm full of mercy and washes our sin. (Max Lucado)

Nothing erodes personal peace more quickly and profoundly than guilt. Could the fact that our no-fault culture has persistently tried to eliminate guilt as an appropriate response and feeling have contributed to the amount of unhappiness there is in a nation filled with blessings? Certainly we can have feelings of guilt that we don't really need to bear, but the true purpose of guilt is to remind us to make things right when we've done wrong with God and others.

Have guilty feelings robbed you of peace? Is the guilt based on a wrongdoing in your life? If so, all you need to do is ask God—and perhaps another person—for forgiveness, and then you will experience His peace again.

Lord, forgive me for any wrongs I've committed.
Restore peace to my life. Amen.

Blessed to Be a Blessing

And do not forget to do good and to share with others, for with such sacrifices God is pleased. (Hebrews 13:16)

Nothing is really ours until we share it. (C. S. Lewis)

As a Christmas present, Michael received a brand-new car from a close friend who had just inherited a large sum of money. Several weeks later, after the holidays, as Michael left the office to go home, a shabbily dressed man stood near his parking spot, admiring his new wheels. "Hey, man, is this your car?" the man asked.

Michael nodded with a gulp. "My friend gave it to me for Christmas."

The man was astonished. "You mean your friend gave it to you, and it cost you nothing? Man, I wish . . ." Michael anticipated what the wish would be—that the man wished *he* had such a generous friend.

"I wish," the man continued to Michael's amazement, "that I could be a friend like that."

Jesus said, "It is more blessed to give than to receive" (Acts 20:35). When we pray for blessings, we ought also to pray that we might use those gifts to bless someone else. What can you bless someone with today, even if it's something small?

Dear Lord, whether I have a lot or a little, show me
someone I can bless today. Amen.

Take the Right Path

We all, like sheep, have gone astray, each of us has turned to his own way; and the Lord has laid on him the iniquity of us all. (Isaiah 53:6)

The word of God hidden in the heart is a stubborn voice to suppress.
(Billy Graham)

It's not that hard to take a wrong turn in life. Doing the wrong thing, if we're honest, has an allure. It's called temptation. When we look around, it's common to spot someone who has gone astray—wayward sons, daughters, friends, and acquaintances fill prisons and homeless shelters, church pews, and cubicles alike.

The good news is that when we repent, God can turn us around and help us find our way again. The better news is that He offers plenty of advice for how to live well in the world so we can avoid going off the rails in the first place. The book of Proverbs alone is a treasure trove of principles for living: work hard, watch the time, don't live just for pleasure, make following God your primary concern. These aren't burdensome rules; they're simply guidelines for living life well and effectively.

Open your Bible and let God lead you today. He'll show you the right path to take.

> Dear Lord, thank You for picking me up and setting
> me on the right path. Give me understanding of Your
> principles for living. Amen.

Book of Books

For the word of the LORD is right and true; he is faithful in all he does.
(Psalm 33:4)

God has placed the work of His Son in the Word and has communicated this Word to us. When we believe in His Word, we are believing in Him. (Watchman Nee)

A Classic Devotion from C. H. Spurgeon

My friends, stand over this volume [the Bible], and admire its authority. This is no common book. It is not the sayings of the sages of Greece; here are not the utterances of philosophers of past ages. If these words were written by a man, we might reject them; but O let me think the solemn thought, that this book is God's handwriting—that these words are God's! Oh, book of books! And wast thou written by my God? Then will I bow before thee. Oh! if you could ever remember that this Bible was actually and really written by God. Oh! if ye had been let into the secret chambers of heaven, if ye had beheld God grasping his pen and writing down these letters—then surely ye would respect them; but they are just as much God's handwriting as if you had seen God write them.[25]

Lord, thank You for speaking to me through Your Word.
Help me to grow in knowledge of it this month. Amen.

Pressed, but Not Crushed

We are hard pressed on every side, but not crushed; perplexed,
but not in despair; persecuted, but not abandoned; struck down,
but not destroyed. We always carry around in our body the
death of Jesus, so that the life of Jesus may also be revealed in
our body. (2 Corinthians 4:8–10)

It is misleading to imagine that we are developed in spite of
our circumstances, for we are developed because of them.
It is mastery in circumstances that is needed, not mastery
over them. (Oswald Chambers)

A beloved husband and father died from cancer after years of chemotherapy and radiation, suffering in horrible ways from the effects of both. During that time, he clung to 2 Corinthians 4:8–10 as a source of hope. He prayed the passage constantly and found that it gave him courage to trust and endure.

He was perplexed, but not in despair. He was not forsaken and not destroyed, because he knew that come what may, the end result would be the same: he would be with Jesus and experience the glorious full manifestation of all His promises! His peace and poise under pressure became the touchstone for his family's faith after he was gone.

The good news is that we too can experience that hope. No matter what you are facing, God will preserve you and give you strength.

Dear God, with You on my side, nothing can destroy or
crush me. Thank You for Your work in my life. Amen.

The Rescue Boat

*Now faith is being sure of what we hope for and certain of
what we do not see.* (Hebrews 11:1)

*The object of hope is a future good which is arduous yet possible to obtain.
It is therefore necessary that the object of hope should be proposed to a
man as something which is possible, in order that he may hope.*
(Thomas Aquinas)

Aboard a ship that was sinking, a woman stood with her blind husband as she grasped for the rescue boat. But an officer pushed the man toward the back of the line, yelling, "Women and children only in these boats!" The wife pleaded with him, explaining that he was blind and that she wouldn't get on the boat if her husband couldn't go with her. The officer then waved them both onto the rescue boat.

The man's hope was in his wife whom he could not see, but he trusted her in faith because he knew her and knew the love she had for him. In the same way, we cannot see God here on earth, but we can hope in what we cannot see because of the promises that He has made to us in His Word.

Lord, I can't see You, but I know You're real and at work in
my life. Thank You for the reassurance of Your presence
and love. Amen.

Your Best You

Whatever you do, do it all for the glory of God. (1 Corinthians 10:31)

And in the end, it's not the years in your life that count. It's the life in your years. (Abraham Lincoln)

*A*ll good things we have are gifts from God. Even the faith with which we respond to God's grace is a gift from Him. All talents and strengths are from Him.

Yet God calls us to use what He has given us. He calls for us to work, acquire, learn, plan, and dream. Some of us aren't comfortable with the thought that God just might be calling us to be ambitious. That doesn't sound godly!

Kindness, love, and service all come first. But what is God telling you to get started or to work on in your life now?

Are you moving forward—or sitting back and relaxing?

Lord, help me walk forward in all You have for me to do.
Thank You for a bright future! Amen.

The Burden Bearer

"For my yoke is easy and my burden is light." (Matthew 11:30)

Who best bear His mild yoke, they serve Him best. (John Milton)

God tells us that He will bear our burdens, making our yoke easy. It is a promise to His children. But in order to experience His rest, we must first give our burdens over to Him. We do that through prayer, confessing that we cannot carry the weight of life without Him. He wants to bear our burdens for us and make our loads light—but only with our permission.

There will be many people in our lives who will offer to carry our burdens. And while they can share in our pain and suffering—and while God often uses others as a means of His grace—people really cannot carry our heaviest burdens for us. They can help, but only Christ can lift the load.

Are you carrying a burden today that is best placed in God's hands?

> Father, what a blessing it is to know that Your love for me is so great that You have promised not only to lighten my load, but to lift it, bearing it for me. Thank You for Your grace and compassion. Amen.

Stay Connected

*"I am the vine; you are the branches. If a man remains in me and I
in him, he will bear much fruit; apart from me you can do nothing."*
(John 15:5)

*God is not in the business of helping the humanly strong become
stronger; rather he takes the weak and makes them strong in himself.*
(Erwin W. Lutzer)

*M*ovement, growth, work, force, and life itself—all require
energy. The power source for the Christian life is connection to Jesus Christ. Jesus paints a picture of a vineyard. It may
spread over acres, but every living branch that bears fruit is connected to the vine.

Often, when we don't feel effective in our service—as spouses,
parents, ministers, volunteers—we focus on techniques. We think
of better methods and programs for making a difference. Maybe
we need to first take a step backward and ask ourselves a few
simple questions: *Am I connected to Jesus Christ? Am I close to
Him? Does He have my faith and love?* It's amazing how everything
else falls into place when those questions are answered positively.

Are you bearing fruit? Are you connected to the vine?

Heavenly Father, I love You and want nothing more
than to be close to You. Amen.

Say Cheese!

On the third day a wedding took place at Cana in Galilee. Jesus'
mother was there, and Jesus and his disciples had also been invited
to the wedding. (John 2:1–2)

The religion that makes a man look sick certainly won't cure
the world! (Phillips Brooks)

The great Bible teacher William Barclay remarked, "A gloomy Christian is a contradiction of terms, and nothing in all religious history has done Christianity more harm than its connection with black clothes and long faces." When people who are without faith look at your face, what do they see? A twinkle in the eye and a smile teasing at the corners of your mouth? Or a dark, sullen anger or unhappiness? Maybe if we wanted to learn to share our faith with the world more effectively, we would spend time in front of the mirror practicing our smiles!

If your feelings are characterized more by gloom than glee today, turn your heart toward God. One of the fruits of the Spirit that He gives to believers is joy (Galatians 5:22). Take a deep breath and pause until the emotions that are swirling around inside you are stilled. Simply set your eyes on Jesus and ask Him to restore your joy. He is more than able to do so. And that's something to smile about.

Father, You are the source of joy in my life. My eyes are on
You. My heart is set on You. I love and adore You. Thank
You for the blessing of Your joy. Amen.

Whatever Is Noble

Finally, brothers, whatever is true, whatever is noble, whatever is right, whatever is pure, whatever is lovely, whatever is admirable—if anything is excellent or praiseworthy—think about such things. (Philippians 4:8)

We scoff at honor and are shocked to find traitors among us. (C. S. Lewis)

To say that our culture is coarse and profane is an understatement. The entertainment industry fills media outlets with a constant barrage of words and images that do little or nothing to edify the soul—if they do not damage it. Paul provides a checklist of virtues we would be wise to dwell on:

- Whatever is noble,
- Whatever is true,
- Whatever is right,
- Whatever is pure,
- Whatever is lovely,
- Whatever is admirable,
- Whatever is excellent or praiseworthy.

Is it time for a personal audit of your thought life? Is it perhaps time to take a "fast" from popular entertainment in order to focus on what is ennobling? There's no better place to start than God's Word.

Lord, thank You for checking my spirit on what I choose to fill my mind with. I turn to thoughts of You and Your Word today. Amen.

Good Things Come to Those Who Wait

Be still before the Lord and wait patiently for him. (Psalm 37:7)

You're in a hurry. God is not. Trust God. (Marie T. Freeman)

They were a young couple in love, and they knew they wanted to be together. But there were a few things standing in the way. She waited for him until he completed his stint in the army, and then he waited for her while she finished college. Then she waited for him a second time, this time waiting out his years in the navy. A total of thirteen years passed before they got married. But by all accounts, theirs was a sweet and contented marriage, one that lasted almost forty-five years.

Some of the best things in life don't happen in an instant; they require waiting. If you're waiting and hoping for God to provide something, don't give up. What He has for you is worth the wait.

God, I know You have good plans for me. I choose
to wait for Your best. Amen.

The Ten Percent Club

One of them, when he saw he was healed, came back, praising God in
a loud voice. He threw himself at Jesus' feet and thanked him—and
he was a Samaritan. (Luke 17:15–16)

God is worthy of our praise and is pleased when we come before Him
with thanksgiving. (Shirley Dobson)

Ten were healed. Only one returned to say thank you to the miracle worker. Does that percentage, only 10 percent, represent those in everyday life who stop to notice and express thanks for the miracles and ordinary blessings bestowed on them? Maybe. But this Scripture passage (Luke 17:11–19) is not about percentages. It's not about numbers—though it is about a number: the number one. The one Samaritan leper who expressed the gratitude of his heart.

Are you numbered with the 10 percent? Are you a kindred spirit with the one who gave thanks? Are you a person who sees miracles and blessings, or who wonders why things never go your way? Join an elite—though not exclusive—group: the 10 percent who savor God's goodness and shout out praise as a result.

God, I never want to neglect to praise You for the ways
You bless me. Open my eyes to Your miracles today. Amen.

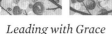

A Special Call

Then I heard the voice of the Lord *saying, "Whom shall I send? And who will go for us?" And I said, "Here am I. Send me!"* (Isaiah 6:8)

The willing feet that go on errands of love, work for Christ.
(Arthur Ingram)

Throughout Scripture we have accounts of men and women who were given special tasks, who received a special call on their lives from God. Abraham was called to leave his home country to become the father of God's people. Samson was called to be a Nazarite—a young man who would never touch fermented wine or have his hair cut—in order to show his commitment to God. James and John were two fishermen whom Jesus called to be His disciples. Paul was blinded and knocked off his horse when Jesus called him to be an ambassador of love. The list goes on and on.

God still calls people today. He asks some people to prepare for a life of dedicated ministry, even to leave a career to serve Him in ministry. There are countless other tasks and calls that God gives that are not universal to all the world or all believers, but are for a specific person. Maybe even you.

When Isaiah worshipped in the temple and felt God's call on his life, his answer was simple: "Here am I. Send me!" (Isaiah 6:8). What will your answer be?

Lord, I want to go where You lead. Thank You for the tasks
You have placed before me. Amen.

The Royal Way of Praying

Cast all your anxiety on him because he cares for you. (1 Peter 5:7)

How often we look upon God as our last and feeblest resource!
We go to Him because we have nowhere else to go. And then we
learn that the storms of life have driven us, not upon the rocks,
but into the desired haven. (George MacDonald)

A Classic Devotion from C. H. Spurgeon

*W*e should have faith enough to believe that the present trouble, about which we are praying, is sent to us in love by God. We should pray concerning our trials in this way:

"Lord, I have this thorn in the flesh. I beseech You, deliver me from it, but meanwhile I bless You for it; for though I do not understand the why or the wherefore of it, I am persuaded there is love within it. Therefore, while I ask You to remove it, so far as it seems evil to me, yet wherein it may to Your better knowledge work for my good, I bless You for it, and I am content to endure it so long as You see fit."

Is not that a sweet way of praying? This is a royal way of praying. Such an amalgam of prayer and thanksgiving is more precious than the gold of Ophir.[26]

Lord, I believe that You love me, no matter what's going
wrong in my life. Help me to rest in Your love in the
midst of difficulties. Amen.

Bear One Another's Burdens

*Carry each other's burdens, and in this way you will
fulfill the law of Christ.* (Galatians 6:2)

*Give me a stout heart to bear my own burdens. Give me a willing
heart to bear the burdens of others. Give me a believing heart to cast
all burdens upon Thee, O Lord.* (John Baillie)

We are not responsible to carry certain burdens of others. In Galatians 6:5, Paul says that "each one should carry his own load." Another translation for the word *load* in that verse would be "backpack." All of us are able to carry a certain amount of weight in life. In fact, doing things for others that they should do for themselves can lead to a cycle of codependence that is unhealthy for the one not pulling his or her own weight—and for the one carrying multiple backpacks.

But there are some burdens that are excessive. They are too heavy for one person to lift alone. Physical disabilities, emotional trauma, and other burdens can crush one's spirit through sheer magnitude. In cases like this, Paul says we can fulfill the law of Christ by helping someone carry the load. Is there someone in your life who needs you to share the love of Christ with him or her? Are you willing to help someone carry that weight?

Lord, I pray for eyes to see the needs around me. Help me
be a burden-bearer, Father God. Amen.

A Deep, Deep Love

And I pray that you, being rooted and established in love, may have power, together with all the saints, to grasp how wide and long and high and deep is the love of Christ. (Ephesians 3:17–19)

> *O the deep, deep love of Jesus!*
> *'Tis a heav'n of heav'ns to me;*
> *And it lifts me up to glory,*
> *With You evermore to be.*
> (Samuel Francis)

When everything around us crumbles, we will always have the love of God. No matter how bad we mess up, no matter how unloved or unlovable we've been, His love endures forever. His love is so deep that it's incomprehensible. Sometimes the lack of love we give and receive makes it hard for us to accept and understand that God truly loves us. But He does, and His grace can help us understand and live out the loving affection our Father has for us.

The song "O the Deep, Deep Love of Jesus," penned by Samuel Francis in the 1800s, describes this vast love of God. Find comfort in the knowledge that God's love is unconditional and irresistible:

'Tis an ocean vast of blessing,
'Tis a haven sweet of rest.

Father, I know that You love me, but sometimes that reality is hard to accept. Help me live in Your love today, and help me share it with others. Amen.

Finding Truth

For the word of God is living and active. Sharper than any double-edged sword, it penetrates even to dividing soul and spirit, joints and marrow; it judges the thoughts and attitudes of the heart. (Hebrews 4:12)

Our claim is that God has revealed Himself by speaking; that this divine (or God-breathed) speech has been written down and preserved in Scripture; and that Scripture is, in fact, God's Word written, which therefore is true and reliable and has divine authority over men. (John Stott)

*O*ne of the prevailing temptations of our pluralistic culture is to see truth as relative. Right and wrong, the attributes of God, the need and nature of salvation—essential beliefs and practices are not considered absolute, but merely suggestive.

Throughout Scripture, we are told that some issues are a matter of personal conscience, so there is plenty of room for debate and personal conviction.

But that doesn't mean all matters—or even most matters—of faith rely on personal conviction. For example, Paul declares that if there is no resurrection of Christ, there is no salvation or promise of heaven available (1 Corinthians 15:12–19). How do we know what is absolute and what involves choice? There is only one sure source of revelation: God's Word. Listen to good preachers and teachers, but never let them take the place of getting to know God's Word for yourself.

Father in heaven, thank You for speaking directly to
me through Your Word. Amen.

A Glorious Hope

He will wipe every tear from their eyes. There will be no more death or mourning or crying or pain, for the old order of things has passed away. (Revelation 21:4)

No two Christians will ever meet for the last time. (author unknown)

*D*eath is not the end for Christians. Oh, no doubt, it is still a time of sharp loss, acute pain, and a throbbing ache that lingers for years and sometimes a lifetime. Perhaps there is no greater sorrow than what is felt over the death of a child.

But woven into the heartache, there is a glorious hope for all who know God and have been redeemed by the blood of Jesus Christ. Death is not the final chapter of life, but rather a doorway into an eternity with God, where every longing of the human spirit is met and fulfilled.

Heaven is a place of no more tears. Death truly is different for God's children.

Father, thank You for the gift of eternal life and the promise of being face-to-face with You in heaven. Amen.

A New You

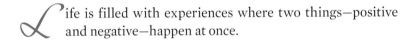

If we have been united with him like this in his death, we will certainly also be united with him in his resurrection. For we know that our old self was crucified with him so that the body of sin might be done away with, that we should no longer be slaves to sin. (Romans 6:5–6)

God specializes in things fresh and firsthand. His plans for you this year may outshine those of the past. He's preparing to fill your days with reasons to give Him praise. (Joni Eareckson Tada)

Life is filled with experiences where two things—positive and negative—happen at once.

- We move to a new location and leave an old location behind.
- A young couple walks down the aisle and exchanges wedding vows, leaving behind their primary family relationships.
- A graduate makes new friends at college but says good-bye to high school classmates.

Some of these experiences are bittersweet. But one experience that includes a negative is only positive: salvation. When we receive new life in Christ, something else, our "old man," that part of us that rebelled against God, is destroyed.

That is one good-bye we will never regret.

Father, thank You for Your redemption and restoration, for making my heart brand-new. Amen.

A Whale of a Storm

"Whoever finds his life will lose it, and whoever loses his life for my sake will find it." (Matthew 10:39)

We know that our reward depends not on the job itself but on the faithfulness with which we serve God. (Pope John Paul I)

*H*e was a faithful prophet of God, full of zeal and integrity. He knew right from wrong. That's why God's call for him to preach to the godless people of Nineveh caught him off guard. He may have had zeal and honor, but compassion and love weren't part of his spirit. So in a fit of anger and rebellion, he disobeyed God and went the opposite direction of Nineveh.

But God was intent that Jonah would follow His command, and He sent a storm and a fish to get him going in the right direction (Jonah 1:1–17).

Jonah's preaching saved a people from destruction—though it never did instill love in his own heart.

The next time a storm forms around you, it just may be an opportunity for you to do something bold for God on behalf of others. After all, those who have survived the storm can bless and help others who are in a storm of their own.

Father, help me to be obedient to Your calling on my life,
and give me eyes of mercy toward others. Amen.

A Fresh Word

Open my eyes that I may see
wonderful things in your law.
(Psalm 119:18)

When you read God's Word, you must constantly be saying to
yourself, "It is talking to me, and about me." (Søren Kierkegaard)

You've heard the joke about marriage: A wife asks her husband if he loves her. He answers, "Of course." She then asks why he never tells her he loves her. He answers, "I told you I loved you twenty years ago and I never changed my mind."

Good marriages need words of affection repeated. Often. Similarly, we need to hear from God every day. The Bible is filled with insights, so when we sit down to read it, often we encounter something brand-new for our spiritual life. But sometimes the very same words, containing the very same truth, speak to us in a new and fresh way. A Bible verse as well known as John 3:16 can be a brand-new reality we realize for the very first time—even though we've heard it hundreds of times before. As you open the pages of God's Word, do so with an open heart and a sense of anticipation. God has something fresh and new to say to you.

Lord, I want to hear You speak through Your Word. Please
show me what You want me to know today. Amen.

An Eternal Impact

*I have been reminded of your sincere faith, which first lived in your
grandmother Lois and in your mother Eunice and, I am persuaded,
now lives in you also.* (2 Timothy 1:5)

*Personal working for souls is good. Giving money is good.
But praying is best of all.* (J. C. Ryle)

What a wonderful heritage in the faith Timothy had. Paul considered this young man more than a protégé; he considered Timothy a son (1 Corinthians 4:17). But Paul knew that Timothy's godly heritage had begun long before he met him. Timothy had a mother and grandmother who prayed for him from his childhood (2 Timothy 1:5). Did you grow up in that kind of family? Even if you didn't, there is a good chance someone prayed for you and was instrumental in your relationship with God.

This raises an even more important question for you to consider. For whom are you praying regularly? Who will say that your prayers gave them the encouragement they needed in a tough time? Whom might you meet in heaven because you would not stop praying for their very soul here on earth?

You have the power to make a difference in the kingdom of God simply by praying for those close to you. Don't miss out on seeing blessings in their lives.

Lord, show me whom I can pray for not just today but
every day as they grow to know You. Amen.

Time to Party

Rejoice in the Lord always. I will say it again: Rejoice! (Philippians 4:4)

*Whence comes this idea that if what we are doing is fun, it can't
be God's will? The God who made giraffes, a baby's fingernails, a
puppy's tail, a crook necked squash, the bobwhite's call, and a young
girl's giggle, has a sense of humor. Make no mistake about that.*
(Catherine Marshall)

*D*o you think of parties as wholly unspiritual? Do you think of time spent enjoying the company of friends as "wasted" or idle?

Jesus Himself was criticized sharply for attending parties. One of His most famous Bible stories was of a son who wandered far from home, squandering all his father had given him. But when he did finally come to his senses and return to his family, the father's immediate response was to throw a huge party to celebrate having his son back home (Luke 15:11–32).

God has created a rhythm to life that involves work and worship, yes, but also play. Sure, some people need to rein themselves in and play a little less. But God has given us reasons to celebrate, and we should devote time to rejoicing as an act of worship. So go ahead and throw that party sooner rather than later. It could be just what you—and your friends—need to draw closer to God.

Dear Lord, You have given me much to celebrate. Thank
You for the chance to do so. Amen.

First Priorities

You Have a Purpose

For we are God's workmanship, created in Christ Jesus to do good works, which God prepared in advance for us to do. (Ephesians 2:10)

Set yourself earnestly to discover what you are made to do, and then give yourself passionately to the doing of it. (Martin Luther King Jr.)

I'm not sure I have a purpose in life. I don't know what I am supposed to do to make the world better.

You might be right. You might not personally have a purpose in life. But there's good news. God has a purpose for you. When He created you, He fashioned you in such a way that you could accomplish things that build His kingdom. But that's not all. There's more good news. Not only did He create you with the ability to accomplish great things, He also prepared specific tasks that would utilize your gifts.

Maybe it's a person only you can reach. Maybe it's a ministry you are supposed to start. Maybe it's a gift of encouragement you are to lavish on hundreds and thousands of people. Look in your heart. Look around you. Ask God to open your eyes. And get busy!

Heavenly Father, open my eyes to the tasks and opportunities You have set before me. Amen.

Falling Stars and Fairies

He who began a good work in you will carry it on to completion
until the day of Christ Jesus. (Philippians 1:6)

What gives me the most hope every day is God's grace; knowing
that his grace is going to give me the strength for whatever I face,
knowing that nothing is a surprise to God. (Rick Warren)

Jiminy Cricket told us that we should wish upon a falling star. Peter Pan said that we just need to believe in fairies.

But we know that we can't really place our hope in a fairy tale. Yet sometimes we do seem a bit naive—maybe even child-like—in the things on which we set our hope. The stock market might be a good investment, but it's no place to build your hopes. Jesus warned us against building our houses on sand (Matthew 7:24–27). Likewise, a strong army can be comforting, but God told Zerubbabel that it's not by might but by His Spirit that the world changes (Zechariah 4:6). It's great to have people we can truly count on. But can we truly place all our hopes in people?

There is only one sure foundation we can build our life on, and that is a relationship with God. With God beside you, your life is never hopeless.

Lord, thank You for walking beside me every step of my
journey. Thank You for Your daily grace that makes all the
difference in my life. Amen.

In View of God's Mercy

Therefore, I urge you, brothers, in view of God's mercy, to offer your bodies as living sacrifices, holy and pleasing to God—this is your spiritual act of worship. (Romans 12:1)

Worship is our response to the overtures of love from the heart of the Father. Its central reality is found "in spirit and truth." It is kindled within us only when the Spirit of God touches our human spirit. (Richard J. Foster)

*P*aul spent the first eleven chapters of Romans establishing the truth that salvation is a gift from God; there is no justification before Him on the basis of our works. He was fighting hard against the idea that legalism is the basis for our faith.

But in chapter 12 of Romans, he showed that good works, obedience, sacrifice, commitment, discipline, and lifestyle are a huge part of what it means to be a Christian. They don't make us children of God, but we do them because we are children of God. Because of God's mercy—His gift of new life through the blood of Jesus—Paul urged us to offer ourselves as living sacrifices.

Have you offered yourself completely to God for His use and purposes in the world?

Heavenly Father, thank You for Your mercy that gave me new life. I give that life to You. Amen.

Your Will Be Done

*"Your kingdom come,
your will be done
on earth as it is in heaven."*
(Matthew 6:10)

*We are trying not so much to make God listen to us as to make
ourselves listen to him; we are trying not to persuade God to do what
we want, but to find out what he wants us to do.* (William Barclay)

A Classic Devotion from John Bunyan

*A*s Christ has taught us, prayer must say, "Your will be done on earth as it is in heaven" (Matthew 6:10); therefore the people of the Lord in humility are to lay themselves and their prayers, and all that they have, at the feet of their God, to be disposed of by him as he in his heavenly wisdom sees best. And never doubting that God will answer the desire of his people in a way that will be most advantageous for them and for his glory. Therefore when the saints pray with submission to the will of God, they are not to doubt or question God's love and kindness to them. But because they are not always wise, and sometimes Satan may take advantage of them, so as to tempt them to pray for that which, if they had it, would neither be to God's glory nor for his people's good.[27]

Lord, I know that You know what's best for me and that You care about me. Please do what's good in my life. Amen.

It Is Well with My Soul

The Lord gives strength to his people;
the Lord blesses his people with peace.
(Psalm 29:11)

It is not too much to say that all real growth in the spiritual life—all
victory over temptation, all confidence and peace in the presence
of difficulties and dangers, all repose of spirit in times of great
disappointment or loss, all habitual communion with God—depend
upon the practice of secret prayer. (author unknown)

*I*n 1873, Horacio Spafford sent his family ahead of him to Europe, planning to join them later. But the ship carrying his wife and four daughters never made it to the U.K. After a collision with another ship, it sank, and Spafford's four daughters with it. His wife survived. Spafford took a ship to France to meet his wife, and when they passed over the site of the shipwreck, the captain showed him the spot where his daughters lost their lives. As he stood, weeping, on the bridge of the ship, God led him to write the words to the classic hymn "It Is Well with My Soul." The opening lines still provide comfort today: "When peace like a river attendeth my way, / When sorrow like sea billows roll, / Whatever my lot, Thou hast taught me to say, / It is well, it is well, with my soul."

Grief and heartache are real. But even amid tragedy, when we accept God's will and loving care, we can experience perfect peace.

God, please strengthen my trust in You so that I can rest in
Your peace during times of tragedy. Amen.

Hope Out Loud

But in your hearts set apart Christ as Lord. Always be prepared to give an answer to everyone who asks you to give the reason for the hope that you have. But do this with gentleness and respect. (1 Peter 3:15)

Those who stand for nothing fall for anything. (Alexander Hamilton)

What's wrong with the world today?" is a perennial topic of discussion. Wars, worldwide strife, death and sickness, natural disasters—ours is truly a hurting world. Is it worse now than ever? That's another topic of conversation and debate! But one thing certainly has not changed in the course of history: the fallen human race needs God.

Perhaps that's why Peter instructed his fellow disciples to be ready to explain the hope that they had. Knowing—and articulating—that it's God who saves us and gives us hope for the future is good for our own spiritual lives. Sharing—articulating—that reason for hope with others offers them what they need to hear and is, again, good for our own souls. Are you able to verbally express the reason you live with hope?

The hope that is in us is not passive; it must be active in order to be effective. Nurture it within yourself, and be ready and able to proclaim it to everyone you know.

God, give me renewed hope in You and the words to say to
share that hope with others. Amen.

Riches of Grace

*In him we have redemption through his blood, the forgiveness of sins,
in accordance with the riches of God's grace.* (Ephesians 1:7)

*Grace is something you can never get but can only be given. There's
no way to earn it or deserve it or bring it about anymore than you
can deserve the taste of raspberries and cream or earn good looks.*
(Frederick Buechner)

God favors you out of His deep, abiding love for you, a love that is not contingent on any effort of yours. Here are some aspects of grace to ponder today:

- Grace provides the gift of salvation, a gift that can't be earned (Ephesians 2:8–9).
- Grace is available to us when we are weak (2 Corinthians 12:9).
- Grace is sufficient for absolutely any need we have—health, finances, relationships, temptations, or any other need (2 Corinthians 12:9).

Whatever need you have in your life today, be assured, God is on your side. He is ready and able to help you as you respond to Him with faith.

> Lord, thank You for grace. It amazes me to know I am Your beloved child. Help me to live in Your grace today. Amen.

The Power of Obedience

Then he took the Book of the Covenant and read it to the people. They
responded, "We will do everything the Lord has said; we will obey."
(Exodus 24:7)

We ought not to be weary of doing little things for the love of God,
who regards not the greatness of the work, but the love with which it
is performed. (Brother Lawrence)

A Classic Devotion from Oswald Chambers

*A*ll God's revelations are sealed to us until they are opened
to us by obedience. You will never get them open by phi-
losophy or thinking. Immediately you obey, a flash of light comes.
Let God's truth work in you by soaking in it, not by worrying
into it. Obey God in the thing He is at present showing you, and
instantly the next thing is opened up. We read tomes on the work
of the Holy Spirit when five minutes of drastic obedience would
make things clear as a sunbeam. We say, "I suppose I shall understand these things some day." You can understand them now: it
is not study that does it, but obedience. The tiniest fragment of
obedience and heaven opens up and the profoundest truths of God
are yours straight away. God will never reveal more truth about
Himself till you obey what you know already. Beware of being
wise and prudent.[28]

Lord, show me where I need to take a step of obedience to
You. And thank You for blessing me when I do so. Amen.

The Battle Suit

Take the helmet of salvation and the sword of the Spirit,
which is the word of God. (Ephesians 6:17)

In opposition to all the suggestions of the devil, the sole, simple,
and sufficient answer is the word of God. This puts to flight all
the powers of darkness. The Christian finds this to be true in his
individual experience. It dissipates his doubts; it drives away his
fears; it delivers him from the power of Satan. (Charles Hodge)

The Bible is referred to as a sword because we use the strength of the Word of God in spiritual battles. The Bible is effective because truth cuts into the falsehood of sin; it causes the sinner to return to God; it wards off the attacks of Satan. The Word fights on.

As we learn the truths of God's Word, we then have possession of the battle gear necessary to fight the enemy of our souls. We have what will cause him to flee: the sword of God's truth. Jesus said, "If you hold to my teaching, you are really my disciples. Then you will know the truth, and the truth will set you free" (John 8:31–32).

God has given us the power we need to live for Him, but we must be willing to call upon Him and ask Him for help. That begins with a commitment to His Word. God will deliver His children as His Word has promised.

Lord, may I ever be ready for battle by learning Your Word. Amen.

God Never Sleeps

He will not let your foot slip—
he who watches over you will not slumber;
indeed, he who watches over Israel
will neither slumber nor sleep.
(Psalm 121:3–4)

I would rather walk with God in the dark than go alone in the light.
(Mary Gardiner Brainard)

A mother and her four-year-old daughter were preparing for bed one night. The child was afraid of the dark, and the mother, on this occasion, felt fearful also.

When the light was out, the child caught a glimpse of the moon outside the window. "Mother," she asked, "is the moon God's light?"

"Yes," answered the mother.

The next question was, "Will God put out His light and go to sleep?"

The mother replied, "No, my child, God never goes to sleep."

Then out of the simplicity of a child's faith, she said these words, which gave reassurance to the fearful mother: "Well, as long as God's light is on, He's awake, and we might as well go to sleep."

Be comforted today by the knowledge that God is always, always watching over you.

Lord, thank You that You will never leave me. Help me to
rest in Your love tonight as I sleep. Amen.

Use Your Talents

Each one should use whatever gift he has received to serve others, faithfully administering God's grace in its various forms. (1 Peter 4:10)

One thing taught large in the Holy Scriptures is that while God gives His gifts freely, He will require a strict accounting of them at the end of the road. Each man is personally responsible for his store, be it large or small, and will be required to explain his use of it before the judgment seat of Christ. (A. W. Tozer)

There is a familiar story of three men who were given varying amounts of talents by their master (Matthew 25:14–30). The man with the most talents did the most. Not surprising. The man with the second most talents came in second place. Not unexpected. The third man did absolutely nothing. Of course. He didn't have enough to make a difference. But when the master saw that he had buried what was given to him, he took it away.

Is that fair? What if he had lost the meager amount on a bad investment? Jesus' story says nothing about being judged on the basis of failing. Judgment is based on doing nothing, burying the talents God has given us.

Has God given you a lot or a little or something in between? Your answer isn't important. All that matters is what you're going to do with what you've got. What investment do you need to make in your world?

Lord, help me to conquer fear and use my talents for good—for You. Thank You for blessing me. Amen.

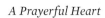

Hindrances to Prayer

Devote yourselves to prayer, keeping alert in it with an attitude
of thanksgiving. (Colossians 4:2 NASB)

When a Christian shuns fellowship with other Christians, the devil
smiles. When he stops studying the Bible, the devil laughs. When he
stops praying, the devils shouts for joy. (Corrie ten Boom)

What keeps you from prayer? Is it worry? Demands on your attention? Boredom? An abundance of entertainment?
Nothing is more important to our spiritual lives than prayer. Jesus taught us to seek the kingdom first (Matthew 6:33), and Paul instructed us to pray without ceasing (1 Thessalonians 5:17). If we desire to follow God, we must pray. So how can you beat those distractions and hindrances?

Try a little separation. Physically remove yourself from your phone, the TV, and reading material. You might choose a verse of Scripture and concentrate on it for a few moments before starting to pray. The hard truth is that all the tricks in the world won't make prayer a piece of cake. Sometimes the choice to direct our attention to talking to God is simply an act of will. But take heart: God wants us to pray, and He can help us overcome any obstacles.

Lord, I do want to pray actively, consistently. Help me clear
the clutter that keeps me from You. Amen.

Pass It On

"In the same way, let your light shine before men, that they may see your good deeds and praise your Father in heaven." (Matthew 5:16)

One drop of water helps to swell the ocean; a spark of fire helps to give light to the world. None are too small, too feeble, too poor to be of service. Think of this and act. (Hannah More)

The concept of "pay it forward" is built on the idea that people have done good things for you that you can't repay directly back to them—but for which you can show gratitude by doing something good for someone who can't repay you. You simply pay forward.

The ultimate expression of paying it forward is what Jesus Christ did for each of us. Even when we were sinners, even when we were enemies with God, He died for us so we could experience eternal life.

How do we pay that gift forward? Simple. We can never repay Him for His sacrificial love toward us, so we share His love with others who need the gift of life. When was the last time you paid it forward?

Dear God, help me to pass on to others the love You so
freely gave to me through Your Son. Amen.

An Invitation to Peace

I will listen to what God the Lord will say;
he promises peace to his people, his saints.
(Psalm 85:8)

Consider Jesus. Know Jesus. Learn what kind of Person it is you
say you trust and love and worship. Soak in the shadow of Jesus.
Saturate your soul with the ways of Jesus. Let Him overwhelm you
with the way He is. (John Piper)

*P*eace is one of those elusive states of mind that run from us when we chase them. We can't get peace when it is our chief goal. Peace is almost always the result of other decisions we make in life: kindness, forgiveness, sober judgment, and many others.

If we want to experience peace, then there is no better place to start than pursuing the One who is the giver of peace, the Prince of Peace, the One whose sacrifice made peace between God and man—as well as man and man—possible in the first place. If you would pursue peace, pursue Jesus. Talk to Him. Listen to Him. Worship Him. Thank Him. Realize He is right beside you, and within you, closer than any human being could ever be to you. Experience peace by experiencing Jesus every day of your life!

Dear God, thank You for sending Jesus to this world to
bring us peace. Thank You that He is in my life now. Amen.

Instant Obedience

On that very day Abraham took his son Ishmael and all those born in his household or bought with his money, every male in his household, and circumcised them, as God told him. (Genesis 17:23)

Obedience is the fruit of faith; patience, the bloom on the fruit.
(Christina Rossetti)

A Classic Devotion from Charles G. Trumbull

*I*nstant obedience is the only kind of obedience there is; delayed obedience is disobedience. Every time God calls us to any duty, He is offering to make a covenant with us; doing the duty is our part, and He will do His part in special blessing.

The only way we can obey is to obey "in the selfsame day," as Abraham did. To be sure, we often postpone a duty and then later on do it as fully as we can. It is better to do this than not to do it at all. But it is then, at the best, only a crippled, disfigured, half-way sort of duty-doing; and a postponed duty never can bring the full blessing that God intended, and that it would have brought if done at the earliest possible moment.

It is a pity to rob ourselves, along with robbing God and others, by procrastination. "In the selfsame day" is the Genesis way of saying, "Do it now."[29]

God, I choose to obey You in all things—right away. Amen.

Joyful Acceptance

I have learned the secret of being content in any and every situation,
whether well fed or hungry, whether living in plenty or in want.
(Philippians 4:12)

God grant me the serenity to accept the things I cannot change,
the courage to change the things I can, and the wisdom to know
the difference. (Reinhold Niebuhr)

We all have things in our lives that we can't change. They run a broad spectrum between minor annoyances, like a family member's persistently annoying behavior, and real tragedies, like the loss of someone close to us.

But even in situations that are beyond our control, we can choose how we respond. The wisdom of the "Serenity Prayer" above reminds us that we can't change some situations and we can't change other people, but we can change ourselves. We can modify our own response to that annoying family member. We can adopt a positive attitude in sticky circumstances. In other words, we can choose joy.

And even during those moments when we can't change our emotions, when grief overwhelms us, we can still choose God. When we do, we are accepting His promise to bring joy into our lives.

Lord, I want to choose joy today. Fill me with Your
Holy Spirit and give me wisdom to respond rightly to
everything in my life. Amen.

Change of Plans

But he took note of their distress
when he heard their cry;
for their sake he remembered his covenant
and out of his great love he relented.
(Psalm 106:44–45)

God does nothing but in answer to prayer. (John Wesley)

It is true to say that God never changes. "Jesus Christ is the same yesterday and today and forever" (Hebrews 13:8). But this verse refers to His nature: He is always good and holy and loving and merciful. It is also true to say that we often ask God to change a situation and instead He changes us. He doesn't always make our burdens smaller; sometimes He makes us stronger.

But sometime our prayers convince God to intervene in a way He would not have had we not prayed. Because of the Hebrew children's flagrant disobedience, God intended to destroy them (Exodus 32:9–10). But Moses prayed that God would not do so, and God changed His mind (vv. 11–14). Have you ever considered that you can convince God to act in a brand-new way because He responds to the urgency of your heart and prayers? This shows that God responds to the prayers of His children.

Father God, thank You for loving me so much that You
take time to listen to my heart, my prayers, and what's on
my mind—and You respond! Amen.

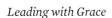

Walking with Peter

Then Peter got down out of the boat, walked on the water
and came toward Jesus. (Matthew 14:29)

What is courage? It is the ability to be strong in trust, in conviction,
in obedience. To be courageous is to step out in faith—to trust and
obey, no matter what. (Kay Arthur)

Okay, he ended up sinking like a rock, but for just a moment Peter did something amazing: he walked on water.

As amazing as that feat was, perhaps just as remarkable is the fact that he left the boat not in shallow water, not on a beautiful, calm day, but in the midst of a storm.

Some argue that an act like that takes stupidity. But really it takes confidence. Not a loud, self-aggrandizing, boastful kind of confidence, but the kind that truly believes a miracle is going to happen. For Peter, that belief was centered on Jesus. He had seen what He had done before and he trusted He would do it again in his life.

How is your sense of trust? Are you ready to walk on water when the next storm comes?

Heavenly Father, I do trust You and put myself in Your hands. I know You can do amazing things in my life! Amen.

Pray for Others

As for me, far be it from me that I should sin against the Lord by failing to pray for you. And I will teach you the way that is good and right. (1 Samuel 12:23)

If we truly love people, we will desire for them far more than it is within our power to give them, and this will lead us to prayer: Intercession is a way of loving others. (Richard J. Foster)

A Classic Devotion from E. M. Bounds

*P*eople must pray, and people must be prayed for. The Christian must pray for all things, of course, but prayers for people are infinitely more important, just as people are infinitely more important than things. Also, prayers for people are far more important than prayers for things because people more deeply involve God's will and the work of Jesus Christ. People are to be cared for, sympathized with, and prayed for, because sympathy, pity, compassion, and care accompany and precede prayer for people.

Our praying concerns not only ourselves, but all people and their greatest interests, and even the salvation of their immortal souls. Praying is a business that takes hold of eternity and the things beyond the grave. It is a business that involves earth and heaven. All worlds are touched by prayer, and all worlds are influenced by prayer.[30]

Father, thank You for the people in my life, and thank
You for knowing their needs. Help me to love others
by praying for them. Amen.

One Hug to Go, Please

Always try to be kind to each other and to everyone else.
(1 Thessalonians 5:15)

*Let us be kind to one another, for most of us are fighting a
hard battle.* (Ian Maclaren)

The restaurant was crowded. A handful of waitresses tried to serve the many guests. A family of four made rude remarks regarding the service, and the father spoke harshly to his server. She rushed to the back and returned with a tray filled with food. On her return trip, a plate fell from her tray and shattered. After a stunned half second, the waitress broke down and cried.

From the next table, a woman stood up without a word and gave the waitress a hug. The waitress cried on her shoulder for a few seconds before cleaning up the dish. When the waitress returned to the family's table, the father apologized to her, and a smile returned to her face.

It's funny how the kind actions of others can bring out the best in people, even during difficult circumstances. Whom can you encourage today?

Lord, help me sow the seeds of peace and
kindness in my life. Amen.

Soaking in the Word

*I lift up my hands to your commands, which I love, and I
meditate on your decrees.* (Psalm 119:48)

*Meditation is the activity of calling to mind, and thinking over, and dwelling
on, and applying to oneself, the various things that one knows about the
works and ways and purposes and promises of God.* (J. I. Packer)

One of the benefits of God's Word is a cleansing and renewing of our minds. How does that happen? Our minds and hearts are pulled away from problems, disappointments, challenges, temptations, failures, resentments, and other negative thoughts and emotions and are redirected to God's thoughts, God's feelings, God's promises, God's principles. But this isn't just an exercise in self-help and guided thoughts. We are told in Hebrews that the Word of God is "living and active" (4:12). God's words aren't just ink on a page or bytes on an electronic device. Because they have been spoken by God Himself, they have a special way of touching us and renewing us in our inner core.

Are you worried, angry, tempted, distracted, resentful? Why not bathe in God's Word right now? Read a passage slowly a couple of times. Ask God to speak to you while you read each time. Memorize a key phrase or two. Repeat those phrases throughout your day. Truly bask and soak in the heart of God as you savor His words to you.

God, today I choose to ignore all distractions and focus
my mind on truths from Your Word. Let Your words sink
deep into my spirit. Amen.

The Creeping Wilderness

He who heeds discipline shows the way to life. (Proverbs 10:17)

*The neglected heart will soon be a heart overrun with worldly
thoughts; the neglected life will soon become a moral chaos; the
church that is not jealously protected by mighty intercession and
sacrificial labors will before long become the abode of every evil
bird and the hiding place for unsuspected corruption. The creeping
wilderness will soon take over that church that trusts in its own
strength and forgets to watch and pray.* (A. W. Tozer)

No great company sets a goal to slide into mediocrity. No
in-love newlyweds plan to divorce down the road. No fit,
muscular athlete figures how to put on a hundred pounds and get
totally out of shape in the next few years. No neighborhood holds
a meeting to outline steps toward a rundown community. No committed, vibrant Christian dreams of a day when he or she will walk
far from God, living a life of joyless compromise.

The common denominator in all the above too-often-true sce-
narios is neglect. The wilderness does not swallow up a great city
in a day; it creeps closer and closer—through neglect.

Prayer. A community of believers. God's Word. These are neglected at great risk to our souls!

Lord, give me diligence to take care of my soul and walk
ever more closely with You. Amen.

What Makes the Difference

Look to the LORD and his strength;
seek his face always.
(1 Chronicles 16:11)

Reach boldly for the miracle. God knows your gifts, your hindrances,
and the condition you're in at every moment. (Bruce Wilkinson)

*A*lready know what you need to do? Already feel a sense of purpose? Already have your eyes on a project or endeavor in your work? Your home life? Your personal development? Your spiritual journey?

Do you already have something to accomplish but fear how you are going to get it done? Whether you will be successful? Whether you have the strength and abilities?

Good! You're in a wonderful place to get started. And there is only one place to start. Turn to God. Tell Him your fears. Tell Him you are not sure you have what it takes. Then ask Him to provide you with His strength, encouragement, and wisdom to get the task done.

Maybe you don't have what it takes. But God does. And that makes all the difference!

Father, thank You for Your strength that meets me where
I am. Please continue to give me grace as I press forward.
Amen.

Invisible Reality

*Hope that is seen is no hope at all. Who hopes for what he
already has? But if we hope for what we do not yet have, we wait
for it patiently.* (Romans 8:24–25)

*I believe in the sun even if it isn't shining. I believe in love
even when I am alone. I believe in God even when He is silent.*
(author unknown)

*H*ow can you prove God is real?

The truth is, even though there are wonderful arguments for the existence of God, you cannot prove His existence. You can point to His world and His works, but He is invisible. Some have heard Him speak in an audible voice, but again, no one has caught God on an audio recorder.

Is this a problem? Is it troubling? Not at all! If God could be seen through a telescope or under a microscope, would He be the almighty God proclaimed in His Word? He is the Creator and as such cannot be studied in the same way as His creation.

Paul wrote, "Hope that is seen is no hope at all" (Romans 8:24). In other words, true hope is for the deeper, more profound realities that require open hearts rather than open eyes.

Lord, thank You for revealing Yourself to me in my heart
and thank You for the faith to see You in my life. Amen.

A Future Hope Changes the Present

We have heard of your faith in Christ Jesus and of the love you have for all the saints—the faith and love that spring from the hope that is stored up for you in heaven and that you have already heard about in the word of truth, the gospel. (Colossians 1:4–5)

In the midst of an ever-changing world, the good news is that the life of faith is anchored by the power, provisions, and promises of God. Circumstances may change, but the future is as sure as the character of God himself. No matter what happens, those who trust in God hope in his word. (Scott Hafemann)

A Classic Devotion from C. H. Spurgeon

*O*ur hope in Christ will animate our hearts to think often of heaven, for all that we can desire is promised there. Nevertheless let it never be said of us, that we are dreaming about the future and forgetting the present; let the future sanctify the present to highest uses. Through the Spirit of God the hope of heaven is the most potent force for the product of virtue; it is a fountain of joyous effort, it is the cornerstone of cheerful holiness. The man who has this hope in him goes about his work with vigor, for the joy of the Lord is his strength.[31]

Lord, thank You for the hope and promise of eternal life with You in heaven. May I find joy in Your Spirit. Amen.

God Hears Our Prayers

Be joyful always; pray continually; give thanks in all circumstances, for this is God's will for you in Christ Jesus. (1 Thessalonians 5:16–18)

If you want to see the rainbow, you must first put up with the rain.
(author unknown)

A farmer who lived near London during World War II wrote to the Scripture Gift Mission requesting prayer that no bombs would fall on his small farm. He enclosed a five-shilling offering. He explained that his harvest had been awful, and he didn't have enough money to bring in water for the parched crops. He could not afford another setback without losing his farm. The secretary of the mission wrote back and said he could not ask that his farm be spared but instead would pray that God's will would be done.

Soon afterward the largest bomb in the German arsenal hit the man's farm. The impact was so big that it unearthed a spring. The spring not only amply watered his farm but also enabled him to share water with his neighbors. And the next year, he enjoyed an abundant harvest. He sent a fifty-pound check to the mission as a thanksgiving offering.

Thank God for unexpected blessings.

Lord, thank You for Your power to work for my good even in the worst of events. I trust You fully to take care of me. Amen.

You Are Forgiven and I Love You

*"Come now, let us reason together," says the LORD. "Though your sins
are like scarlet, they shall be as white as snow; though they are red as
crimson, they shall be like wool." (Isaiah 1:18)*

*Forgiveness is the answer to the child's dream of a miracle by which
what is broken is made whole again, what is soiled is again made
clean. (Dag Hammarskjold)*

Several years ago in Spain, a father named Juan had become
estranged from his son, Paco. After more than a year spent
apart, Juan set off to find his son. He searched for months to no
avail.

In a last, desperate effort to find him, the father put a full-page
ad in a Madrid newspaper. It read: "Dear Paco, meet me in front of
this newspaper office at noon on Saturday. You are forgiven. I love
you. Your father."

On Saturday, eight hundred different young men named Paco
showed up, all seeking forgiveness and love from their fathers.

Our world is hungry for reconciliation. The good news is that
a message of acceptance and forgiveness, an offer of peace, can
go a long way. With whom can you share God's acceptance today?

God, thank You that You reach out to us. I pray
that You would use me to create reconciliation
and peace in my world. Amen.

By Grace Alone

But by the grace of God I am what I am, and his grace to me was not without effect. (1 Corinthians 15:10)

Yes, God's grace is always sufficient, and His arms are always open to give it. But, will our arms be open to receive it? (Beth Moore)

A Classic Devotion from Andrew Murray

Law demands; grace bestows. Law commands, but gives no strength to obey. Grace promises and performs, doing everything for us. Law burdens, casts down, and condemns. Grace comforts, makes strong and glad. Law appeals to self to do its utmost; grace points to Christ to do all. Law requires effort and strain, urging us toward a goal we can never reach. Grace works all of God's blessed will in us. I pointed out to [a man I knew] how his first step should be to completely accept his failure and his inability, as God had been trying to show him, instead of striving against it. With this acceptance and confession, he could sink down before God in utter helplessness. There he would learn that, unless grace gave him deliverance and strength, he could never do better than he had done, and that grace would, indeed, work all for him. He must come out from under law, self, and effort, taking his place under grace and allowing God to do all.[32]

Lord, I know that when I am weak, I am strong in You. Thank You for the grace that makes serving You a joy. Amen.

The Blessing of Obedience

*Get yourself ready! Stand up and say to them whatever
I command you. (Jeremiah 1:17)*

*The gospel alone is sufficient to rule the lives of Christians
everywhere. Any additional rules made to govern men's conduct
added nothing to the perfection already found in the Gospel of
Jesus Christ. (John Wycliffe)*

*E*ric Liddell, known as the "Flying Scotsman," was an Olympic runner—and a minister of the gospel. He took a strong stand when he refused to compete in a race because the meet was held on a Sunday. Rather than running, Eric was at church preaching as the games continued without him. He was faithful to what he knew was God's will for his life. Since that day in 1924, his testimony has ministered to thousands of people, young and old.

Eric later went on to win the 400-meter race at the 1924 Summer Olympics held in Paris; he chose to honor God with his decisions, and he was blessed with success. His passion for running was evident, but his love and commitment to Christ, who gave him the ability to run, were foremost in his heart and mind.

When you know God's will in a specific area of your life, do you obey? Do you receive the blessing He has for you?

Father, I am not always quick to obey. Help me to see the
wisdom and experience the riches of living for You! Amen.

Harvest Time

He makes grass grow for the cattle,
and plants for man to cultivate—
bringing forth food from the earth . . .
and bread that sustains his heart.
(Psalm 104:14–15)

We know that our reward depends not on the job itself but on the
faithfulness with which we serve God. (Pope John Paul I)

*E*very year, farmers go into a flurry of activity when harvest time arrives. The memory of the long hours of hard labor necessary to guarantee a good crop seems to fade in the distance. They feel pride at seeing the finished results of all their work— grain, vegetables, and livestock that will feed many people.

We all experience harvest times in our lives, whether we own a farm or can't keep a houseplant alive. We must work hard toward our goals, whether they're professional, personal, or spiritual. But if we're persistent and diligent, we'll experience a harvest; we'll reap rewards from our labors. And that's a very special kind of joy, the thrill of hard work paying off.

God, give me diligence to keep working so that I might see
fruit in my life and in the lives of others. Amen.

The Good Shepherd

"My sheep listen to my voice; I know them, and they follow me."
(John 10:27)

I know not the way God leads me, but well do I know my Guide.
(Martin Luther)

*I*n John 10, Jesus gives us plenty of reasons that we should trust Him and follow Him:

- Verse 10: He has come to give us abundant life. What awaits us when we follow Him are green pastures and abundant provision for our needs.
- Verse 11: He lays down His life for us. He always has our best interests at heart and serves us sacrificially.
- Verse 14: He knows us. He knows what's really best for us.
- Verse 28: He is strong enough to protect us.

We couldn't ask for a better Shepherd, always ready to guide and protect. Have you thanked Him today? Are you following Him now?

Lord, thank You for Your goodness to me. I love You. Amen.

Bold Faith

*"I tell you the truth, if you have faith as small as a mustard seed, you
can say to this mountain, 'Move from here to there' and it will move.
Nothing will be impossible for you."* (Matthew 17:20)

*Faith and works are bound up in the same bundle. He that obeys
God trusts God; and he that trusts God obeys God. He that is
without faith is without works; and he that is without works is
without faith.* (C. H. Spurgeon)

A Classic Devotion from Martin Luther

*F*aith is a living, bold trust in God's grace, so certain of God's
favor that it would risk death a thousand times trusting in it.
Such confidence and knowledge of God's grace makes you happy,
joyful and bold in your relationship to God and all creatures. The
Holy Spirit makes this happen through faith. Because of it, you
freely, willingly, and joyfully do good to everyone, serve everyone,
suffer all kinds of things, love and praise the God who has shown
you such grace. Thus, it is just as impossible to separate faith and
works as it is to separate heat and light from fire! Ask God to work
faith in you, or you will remain forever without faith, no matter
what you wish, say or can do.[33]

Lord, I pray that my faith would show up in my life through
good works for You. Amen.

Rest for the Weary

My soul clings to you;
your right hand upholds me.
(Psalm 63:8)

Pray, and let God worry. (Martin Luther)

A badly broken foot landed Patti in a wheelchair on an international trip. Instead of sightseeing, she spent her time in a hospital bed—definitely not where she wanted to be. But Patti found that because she wasn't able to be as active, she had more time to spend with the Lord and listen to His message for her life:

> I had the opportunity to rest in Him and rely on Him for healing in my soul as well as my body. God used the nine months of recovery and physical therapy to draw my heart near to His.

The Bible tells us that we will experience trials and tribulations in life and that when we do, we have a choice to make. We can either endure the time by basking in pity—or we can look upon the trial as an opportunity to invite Christ to do new work in our hearts. The latter brings with it joy and peace and a sense of satisfaction in knowing even tough times are not wasted.

Father, thank You for helping me respond to You when
life is tough—and for making this a time to grow into the
person You want me to be. Amen.

God's Love Commended to Us

But God demonstrates his own love for us in this: While we were still sinners, Christ died for us. (Romans 5:8)

If we want proof of God's love for us, then we must look first at the Cross where God offered up His Son as a sacrifice for our sins. Calvary is the one objective, absolute, irrefutable proof of God's love for us. (Jerry Bridges)

A Classic Devotion from Charles Grandison Finney

So long as we think of God only as One to be feared, not to be loved, there will be a prejudice against Him as more an enemy than a friend. Yet, God would lead us to serve Him in love and not in bondage. He would draw us forth into the liberty of the sons of God. He loves to see the obedience of the heart. He would inspire love enough to make all our service free and cheerful and full of joy.

If you wish to make others love you, you must give them your love. Show your servants the love of your heart, so will you break their bondage, and make their service one of love. In this way God commends His love towards us in order to win our hearts to Himself, and thus get us ready and fit to dwell forever in His eternal home.

His ultimate aim is to save us from our sins that He may fill us forever with His own joy and peace.[34]

Lord, help me to serve You with joy. Amen.

Peace and Encouragement

A Sure Foundation

Those who trust in the Lᴄᴀᴀ are like Mount Zion, which cannot be shaken but endures forever. (Psalm 125:1)

God is the only one who can make the valley of trouble a door of hope. (Catherine Marshall)

*D*uring the Great Depression, many people lost hope in the government, their churches, their families, and even God as the downward spiral of economic disaster engulfed everything they owned. People who had previously been considered upper-middle class found themselves standing in soup lines. Those who had ordered their lives around money faced dismal futures, and suicides became common.

Sound familiar? Is it possible that living in a prosperous society tempts us to put our hope in the wrong things?

The truth is that no earthly thing deserves our trust; recent economic woes and front-page scandals demonstrate once again that even the most stable institution, person, or system can fail. But when we place our hope in God, we find His protection and renewal even in the deepest valleys of our lives on earth. He alone is a worthy foundation on which to build our lives.

Lord, You are the One who holds my life in Your hands.
Today I put my trust in You. Amen.

An Emergency Called Complacency

Let us throw off everything that hinders and the sin that so easily entangles. (Hebrews 12:1)

Here lies the tremendous mystery—that God should be all-powerful, yet refuse to coerce. He summons us to cooperation. We are honored in being given the opportunity to participate in His good deeds.
(Elisabeth Elliot)

Complacency is a blight that saps energy, dulls attitudes, and causes a drain on the brain. The first symptom is satisfaction with things as they are. The second is rejection of things as they might be. "Good enough" becomes today's watchword and tomorrow's standard. Like water, complacent people follow the easiest course—downhill. They draw false strength from looking back.

But God has given us certain responsibilities that require attention and action on our part. Our lives need upkeep, and we must be careful not to neglect these matters that require a non-complacent vigilance of attitude. Priority one is making sure we are following God. He does not force us to choose Him. But when we do, we experience His blessing.

God, I want to keep my life in line with You. Fill me with Your Holy Spirit and grant me diligence to keep following Your will. Amen.

Never Give Up

*I prayed for this child, and the L*ord* has granted me what I asked of him. So now I give him to the L*ord*.* (1 Samuel 1:27–28)

In all moods and in all seasons, pour out the soul in prayer and supplication with thanksgiving, and if the Spirit groans in intercession do not be afraid of the agony of prayer. (Bruce Wilkinson)

*H*annah loved the Lord and was a woman of good report. But she was barren, which in her culture made her something of an outcast. She prayed faithfully and diligently for years, crying out to God for a child. And then one day it happened. She bore a son and named him Samuel. Soon she did something that seems counter-intuitive: she took Samuel to the priest in Shiloh and left him there. Because God had blessed her with a child, she gave him back to God. In the end, God gave Hannah and her husband other children, and Samuel became one of the greatest figures in Israel's history.

Often we have to wait for the things we most deeply want. There are times when we have to accept no as an answer to prayer; but there are other times when we'll be blessed if we keep knocking, seeking, and asking. And what we receive will be a blessing not only for ourselves but for others as well.

God, I know that You see the desires of my heart. Today I bring them before You and determine to continue doing so, knowing that You are good. Amen.

Sing Praises

As they began to sing and praise, the Lord set ambushes against the men . . . who were invading Judah, and they were defeated.
(2 Chronicles 20:22)

In praise my soul ascends to self-forgetting adoration, seeing and praising only the majesty and power of God, His grace and redemption. (Ole Kristian O. Hallesby)

A Classic Devotion from Mrs. Charles E. Cowman

*O*h, that we could reason less about our troubles, and sing and praise more! There are thousands of things that we wear as shackles which we might use as instruments with music in them, if we only knew how.

Those men that ponder, and meditate, and weigh the affairs of life, and study the mysterious developments of God's providence, and wonder why they should be burdened and thwarted and hampered—how different and how much more joyful would be their lives, if, instead of forever indulging in self-revolving and inward thinking, they would take their experiences, day by day, and lift them up, and praise God for them.

We can sing our cares away easier than we can reason them away. Sing in the morning. The birds are the earliest to sing, and birds are more without care than anything else that I know of.[35]

Dear God, teach me to praise You and unburden myself by remembering Your goodness to me. Amen.

Faithfulness in the Pit

To the One who remembered us in our low estate
His love endures forever.
and freed us from our enemies,
His love endures forever.
(Psalm 136:23–24)

Each of us may be sure that if God sends us on stony paths He will provide us with strong shoes, and He will not send us out on any journey for which He does not equip us well. (Alexander Maclaren)

In Genesis 39:1–23, we read the fascinating story of Joseph. This handsome, brilliant, favorite son was sold into slavery by his own brothers and became a servant of Potiphar, an Egyptian army commander. Potiphar was so impressed with Joseph that he entrusted all he had to Joseph's care. But when Joseph rejected Potiphar's wife's advances, she took revenge by accusing Joseph of trying to rape her. Predictably, Potiphar had Joseph thrown in jail.

But because Joseph was a man who loved the Lord faithfully, God blessed him even in the pit of prison. Many years and events later, Joseph was made ruler over Egypt.

Heavenly Father, You are with me and provide everything I need, even in the darkest pits of life. Amen.

God with Us

The LORD your God is with you,
he is mighty to save.
He will take great delight in you,
he will quiet you with his love,
he will rejoice over you with singing.
(Zephaniah 3:17)

The God of Christians is a God of love and comfort, a God who fills
the soul and heart of those whom he possesses, a God who makes
them conscious of their inward wretchedness, and his infinite mercy.
(Blaise Pascal)

We live in a fast-paced, busy, media-saturated, noisy world. Is it any wonder that we really do need a quiet time every day? A time for prayer and God's Word? Because it's too easy to let the noise and activity of modern life cloud and obscure the reality that God is present and in our midst.

How different our lives would be if we walked each step and breathed each breath with the knowledge that God is right beside us. Rejoicing with us. Correcting us. Encouraging us. Loving us.

Do you slow down long enough to sense God's nearness to you?

Lord, thank You for being there for me, for being present
in all the moments of my life. Forgive me when I get too
busy to acknowledge You. Amen.

Love Is Costly

"My command is this: Love each other as I have loved you."
(John 15:12)

Whoever loves much, does much. (Thomas à Kempis)

*H*e had little himself, but he knew that the young Chinese mother he encountered had nothing at all. The woman looked so weak from starvation. He wondered if she would live through the night. She held a tiny baby girl in her arms. He handed the mother all the food he had, a cooked sweet potato. The young mother took a bite of the potato, chewed it carefully—and then pressed the warm food into her baby's mouth. She repeated the process again and again, not keeping a single bite for herself. Sadly, the mother died during the night. But the little girl lived.

Jesus said, "Greater love has no one than this, than to lay down one's life for his friends" (John 15:13 NKJV). He Himself went on to give His life so that we could live eternally with Him. We may never have to die for someone we love. But with God's help, we can learn to love others sacrificially, reflecting His perfect love.

Dear Lord, help me love others the way You
have loved me. Amen.

Never Fear

So do not fear, for I am with you; / do not be dismayed, for I am your God. / I will strengthen you and help you; / I will uphold you with my righteous right hand. (Isaiah 41:10)

If the Lord be with us, we have no cause of fear. His eye is upon us, His arm over us, His ear open to our prayer, His grace sufficient, His promise unchangeable. (John Newton)

*T*he fear reaction is wired into our brains, a part of our physiology. It's what triggers our fight-or-flight reaction, which can save our lives during sudden life-threatening circumstances. But fear is also an emotion that can interrupt our spiritual progress—and our lives in general—when it slips out of our control.

John, Jesus' "beloved disciple," contrasts fear and love in 1 John 4:18—the two are complete opposites. And if God is love, He is the solution to out-of-control fear. Whatever you're afraid of, surrender that fear to God. If you're afraid of the past, remember that He makes all things new. If you dread the future, meditate on His providence and plans for you. And if you fear dying or losing someone, remember that He has conquered death and His grace is sufficient for every need.

Fear can be a formidable foe. But God is truly able to help us expel it from our lives.

Father, I know that You can do anything. I ask for Your Spirit to fill me with Your love so that I might be free from fear. Amen.

Tips for Reading and Studying Scripture

For they received the message with great eagerness and examined the Scriptures every day to see if what Paul said was true. (Acts 17:11)

Absorb the Word into your system by dwelling on it, pondering it, going over it again and again in your mind, considering it from many different angles, until it becomes part of you. (Nancy Leigh DeMoss)

A Classic Devotion from Thomas Boston

- Follow a regular plan in reading [the Scriptures], that you may be acquainted with the whole; and make this reading a part of your private devotions.
- Set a special mark, however you find convenient, on those passages you read, which you find most suitable to your case, condition, or temptations. . . . It will be profitable often to review these.
- Read with a holy attention, arising from the consideration of the majesty of God, and the reverence due to him. This must be done with attention, first, to the words; second, to the sense; and, third, to the divine authority of the Scriptures.
- Let your main purpose in reading the Scriptures be practice, and not bare knowledge. Read that you may learn and do.[36]

Lord, I want Your Word to make a difference in my life. Teach to me to read and study it so that I might grow in You. Amen.

Enduring Joy

Let us fix our eyes on Jesus, the author and perfecter of our faith,
who for the joy set before him endured the cross, scorning its shame,
and sat down at the right hand of the throne of God. (Hebrews 12:2)

Christ came to take away our sins, to roll off our curse, to unbind
our chains, to open our prison house, to cancel our debt; in a word, to
give us the oil of joy for mourning, the garment of praise for the spirit
of heaviness. Is not this joy? (Octavius Winslow)

The perfect picture of joy is found in the life of Jesus. And what an amazing, active, buoyant, effective, fulfilling life He lived. But we don't see the full measure of His joy in the miracle of turning water to wine at a wedding or in the feeding the five thousand. Amazingly, we don't see Jesus' joy in full bloom until the darkest moment of his life: "for the joy set before him [he] endured the cross" (Hebrews 12:2).

In John 15:11 we read that Jesus spoke to His disciples, "I have told you this so that my joy may be in you and that your joy may be complete." In His final instructions He was teaching those He loved how to have the same joy He had through closeness to God the Father. But it was on the cross that He paid the price that made this joy possible.

Next time you struggle with finding a sense of joy, simply consider Jesus.

Lord, thank You for the cross that saves me and brings me
to You, for the joy of knowing You. I love You. Amen.

Costly Grace

*"Anyone who does not carry his cross and follow me
cannot be my disciple."* (Luke 14:27)

*Grace is never cheap. It is absolutely free to us, but infinitely
expensive to God.* (Jerry Bridges)

A Classic Devotion from Dietrich Bonhoeffer

Costly grace is the treasure hidden in the field; for the sake of it a man will gladly go and sell all that he has. It is the pearl of great price which the merchant will sell all his goods to buy. It is the kingly rule of Christ, for whose sake one will pluck out the eye which causes him to stumble; it is the call of Jesus Christ at which the disciple leaves his nets and follows him.

Such grace is costly because it calls us to follow, and it is grace because it calls us to follow Jesus Christ. It is costly because it costs a man his life, and it is grace because it gives a man the only true life. It is costly because it condemns sin, and grace because it justifies the sinner.

Grace is costly because it compels a man to submit to the yoke of Christ and follow him; it is grace because Jesus says: "my yoke is easy and my burden light."[37]

Lord, thank You for grace. May I never take it for granted; may I always remember with reverence what it cost You. Amen.

In the Beginning

In the beginning God created the heavens and the earth.
(Genesis 1:1)

All glory comes from daring to begin. (Eugene F. Ware)

*W*hen we discuss the economy and new jobs, entrepreneurs and small business owners are always mentioned. Those brave souls leave the security of an established company—and a regular paycheck—to start a new venture.

We can admire men and women who dare to embark on a bold new beginning, but the ultimate Entrepreneur, the original Entrepreneur, the One who gave the most to accomplish the most, is none other than God, the Creator of the universe and all that is. Now that's a business story, a love story, and a grand adventure rolled into one.

When was the last time you praised God the Creator? When was the last time you thanked God for creating you?

God, I'm in awe of Your creativity. I ask You for a heart of gratitude for the world You have given me and for creating me the way You did. Amen.

A Prayerful Heart

God Still Speaks

My sheep listen to my voice; I know them, and they follow me.
(John 10:27)

*Stay within whispering distance. If you stray, you won't
hear His voice.* (author unknown)

*T*hroughout the Bible, God interacts intimately with those who seek Him. He whispered to the prophet Samuel as a young boy. He spoke directly to and through the prophets. He wrestled with Jacob. He called David a man after His own heart and sent His angel Gabriel to greet Mary as someone "highly favored." And as Jesus, He walked among us, just as He did with Adam and Eve in the garden of Eden.

Thousands of years later, God is still speaking. He longs to hear from us, His children, in prayer, and He wants to speak back to us. Relationships thrive on communication—regular, quality communication. Through prayer and listening to God through His word, we can experience a loving, thriving relationship with none other than God Himself.

Lord, thank You that You speak to us and seek us
out. Thank You for knowing me. Teach me to listen
to and follow You. Amen.

A Shared Hope

And let us consider how we may spur one another on toward love and good deeds. Let us not give up meeting together, as some are in the habit of doing, but let us encourage one another—and all the more as you see the Day approaching. (Hebrews 10:24–25)

The Bible knows nothing of solitary religion. (John Wesley)

Church attendance is down in America. Fewer people attend, and those who attend do so less often. This may be due to more Sunday morning activity options, irrelevant churches or churches that fail to engage their congregations, or the growth of a post-Christian generation.

Whether you agree or disagree with any of these reasons, one thing is certain: the writer to the Hebrews said that meeting together is essential for the spiritual vitality of believers. He warns that there is a day of judgment coming when it is going to be difficult to live the Christian life, and we need to encourage one another and spur one another on to good deeds.

Do you have a place where you regularly meet with other believers for spiritual growth and encouragement?

Dear Father, help me to commit myself to the body of
Christ and help others to grow in their faith—while I grow
in my faith too. Amen.

No Worries

"Are not two sparrows sold for a penny? Yet not one of them will fall to the ground apart from the will of your Father. And even the very hairs of your head are all numbered. So don't be afraid; you are worth more than many sparrows." (Matthew 10:29–31)

Every evening I turn my worries over to God. He's going to be up all night anyway. (Mary C. Crowley)

It is believed by some that worrying is a sin. Do you believe that? How could such a natural and common emotion be a violation of God's will?

Without attempting to answer that question, all of us can argue that worry is rarely, if ever, helpful—and it is usually detrimental to our quality of life. Worry is bad for our physical health, bad for our mental health, and it doesn't change anything.

Fundamentally, worry is a lack of faith in God and His protection and provision in our lives. That's why some call it a sin. It is true that He doesn't promise to make everything turn out the way we want it to. But He does promise to meet all our needs and to never forsake us.

Will you believe Him? If so why worry? With God beside us, there are no real worries.

God, You clothe and feed all the birds outside my window,
so I know You care for me. Amen.

An Obedient Surrender

"Therefore everyone who hears these words of Mine and acts on them, may be compared to a wise man who built his house on the rock. And the rain fell, and the floods came, and the winds blew and slammed against that house; and yet it did not fall, for it had been founded on the rock." (Matthew 7:24–25 NASB)

Unless he obeys, a man cannot believe. (Dietrich Bonhoeffer)

A Classic Devotion from Andrew Murray

*Y*ou know in daily life what absolute surrender is. You know that everything has to be given up to its special, definite object and service. I have a pen in my pocket, and that pen is absolutely surrendered to the one work of writing, and that pen must be absolutely surrendered to my hand if I am to write properly with it. If another holds it partly, I cannot write properly. This coat is absolutely given up to me to cover my body. The Temple of Solomon was absolutely surrendered to God when it was dedicated to Him. And every one of us is a temple of God, in which God will dwell and work mightily on one condition—absolute surrender to Him. God claims it, God is worthy of it, and without it God cannot work His blessed work in us. God not only claims it, but God will work it Himself.[38]

Lord, today I choose to surrender to You completely. Amen.

Consistently and Persistently

*Then Jesus told his disciples a parable to show them that they should
always pray and not give up.* (Luke 18:1)

*Prayer is not overcoming God's reluctance, but laying hold
of His willingness.* (Martin Luther)

*J*esus spoke in many parables to teach His followers about living
in the kingdom of God. In one parable, He told them about a
widow who came before a judge with a grievance. She constantly,
continually requested that the judge protect her from her adversary. The judge always refused to grant the widow's request, but
she was persistent until finally the judge said, "Even though I don't
fear God or care about men, yet because this widow keeps bothering me, I will see that she gets justice, so that she won't eventually
wear me out with her coming!" (Luke 18:4–5).

Salespeople know you have to knock on doors persistently
and consistently to close a sale. Teachers know repetition is a
necessary ingredient if students are to retain what they learn.
Constantly coming to God doesn't pester Him, but it does keep our
own focus on Him.

Heavenly Father, thank You for the invitation to
come to You in prayer on a daily, hourly, and even
moment-to-moment basis. Amen.

Remember to Remember

*I will remember the deeds of the LORD; yes, I will remember
your miracles of long ago.* (Psalm 77:11)

Memory keeps gratitude fresh and gratitude keeps faith fruitful.
(Dale Ralph Davis)

The concept of remembering is an important biblical theme. The command not to forget is given more than four hundred times. We are to remember the wonders of God's creation and works of His hands (Deuteronomy 4:32); that the world belongs to God (Psalm 50:10); the deliverance of His people from captivity (Deuteronomy 5:15); and the sacrificial gift of Jesus Christ on the cross (1 Corinthians 11:25).

Remembering is not just about looking at the past. It is about facing the future with confidence. Remembering keeps us from falling into the sin of ingratitude—we remember all that God has done for us and don't take pride in our own abilities and accomplishments. Remembering also gives us encouragement for tough times—we remember that times have been tough before and God helped us through them, and we know in our hearts He will do so again.

Today have you remembered to remember?

God, You have done so much for me. Today I choose to
reflect on Your goodness in my past with hope for the
present and future. Amen.

Turnaround

"I tell you, no! But unless you repent, you too will all perish."
(Luke 13:3)

A pessimist sees the difficulty in every opportunity; an optimist sees the opportunity of every difficulty. (Winston Churchill)

*I*s it fair to say we live in a lax, permissive, indulgent age? That doesn't include everybody, of course, but many of us put pleasure before discipline in our own habits, our child rearing, and our attitudes toward the behavior of others.

Part of this prevailing attitude is due to our desire not to be judgmental. That is a good impulse. But some of it comes from being too comfortable in our relative wealth and easy lifestyle!

Repentance is turning away from sin and going in the opposite direction. Not all of our choices deal with sin; nevertheless, the wise person incorporates discipline and even self-denial to grow toward maturity.

In what ways do you need more discipline in your life?

Dear God, it is by Your grace I am saved, but thank You for giving me the power to make decisions that help me grow and become stronger. Amen.

The Greatest of These

*And now these three remain: faith, hope and love. But the
greatest of these is love.* (1 Corinthians 13:13)

*All the fruits of the Spirit . . . are summed up in charity, or Christian
love; because this is the sum of all grace.* (Jonathan Edwards)

Some Scripture is so clear it needs no interpretation or comment! Take a moment to prayerfully read through the famous
"love chapter" from the apostle Paul:

> If I speak in the tongues of men and of angels, but have not love,
> I am only a resounding gong or a clanging cymbal. If I have the
> gift of prophecy and can fathom all mysteries and all knowledge, and if I have a faith that can move mountains, but have
> not love, I am nothing. If I give all I possess to the poor and surrender my body to the flames, but have not love, I gain nothing.
>   Love is patient, love is kind. It does not envy, it does not
> boast, it is not proud. It is not rude, it is not self-seeking, it is
> not easily angered, it keeps no record of wrongs. Love does not
> delight in evil but rejoices with the truth. It always protects,
> always trusts, always hopes, always perseveres. (1 Corinthians
> 13:1–7)

Dear God, thank You for all the talents and gifts You have
given me. But thank You most of all for love. Help love to
grow in me every day. Amen.

Paid in Full

And God is able to make all grace abound to you, so that in all things at all times, having all that you need, you will abound in every good work. (2 Corinthians 9:8)

We are never more like God than when we give. (Charles Swindoll)

*A*long with many others, the Litt family suffered lean times during the Great Depression. In order to keep food on the table, Mr. Litt reluctantly opened a charge account with the neighborhood grocer.

When she turned sixteen, Kathryn Litt went to work at the five-and-dime store to help with family expenses. And out of admiration for the many sacrifices he had made, she also wanted to give her dad a great birthday present, something he hadn't received in several years.

After receiving her first paycheck, she burst through the front door in excitement and handed her father a carefully wrapped present. He couldn't hide his tears when he found inside a neat stack of receipts from the grocery store, all marked "paid in full."

During times of trouble, it's tempting to draw inward in fearful selfishness. But when we react to difficulties with unselfish acts, we make life beautiful—for ourselves and for others, even in the worst of times.

Lord, help me to trust You so much that I am able to give freely to others even in the midst of my own troubles. Amen.

Our Inheritance

"I do not give to you as the world gives. Do not let your hearts be troubled and do not be afraid." (John 14:27)

This blessed friend is Jesus; it is his will and plan that we hang on to him, and hold tight always, in whatever circumstances.
(Julian of Norwich)

A Classic Devotion from D. L. Moody

*D*id you ever think that when Christ was dying on the cross, He made a will? Perhaps you have thought that no one ever remembered you in a will. You have been remembered, if you are in the kingdom. Christ remembered you in His will. He willed His body to Joseph of Arimathea, He willed His mother to John, the son of Zebedee—and what a legacy it was! Better than bonds and stocks—and He willed His Spirit back to His Father. But to His disciples He said, "My peace, I leave that with you; that is my legacy. My joy, I give that to you." "My joy," think of it! "My peace give I unto you"—not our peace, but His peace!

Christ rose to execute His own will. If He had left us a lot of gold, thieves would have stolen it in the first century; we never would have got it; but He left His peace and His joy for every true believer.[39]

God, thank You for Your many blessings, including the inheritance of peace. Amen.

Through the Ages

*The statutes of the L*ORD *are trustworthy,*
making wise the simple.
*The precepts of the L*ORD *are right,*
giving joy to the heart. (Psalm 19:7–8)

It is not at all incredible, that a book which has been so long in
the possession of mankind should contain many truths as yet
undiscovered. (Bishop Butler)

*N*o other book has had a greater influence on the course of history than God's Word. Consider the testimony of greats from previous generations:

- George Washington: "It is impossible to rightly govern the world without God and the Bible."
- Abraham Lincoln: "Take all of [the Bible] that you can by reason and the balance by faith, and you will live and die a better man."
- Daniel Webster: "If there is anything in my thoughts or style to commend, the credit is due to my parents for instilling in me an early love of the Scriptures."

What is your testimony on the importance of God's Word?

Lord, help me to place the kind of priority on Your Word
that reflects my trust in You—and that sows seeds of
greatness in me. Amen.

A Fountain of Joy

Though you have not seen him, you love him; and even though
you do not see him now, you believe in him and are filled with an
inexpressible and glorious joy. (1 Peter 1:8)

When I met Christ, I felt that I had swallowed sunshine.
(E. Stanley Jones)

A Classic Devotion from D. L. Moody

*H*appiness is caused by things that happen around me, and circumstances will mar it; but joy flows right on through trouble; joy flows on through the dark; joy flows in the night as well as in the day; joy flows all through persecution and opposition. It is an unceasing fountain bubbling up in the heart; a secret spring the world can't see and doesn't know anything about. The Lord gives His people perpetual joy when they walk in obedience to him.

Joy is love exalted; peace is love in repose; long-suffering is love enduring; gentleness is love in society; goodness is love in action; faith is love on the battlefield; meekness is love in school; and temperance is love in training. The world does not understand theology or dogma, but it understands love and sympathy.[40]

God, thank You for the joy You offer me, a joy
that transcends all circumstances. Help me walk
closely with You. Amen.

By Prayer

You do not have, because you do not ask God. (James 4:2)

Prayer is the way and means God has appointed for the communication of the blessings of His goodness to His people. (Arthur W. Pink)

God blesses us every day with things we don't necessarily ask for, things we might take for granted: a place to live, fresh air, the beauty of nature, friends, and family. But for some blessings, He chooses to make us part of the process by encouraging us to ask for what we need and want. And the truth is that we experience life and blessings more fully when we look to God for all our wants and needs, either by expressing gratitude or petitioning Him for our needs.

If you're hurting for something today, ask God for it. And if you're not, thank Him for what you have. You'll find your life more richly blessed—even if only from an improved attitude. Best yet, your whole being will be permeated with an awareness of God's presence and goodness.

Lord, thank You for blessing me. Help me open my heart
and needs to You today. Amen.

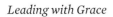

You've Been Sent

Moses said to God, "Suppose I go to the Israelites and say to them, 'The God of your fathers has sent me to you,' and they ask me, 'What is his name?' Then what shall I tell them?" God said to Moses, "I AM WHO I AM. This is what you are to say to the Israelites: 'I AM has sent me to you.'" (Exodus 3:13–14)

Lord, make my life a window for Your light to shine through and a mirror to reflect Your love to all I meet. (Robert Schuller)

*M*oses was raised and educated in Pharaoh's court as a young nobleman. But when God called him to lead his people out of slavery, he was terrified. He was afraid to speak, much less lead. He had good excuses. He stuttered. He had a criminal past. He had been abandoned by his mother as a baby.

But then he saw God in a burning bush. One by one his excuses were stripped away. His doubts and questions were answered as only God can answer. And he, a refugee far from home, was sent with a message from God.

You've been sent too. With a message from God. No excuses. No giving in to fear. Are you ready to say yes?

Dear God, I want to be willing to heed Your call. Show me what You would have me do to share Your love with the world. Amen.

Praying Scripture

*I pray also that the eyes of your heart may be enlightened in order
that you may know the hope to which he has called you, the riches of
his glorious inheritance in the saints.* (Ephesians 1:18)

*The richness of God's Word ought to determine our prayer, not the
poverty of our heart.* (Dietrich Bonhoeffer)

*J*ames, the brother of Jesus, tells us, "The effective, fervent prayer
of a righteous man avails much" (5:16 NKJV). When we face hard
times, prayer can sustain us like nothing else—both the prayers of
others and the continual prayers we offer for our own situation.

Perhaps one of the most effective ways to pray powerfully is
to pray the words of Scripture. Just as Jesus responded to temptation with Scripture, so we can experience spiritual victory with
the Word of God.

Pray God's promises and ask for their fulfillment in your life.
Pray that those close to you would follow God's path for them.
Pray for His kingdom to come, His will to be done on earth as it
is in heaven. There can be no better words of comfort, strength,
healing, love, and hope than the very words and thoughts of God
as revealed in His Word.

Father, thank You for Your powerful Word. I pray that my
prayer life would become more powerful and effective.
May my prayers move hearts and mountains. Amen.

Forgive to Live

Therefore, as God's chosen people, holy and dearly loved, clothe yourselves with compassion, kindness, humility, gentleness and patience. Bear with each other and forgive whatever grievances you may have against one another. Forgive as the Lord forgave you.
(Colossians 3:12–13)

Learning how to forgive and forget is one of the secrets of a happy Christian life. (Warren Wiersbe)

Grudges and grievances. We feel them; we welcome them; we ponder them; they grow; they make themselves at home in our lives. It's almost as if we enjoy them and the drama they bring—but ultimately they sap energy, joy, peace, and spiritual vitality. In fact, we end up being judged in the same way we judge others (Matthew 7:2). What we think is going to protect our very selves is the thing that gnaws at it.

The antidote is simple. Not easy, but simple. It's forgiveness. Not holding someone's wrongs against them, considering their slights and disregard as if they were never done against us. *I forgive you.* A simple phrase. A different task. But a task empowered and rewarded by God!

Lord, I forgive others as You have forgiven me. Amen.

This Is My Song

He restores my soul.
He guides me in paths of righteousness
for his name's sake.
(Psalm 23:3)

If perfect earthly sight were offered me tomorrow I would not accept it. I
might not have sung hymns to the praise of God if I had been distracted
by the beautiful and interesting things about me. (Fanny Crosby)

*F*anny Crosby, blinded at six weeks old in 1820, was raised by her mother and grandmother. Throughout her life, she always maintained her faith in God's goodness. She never believed that He was punishing her, and she believed that if she kept her heart open to Him, He would lead her.

As a seven-year resident of a school for the blind, she learned to sing and to play the piano and guitar. She went on to spend her entire life serving the Lord through poetry and music, writing such beloved hymns as "Blessed Assurance" and "Jesus Is Tenderly Calling You Home," which are still sung by millions today.

Even when we find ourselves hindered by our circumstances, God can use us where we are. If we will just keep trusting Him, we will have many reasons to proclaim, "This is my story, this is my song, praising my Savior all the day long."

Make me ready to serve You, God. Amen.

Go with Joy

You will go out in joy
and be led forth in peace;
the mountains and hills
will burst into song before you,
and all the trees of the field
will clap their hands.
(Isaiah 55:12)

Attitude is a little thing that makes a big difference.
(Winston Churchill)

*B*ad habits are easier to form than good habits. It's easier to wallow in a bad attitude than to change the way we look at life in a positive way. Those principles are true of both groups and individuals.

What is the attitude of the various groups you belong to? Your neighborhood friends? Your work department? Your family? Your church? Is there a spirit of negativity and complaining—or a spirit of joy? Most important, what attitude do you bring to the table?

Are you positive or negative? Do you go forth into the world with a contagious joy—where even mountains and hills "burst into song"—or do you succumb to a prevailing negativity? The choice is yours!

Dear God, help me to take joy into every situation and
every meeting I have today. Amen.

Carry Your Cross

"If anyone would come after me, he must deny himself and take up his cross and follow me." (Mark 8:34)

The only lasting treasure is spiritual; the only perfect freedom is serving God. (Malcolm Muggeridge)

A Classic Devotion from Alexander Smellie

The cross which my Lord bids me take up and carry may assume different shapes. I may have to content myself with a lowly and narrow sphere, when I feel that I have capacities for much higher work. I may have to go on cultivating year after year, a field which seems to yield me no harvests whatsoever. There are many crosses, and every one of them is sore and heavy. None of them is likely to be sought out by me of my own accord. But never is Jesus so near me as when I lift my cross, and lay it submissively on my shoulder, and give it the welcome of a patient and unmurmuring spirit.

He draws close, to ripen my wisdom, to deepen my peace, to increase my courage, to augment my power to be of use to others, through the very experience which is so grievous and distressing, and then I grow under the load.[41]

Lord, I choose to take up my cross and follow You. Thank You for being close to me when I do so. Amen.

All His Benefits

Praise the Lord, O my soul,
and forget not all his benefits.
(Psalm 103:2)

Love is the child of gratitude. Love grows as gratitude is felt, and
then breaks out into praise and thanksgiving to God: "I love the Lord
because he hath heard my voice and my supplication."
(E. M. Bounds)

*I*n Psalm 103, the psalmist urges us to praise God for all the things He does for us:

- He forgives our sins and heals our sicknesses (v. 3).
- He saves us from the messes we get into (v. 4).
- He gives us good gifts (v. 5).
- He has compassion on us as His children (v. 13).

One possible cause of feelings of anxiety and lack in our lives is that we trust in something—ourselves, money, another person—more than we trust in God. In times like these, we need to let the truth sink into our hearts: God is more than enough. He lovingly meets our every need. Step one to living joyfully and thankfully in His grace is acknowledging His goodness.

Lord, You do so much for me. You are all I need. Amen.

Love Is the Winner

"But I tell you: Love your enemies and pray for those
who persecute you." (Matthew 5:44)

Nature teaches us to love our friends, but religion our enemies.
(Thomas Fuller)

*D*avid Wilkerson's best-selling book, *The Cross and the Switchblade*, is the account of his dramatic and sometimes traumatic encounters with Nicky Cruz, leader of a notorious New York City gang of thugs, the Mau Maus. Ultimately, it is a story of love winning over hate.

One night, when Cruz threatened to use his knife to cut up Wilkerson, he was shocked to hear the preacher tell him that if he did, every piece of his body would scream out how much God and Reverend Wilkerson loved him. That message of love in the face of the hate that ruled his life would not leave the heart and mind of Cruz. And now, for more than fifty years, he has walked with God, serving in ministry, telling thousands upon thousands about the power of God's love and how it can transform even the wickedest of sinners.

Hate is powerful and destructive, but love truly is the winner.

Lord, Your love can transform anyone, and I'm grateful that
it has transformed me. Help me be a conduit of Your love
in someone's life this week. Amen.

Prayer Changes Things

Nothing is impossible with God. (Luke 1:37)

When we call on God, He bends down His ear to listen, as a father bends down to listen to his little child. (Elizabeth Charles)

A Classic Devotion from Oswald Chambers

*W*e grouse before God, we are apologetic or apathetic, but we ask very few things. Yet what a splendid audacity a childlike child has! Our Lord says—"Except ye become as little children." Ask, and God will do. Give Jesus Christ a chance, give Him elbow room, and no man will ever do this unless he is at his wits' end. When a man is at his wits' end it is not a cowardly thing to pray, it is the only way he can get into touch with Reality. Be yourself before God and present your problems, the things you know you have come to your wits' end over.

It is not so true that "prayer changes things" as that prayer changes me and I change things. God has so constituted things that prayer on the basis of Redemption alters the way in which a man looks at things. Prayer is not a question of altering things externally, but of working wonders in a man's disposition.[42]

Lord, sometimes I feel overwhelmed and unsure of how things are going to turn out. But I know that You hear my cries to You. Help me bring problems to You completely. Amen.

God's Plans

"For I know the plans I have for you," declares the Lord,
"plans to prosper you and not to harm you, plans to give you
hope and a future." (Jeremiah 29:11)

If we do not lay out ourselves in the service of mankind whom
should we serve? (John Adams)

As a young man, William Carey worked as a shoemaker living in London. He was fascinated by explorers and missionaries, anyone who traveled to foreign lands. His interest in other cultures soon became a deeply felt compassion for the lost and needy of the whole world. Some reported that on the walls of his shop, he hung hand-drawn maps of other countries, annotated with information he found about the climate, diet, and religions of various areas of the world. He built a globe from scraps of leather left over from the shoes he made, and he regularly prayed over it for the people of each country that he thought had never heard the gospel message. And later in life, he became a missionary to India and served many with the message and love of Christ.

Whether or not we serve on an overseas mission field, God has given all of us a calling. How do you find out what yours is? You can probably find it in your areas of interest. You might not think your passions in life are very useful; but in God's hands, they can be used to help and serve others.

Lord, show me what I can do to serve You by serving
others, and give me joy in doing it. Amen.

Two Brothers

"For whoever does the will of my Father in heaven is my brother and sister and mother." (Matthew 12:50)

Give God an inch, and He'll take a mile, encouraging and strengthening you each step of the way. (Joni Eareckson Tada)

The Bible is filled with famous brothers. Cain and Abel. Jacob and Esau. Peter and Andrew. The prodigal and his older brother. But there are two unnamed brothers whom Jesus introduced in a parable (Matthew 21:28–31). Their father gave each an assignment. One had a great attitude and immediately told his father, "No problem, I'm on it." The other brother moaned and complained and said, "No way." At the end of the day, the one with a great attitude had done a great job and the one with a bad attitude was still pouting and sullen. Right?

Wrong! The first brother got distracted and never got started. The other brother thought better of his refusal and got the job done. Jesus asked, "Which one obeyed?" Easy: the one who got it done.

A good attitude is better than a bad attitude, but actions still speak louder than words. Have a bad attitude over a task God has placed before you? Just get busy and it'll disappear before you know it.

God, sometimes there's a certain joy missing in my efforts to obey You. But I do want to live in a way that pleases You. Teach me to obey whether or not I feel like it. Amen.

Don't Let the Grass Grow

Be joyful in hope, patient in affliction, faithful in prayer.
(Romans 12:12)

Be sure no time is so well spent as that which a man spends on his knees. (J. C. Ryle)

The story is told that in Africa, members of one tribe that had converted to Christianity staked out their own space in the thicket surrounding their village for prayer time. Gradually, they wore down paths in the grass that led to their prayer spot. If a believer began to neglect prayer, his fellow Christians would kindly point out, "Brother, the grass grows on your path."

Has the grass grown on your path? Do you struggle with the discipline of regular prayer? If you're willing to make the effort, you'll reap rewards of spiritual growth. Wherever you are—whether you already have a well-established prayer time or struggle just to whisper a few words a day—begin adding a little extra time in prayer to your day. Doing so will help you see everything else in your day through the lens of God's love and presence.

Lord, sometimes I struggle to make time to meet with You.
I pray that You would strengthen my resolve to spend
quality time with You in prayer. Amen.

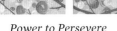

Big Faith

By faith Abraham, when called to go to a place he would later receive
as his inheritance, obeyed and went, even though he did not know
where he was going. (Hebrews 11:8)

One needs the sweetness to start one on the spiritual life but,
once started, one must learn to obey God for his own sake, not
for the pleasure. (C. S. Lewis)

God had promised to lead Abraham to a place called Canaan, a "land of promise." Even when things looked bleak—enemies everywhere, a difficult nephew, his and his wife's inability to have children—Abraham obeyed. And ultimately, despite the obstacles to overcome, he saw God's promise in his life fulfilled.

You may feel as if God is calling you into what looks like a forsaken desert. You may not be sure how God's promises will be fulfilled. But like Abraham, you can safely obey because even though you might not know where you're going, you do know who is leading you. And you know that He has never failed yet.

God, I know that You are trustworthy. I choose to
follow You today. Amen.

Thank God for Happiness

Is any one of you in trouble? He should pray. Is anyone happy?
Let him sing songs of praise. (James 5:13)

All our life is a celebration for us; we are convinced, in fact, that God
is always everywhere. We sing while we work . . . we pray while we
carry out all life's other occupations. (Saint Clement of Alexandria)

*I*nto every life a little rain must fall. Sometimes things just go wrong. But sometimes things go right. And when they do, James says, we should praise God.

What's going right in your life today—what is making you happy? Is there a relationship in your life that's thriving? Do you have the simple blessings of a job and reliable transportation to work? Have you found an activity or service opportunity that brings you joy? You might have to do a little looking around and count your blessings; sometimes those little reasons for joy and gratitude get overlooked. But when you find something to be happy about, be happy.

When we find ourselves in trouble, we need to turn to God for help and strength. But when things are going well, we still need to turn to God. He deserves our thanksgiving for the good things He gives us.

Lord, You have given me so many reasons to be happy.
Today I want to express my joy as praise to You. Amen.

Bigger than You

If anyone serves, he should do it with the strength God provides, so that in all things God may be praised through Jesus Christ. To him be the glory and the power for ever and ever. Amen. (1 Peter 4:11)

The smallest things become great when God requires them of us; they are small only in themselves; they are always great when they are done for God, and when they serve to unite us with Him eternally.
(François Fénelon)

*I*t was only a couple of pennies, but her gift continues to give through the centuries as a model of humble and generous sharing. She was a widow who didn't give with fanfare or from a surplus overflow. But she gave from her heart and God made something tiny grow into something large and beautiful (Mark 12:41–43).

A young boy shared a little bread and a few fish and it fed thousands. God knows how to multiply! It doesn't matter what size your gift is. You might not have much money or influence; you may not have tremendous talents or gifts; you might feel as though you're out of energy right now. But if you give out of a loving heart, a humble heart, a compassionate heart, God can take something small and turn it into something great.

Dear God, thank You for taking what I bring to the table
and making something great out of it. Amen.

Hope in Your Word

How sweet are your words to my taste,
sweeter than honey to my mouth!
(Psalm 119:103)

The longer you read the Bible, the more you will like it; it will grow
sweeter and sweeter; and the more you get into the spirit of it, the
more you will get into the spirit of Christ. (William Romaine)

A Classic Devotion from King David

*Y*our word is a lamp to my feet and a light for my path. I have taken an oath and confirmed it, that I will follow your righteous laws. I have suffered much; preserve my life, O Lord, according to your word. Accept, O Lord, the willing praise of my mouth, and teach me your laws. Though I constantly take my life in my hands, I will not forget your law. The wicked have set a snare for me, but I have not strayed from your precepts. Your statutes are my heritage forever; they are the joy of my heart. My heart is set on keeping your decrees to the very end. I hate double-minded men, but I love your law. You are my refuge and my shield; I have put my hope in your word.[43]

Lord, I come to Your Word today wanting to make it part
of me and to delight in it my whole life. Help me to follow
You by following Your Word. Amen.

One Love

Each of you should look not only to your own interests, but also to the interests of others. (Philippians 2:4)

He who is filled with love is filled with God Himself. (St. Augustine)

There is no "new and improved" magical formula that will make your marriage better in only seven days. It is only when both husband and wife begin to practice the biblical principle of "mutual submission" (Ephesians 5:21) that love and a marriage can soar. Submission, one of the most difficult habits to cultivate in our self-centered society, simply means: "I love you so much that I will look out for your interests before I look out for mine."

God's plan for your life includes personal fulfillment, success, and happiness. But He also asks His children to be strong enough to take the initiative in loving and serving others. Even your spouse! And if you're not married, there are still many people in your life whom you can serve in love.

The good news is that love is still the most poignant and powerful force in the world. So whether your marriage is healthy and thriving, in need of some fine-tuning, or in a serious crisis, express to your spouse the love that God has so generously lavished on you—and watch God rekindle the flames of love and romance.

Lord, You love the church—your children—as a
husband loves his bride. Help me to love those closest
to me with Your love. Amen.

Learning to Wait for God's Best

> *O Lord Almighty,*
> *blessed is the man who trusts in you.*
> (Psalm 84:12)

> *God has wisely kept us in the dark concerning future events*
> *and reserved for himself the knowledge of them that he may*
> *train us up in a dependence upon himself and a continued*
> *readiness for every event.* (Matthew Henry)

Children can be impulsive and often want everything "now!" (So can grownups!) It is the wise parent who does not give in to every demand, but rather keeps some things on hold until the time is right.

God deals with us the same way. He makes every good thing available to His children—but only at the right time. He trains us to trust Him—even when we want something right now—so that we will become mature, Christlike adults who are better able to appreciate and enjoy His blessings. He also keeps us from greedy self-centeredness by answering some of our requests with a firm no.

To try and move ahead of God's perfect plan for us is to deny Him the privilege of teaching us and watching us grow to be like Him.

> Father, God, how grateful I am for the blessing of Your
> hand of guidance. Help me to wait for You. Amen.

Unbeatable Joy

He chose us in him before the creation of the world to be holy and blameless in his sight. In love he predestined us to be adopted as his sons through Jesus Christ, in accordance with his pleasure and will.
(Ephesians 1:4–5)

Resolve to keep happy and your joy and you shall form an invincible host against difficulties. (Helen Keller)

Someone may think he or she can put you in your place with a sarcastic slam in your direction, a joke at your expense, an unfair criticism, or some other form of putdown. But no one can make you feel bad about yourself if you march into life with an unconquerable joy—a joy that looks in the face of hardship and opposition and smiles.

Where does that joy come from? How can you develop that inner peace and confidence that doesn't allow the pettiness of life to rob you of joy? Simple. It's coming to the point in life that you know beyond a shadow of a doubt that the only opinion that really matters is that of your heavenly Father. Since He loves you so much, you have much to be joyful for!

God, I walk in joy today, knowing You know me
best and love me most. Amen.

Joyful Obedience

Submit yourselves, then, to God. Resist the devil, and he will flee from you. Come near to God and he will come near to you. (James 4:7–8)

I know the power obedience has of making things easy which seem impossible. (Saint Teresa of Avila)

A Classic Devotion from Thomas à Kempis

*I*t is a very great thing to obey, to live under a superior and not to be one's own master, for it is much safer to be subject than it is to command. Many live in obedience more from necessity than from love. Such become discontented and dejected on the slightest pretext; they will never gain peace of mind unless they subject themselves wholeheartedly for the love of God. Go where you may, you will find no rest except in humble obedience to the rule of authority. Dreams of happiness expected from change and different places have deceived many.[44]

Lord, help me to find contentment in obeying
You and others. Amen.

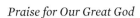

The Way to Worship

Worship the Lord with gladness;
Come before him with joyful songs.
(Psalm 100:2)

Just as an indescribable sunset or a breathtaking mountaintop vista
evokes a spontaneous response, so we cannot encounter the worthiness
of God without the response of worship. (Donald Whitney)

When we recognize all that God has done for us and given us, the right response is to worship. Psalm 100 offers us a powerful primer for true worship:

- "Shout for joy to the Lord" (v. 1). Worship should be enthusiastic and engage our whole hearts and minds.
- "It is he who made us, and we are his" (v. 3). Here David affirms that God is our Creator and we depend on Him.
- "For the Lord is good and his love endures forever; his faithfulness continues through all generations" (v. 5). True worship expresses gratitude and praise to God.

Now might be a good time to read slowly through all of Psalm 100 as a reminder of how to worship and why God deserves our praise. One of the joys of knowing God is the privilege of entering "his gates with thanksgiving and his courts with praise" (v. 4).

God, teach me to praise and worship You. Amen.

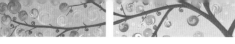

Changing Names

Then Saul, who was also called Paul, filled with the Holy Spirit . . .
(Acts 13:9)

Prayer is the risen Jesus coming in with His resurrection power,
given free rein in our lives, and then using His authority to enter any
situation and change things. (Ole Kristian O. Hallesby)

He was educated at the highest levels in both law and theology. He was an international traveler, aware and sophisticated in the ways of the world. A young leader with all the right connections, he was climbing the career ladder at a rapid pace. Devout. Respected. Even feared. But he was a man at war with himself. He was Saul.

On his way to Damascus, a trip where he planned to strike a violent blow against this new branch of the Jewish faith that was spreading like wildfire, he encountered the risen Christ. He was struck blind, and Jesus spoke to him in an audible voice: "Saul! Saul! Why do you persecute me?" (Acts 22:7).

From that moment, the persecutor became a preacher; the man who was filled with turmoil came to inner peace. Saul was renamed by God Himself and became Paul. Meeting the risen Lord changes everything!

Thank You for giving me a new life and new heart
when I met You, God. Amen.

Right Desires

You do not have, because you do not ask God. When you ask, you do not receive, because you ask with wrong motives, that you may spend what you get on your pleasures. (James 4:2–3)

Each time, before you Intercede, be quiet first, and worship God in His glory. Think of what He can do, and how He delights to hear the prayers of His redeemed people. Think of your place and privilege in Christ, and expect great things! (Andrew Murray)

A Classic Devotion from C. H. Spurgeon

*M*an is a creature abounding in wants. He is ever restless. At the same time, there are desires in Christians also. To rob the saints of their desires would be to injure them greatly, for by their desires they rise out of their lower selves. Believers desire the best things: things that are pure and peaceful, admirable and elevating. They desire God's glory. . . . Desires from the Spirit of God stir the renewed nature, exciting and stimulating it. They make the believer groan in anguish until he can attain the things that God has taught him to long for.

If God will give for the asking but we remain poor, who is to blame? Is not our blame most grievous? Does it not look as if we are out of touch with God when we will not even ask a favor of Him?[45]

Lord, thank You for Your goodness in hearing my prayers.
I bring all my hopes, wishes, and disappointments to
You today, God. Amen.

Serving the Poor

There will always be poor people in the land. Therefore I command you to be openhanded toward your brothers and toward the poor and needy in your land. (Deuteronomy 15:11)

We cannot do great things on this earth, only small things with great love. (Mother Teresa)

*T*he motto "Give a man a fish and he will eat for a day; teach a man to fish and he will eat for a lifetime" forms a foundation for the work of many charities and ministries as they strive to help the people they serve become self-sufficient. So many of the poor in our midst need not just food for today but encouragement, compassion, and a mentor to help them meet their challenges for a brighter tomorrow. So, as we try to follow the Bible's command to look after the poor, we should pray for wisdom about ways we might best help someone move to a new level in life.

There's nothing wrong with giving money. Most service agencies rely on donations. But don't be afraid to get a little dirty, to get creative with your giving. Pick up a few extra groceries for a food pantry while you're at the store. Serve a few hours a week at a homeless shelter. Give your time to mentor a child at risk. Whatever you do, ask God to help you meet the deepest needs of those around you.

Father, I'm in awe of Your compassion for the poor. Show me how to reach out to others with Your compassion and love this month. Amen.

Pulling Through

"Everything is possible for him who believes." (Mark 9:23)

Faith in faith is pointless. Faith in a living, active God moves mountains. (Beth Moore)

*H*is football career was legendary. He played for one of the most tradition-rich high schools in the state and even the nation. Even before his first college game, he ended up pictured on the front of a Wheaties box. He was a two-time All-American for Ohio State and went on to have a long, award-filled NFL career, even overcoming a broken neck to extend his playing days.

But the biggest challenge of his life came when doctors diagnosed his wife with an aggressive malignant cancer. With the same passion he showed on the football field, he prayed and stood by his wife—leaving professional football for a year to be by her side. When she lost her hair from chemotherapy, he went with his two children to the barber so that all members of the family had shaven heads in a display of team solidarity. With faith and determination, the family pulled together as Mom battled with cancer for more than a decade before finally succumbing to the disease.

Life will very often call for us to respond with strength and perseverance. Fortunately, when we put our faith in God, He can supply all the strength we need.

Lord, help me to tackle my life's challenges and responsibilities with unshakable faith in You. Amen.

All I Need

*And my God will meet all your needs according to his glorious riches
in Christ Jesus.* (Philippians 4:19)

*People, places, and things were never meant to give us life. God alone
is the author of a fulfilling life.* (Gary Smalley and John Trent)

A Classic Devotion from George Müller

*A*ll believers, according to the will of God concerning them
in Christ Jesus, may cast, and ought to cast, all their care
upon Him who careth for them, and need not be anxiously concerned about anything.

My Lord is not limited; He can again supply. How truly precious it is that every one who rests alone upon the Lord Jesus for
salvation, has in the living God a father, to whom he may fully un-
bosom himself concerning the most minute affairs of his life, and
concerning everything that lies upon his heart! Dear reader, do you
know the living God? Is He, in Jesus, your Father? Be assured that
Christianity is something more than forms and creeds and ceremo-
nies: there is life, and power, and reality, in our holy faith. If you
never yet have known this, then come and taste for yourself.[46]

God, I know that You can provide all I need. Today I
bring all my worries to You. Amen.

Thanking God

> *Keep me safe, O God,*
> *for in you I take refuge.*
> *I said to the LORD, "You are my Lord;*
> *apart from you I have no good thing."*
> (Psalm 16:1–2)

Nothing taken for granted; everything received with gratitude;
everything passed on with grace. (G. K. Chesterton)

When a mother in a drunken stupor lit up a cigarette, not coherent enough to think of her children's safety, she set fire to their little shanty home. When she escaped, she abandoned it—and the children. Fortunately, all the children made it out of the house alive and actually lived in the yard near the charred remains of their home for several days until the police found them. They were taken to a Christian children's home to live. And there their lives were turned around. Notably, these children—now grown and married—are marked by a deep sense of gratitude. They have endured more heartbreak than most, and having escaped and moved on to a better life, they are grateful to God for seeing them through.

Your life's tragedies may not be as difficult and dramatic as what this family faced. But if you have a relationship with God, your life has been touched for the better. Have you said thank you today?

God, I have seen You turn around even the worst
situations. Thank You for Your work in our lives, and thank
You for saving me. Amen.

A New Song

*Sing to the L*ORD *a new song;*
*sing to the L*ORD*, all the earth.*
*Sing to the L*ORD*, praise his name;*
proclaim his salvation day after day.
(Psalm 96:1–2)

Rejoice, my heart, be glad and sing,
A cheerful trust maintain;
For God, the Source of everything,
Thy portion shall remain.
(Paul Gerhardt)

A Classic Devotion from Saint Augustine

Sing to the Lord a new song; his praise is in the assembly of the saints. We are urged to sing a new song to the Lord, as new men who have learned a new song. A song is a thing of joy; more profoundly, it is a thing of love. Anyone, therefore, who has learned to love the new life, has learned to sing a new song, and the new song reminds us of our new life.

The new man, the new song, the new covenant, all belong to the one kingdom of God, and so the new man will sing a new song and will belong to the new covenant.[47]

Lord, You have given me a blessed new life. May my every
word and action be a song of praise to You. Amen.

The Language of Love

Carry each other's burdens, and in this way you will fulfill the law of Christ. (Galatians 6:2)

I have found the paradox that if I love until it hurts, then there is no hurt, but only more love. (Mother Teresa)

Author Leo Buscaglia told about a contest he was asked to judge. The purpose of the contest was to find the most caring child.

The winner was a four-year-old child whose elderly next-door neighbor had recently lost his wife. Upon seeing the man cry, the little boy went into the old gentleman's yard, climbed onto his lap, and just sat there.

When his mother asked him what he had said to the neighbor, the little boy said, "Nothing, I just helped him cry."

The Bible tells us to mourn with those who mourn and rejoice with those who rejoice (Romans 12:15). We all have burdens to bear. But one of the ways God helps us bear them is by sending us the loving comfort of other people. If you want to experience and live out God's love for you, make your heart available both to receive love and companionship from others and to be a loving presence in someone else's life.

Father, thank You for the gift of love that You bring
through others. Send me to someone I can
encourage today. Amen.

With Help from the Holy Spirit

Do you not know that your body is a temple of the Holy Spirit, who is in you, whom you have received from God? (1 Corinthians 6:19)

O Holy Spirit of God, abide with us; inspire all our thoughts; pervade our imaginations; suggest all our decisions; order all our doings. Be with us in our silence and in our speech, in our haste and in our leisure, in company and in solitude, in the freshness of the morning and in the weariness of the evening; and give us grace at all times humbly to rejoice in Thy mysterious companionship. (John Baillie)

A Classic Devotion from Oswald Chambers

*W*e realize that we are energized by the Holy Spirit for prayer; we know what it is to pray in the Spirit; but we do not so often realize that the Holy Spirit Himself prays in us prayers which we cannot utter. When we are born again of God and are indwelt by the Spirit of God, He expresses for us the unutterable. . . .

Have we recognized that our body is the temple of the Holy Ghost? If so, we must be careful to keep it undefiled for Him. We have to remember that our conscious life, though it is only a tiny bit of our personality, is to be regarded by us as a shrine of the Holy Ghost. He will look after the unconscious part that we know nothing of; but we must see that we guard the conscious part for which we are responsible.[48]

Lord, thank You that Your Spirit is within me, helping me and drawing me closer to You. Amen.

Serving and Communion

But Martha was distracted by all the preparations that had to be made. She came to him and asked, "Lord, don't you care that my sister has left me to do the work by myself? Tell her to help me!"
(Luke 10:40)

In the service of the Lord, it is not where but how you serve.
(J. Reuben Clark)

*M*artha was just doing what she knew to do, what seemed natural to her: preparing the house and a meal for her dinner guests. Her sister, Mary, chose to sit at the feet of Jesus and listen to Him teach. At some point, it must have become too much for Martha, and she burst out angrily, asking Jesus to tell Mary to help her. But instead, He told her, "Martha, Martha . . . you are worried and upset about many things, but only one thing is needed. Mary has chosen what is better, and it will not be taken away from her" (Luke 10:41–42).

God does not discourage us from serving others with hospitality and seemingly mundane chores. But like Martha, we must guard against the tendency to get preoccupied and bogged down in our responsibilities, forgetting the One we are ultimately serving. When our service becomes a burden or a distraction from communion with God, we know we need to realign our priorities.

God, thank You for the privilege of serving You, but thank
You even more for the joy of simply being in Your presence.
Help me keep my eyes on You even as I serve. Amen.

Happy Thoughts

Be transformed by the renewing of your mind. (Romans 12:2)

Seek to cultivate a buoyant, joyous sense of the crowded kindnesses of God in your daily life. (Alexander Maclaren)

*B*etween personnel problems and cranky patients, Amy experienced considerable stress in her job as a nurse. Some of her frustration went home with her. Although she tried to spare her kids from her moods, four-year-old Brad took notice when her nerves were ragged. One evening, before she left for the night shift at the hospital, the child seemed sad as he hugged her good-bye. But suddenly his face seemed to brighten with an idea and he said, "Mom, while you're at work, think happy thoughts."

With a smile, she said, "Thanks, Brad, I will." And that night she did just that—for Brad. But that night's shift went so much better than usual that she soon found herself thinking happy thoughts for herself.

All of us have reasons for joy—an activity we love, a fun-loving friend, or in Amy's case, a tenderhearted young child waiting for her at home. When we choose to dwell on those delightful things in life, we find that joy fills us a little more easily, even during tough days.

God, today I choose, with Your help, to think about the good things in my life. Thank You for the joy You have given me. Amen.

Practice Makes Perfect

Whatever you have learned or received or heard from me, or seen in me—put it into practice. And the God of peace will be with you.
(Philippians 4:9)

Faith is an activity; it is something that has to be applied.
(Corrie ten Boom)

You're not really a soccer player unless you actually play soccer. You're not a writer if you don't put ink on a page or start typing at a keyboard. And you're not a pianist if you never play the piano. In much the same way, faith is a practice. It is active. And it can be strengthened or weakened, depending on how little or much we practice it.

There are many ways to practice faith, like attending church or joining a Bible study; serving the needy or visiting prisoners; tithing and even giving sacrificially when the economy is tough. Spiritual disciplines like prayer and fasting can also nurture your faith and spirit. Practicing your faith doesn't have to be complicated or have a long list of regulations. All it takes is a little effort and initiative on your part.

Practice makes perfect because that is when we live as God intended us to live.

God, please teach me to discipline myself and
practice my faith. Amen.

Ready for Anything

That is how it continued to be; the cloud covered it, and at night it looked like fire. (Numbers 9:16)

Faith and obedience are inescapably related. There is no saving faith in God apart from obedience to God, and there can be no godly obedience without godly faith. (John MacArthur)

A Classic Devotion from Alexander Maclaren

*W*e need to hold the present with a slack hand, so as to be ready to fold our tents and take to the road if God will. We must not reckon on continuance, nor strike our roots so deep that it needs a hurricane to remove us. To those who set their gaze on Christ, no present from which He wishes them to remove can be so good for them as the new conditions into which He would have them pass. It is hard to leave the spot, though it be in the desert, where we have so long encamped that it has come to look like home. But we must set ourselves to meet the God-appointed change cheerfully, in the confidence that nothing will be left behind which it is not good to lose, nor anything met, which does not bring a blessing, however its first aspect may be harsh or sad.[49]

Heavenly Father, help me to not get so comfortable with my life that I can't move on to new opportunities You set before me. Give me the kind of faith that is ready to go when You call my name! Amen.

Love Beyond Reason

"You did not choose me, but I chose you." (John 15:16)

He chose us because He loves us, and He loves us because He loves us. He does not love us because we are lovable, but only because He is love. (John Stott)

Throughout the Old Testament, God spoke to His people through prophets. Some of the prophets were great orators. Others, such as Hosea, communicated truth about God's love and judgment through dramatic events in their own lives.

Hosea was married to an unfaithful wife. She bore the sons of other men. She left him and lived as a prostitute. When she lost her beauty and charm and was sold into slavery, what did Hosea do?

The unthinkable, of course. He acted like God.

He went to the market to redeem her. He bought her not as a slave but to make her his wife once again. In this act of supreme commitment and mercy, Hosea showed God's people that God still loved them—even though they were not faithful to Him. He loves us the same way too!

Heavenly Father, Your love never fails. Thank You for redeeming me when I was not faithful to You. Amen.

The Value of Hard Work

The plans of the diligent lead to profit. (Proverbs 21:5)

He who labors diligently need never despair, for all things are accomplished by diligence and labor. (Menander)

Scripture tells us to rely on God and wait for Him. It tells us that He has blessings for us that we can't earn and that He loves to give gifts to His children.

But there's another principle in the Bible that we shouldn't ignore: the principle of hard work. The book of Proverbs instructs us to look to the ant, who has no "overseer or ruler, yet it stores its provisions in summer and gathers its food at harvest" (6:7–8). If we want a bright future—if we want to enjoy benefits in the short-term as well as the long-term—we have to put our noses to the grindstone and do some work.

So while it's important to wait on God and look to Him for provision, perhaps one of the best things to do while we're waiting is work hard.

Dear Lord, thank You for the blessings in my life. Give me a spirit of diligence and commitment to the tasks in front of me. Amen.

Every Moment

In repentance and rest is your salvation,
in quietness and trust is your strength.
(Isaiah 30:15)

Let this be your chief object in prayer, to realize the presence of your
heavenly Father. Let your watchword be: Alone with God.
(Andrew Murray)

A Classic Devotion from Brother Lawrence

*A*ll consists in one hearty renunciation of everything which we are sensible does not lead to God; that we might accustom ourselves to a continual conversation with Him, with freedom and in simplicity. . . . We need only to recognize God intimately present with us, to address ourselves to Him every moment, that we may beg His assistance for knowing His will in things doubtful, and for rightly performing those which we plainly see He requires of us, offering them to Him before we do them, and giving Him thanks when we have done. . . .

Without being discouraged on account of our sins, we should pray for His grace with a perfect confidence, as relying upon the infinite merits of our Lord. . . .

God always [gives] us light in our doubts, when we [have] no other design but to please Him.[50]

God, thank You for always being near me, providing grace.
Walking with You will lead me to peace. Amen.

Love in Deed

If anyone has material possessions and sees his brother in need but has no pity on him, how can the love of God be in him? (1 John 3:17)

If you can't feed a hundred people, then feed just one.
(Mother Teresa)

Actions speak louder than words. We all know this common bit of wisdom, and few would disagree with it. But how many of us still struggle to implement this principle in our lifestyles? How many of us rationalize our lack of love in action on the basis of our fine intentions and words?

Maybe the needs around us are so great that we simply don't know where to start. But perhaps the biggest reason we don't help others in love is that we are too focused on our own needs, wants, and comforts.

Is God's love in you being choked off because it is bottled up? We stem the input when we put a dam in front of the output. How do you reactivate the flow of God's love in your life? He will do it for you. Your job is simply to meet a need right in front of your eyes.

Dear God, thank You for the opportunities You put before me to share Your love. Amen.

True Joy

In all my prayers for all of you, I always pray with joy. (Philippians 1:4)

Joy is not the absence of trouble but the presence of Christ.
(William Van der Hoven)

*P*aul's letter to the Philippians is considered the book of joy in the New Testament. Writing from a prison in Rome, Paul gave these characteristics of true joy:

- True joy is found in bonds of fellowship: "In all my prayers for all of you, I always pray with joy because of your partnership in the gospel" (1:4–5).
- True joy grows proportionally with love: "And this is my prayer: that your love may abound more and more in knowledge and depth of insight" (1:9).
- True joy is based on righteous living: "So that you may be able to discern what is best and may be pure and blameless until the day of Christ, filled with the fruit of righteousness that comes through Jesus Christ" (1:10–11).
- True joy brings glory to God: "To the glory and praise of God" (1:11).

Are you experiencing God's joy today?

Lord, help me to experience true joy. Amen.

Sincere Faith

The goal of this command is love, which comes from a pure heart and a good conscience and a sincere faith. (1 Timothy 1:5)

It is just as important to trust God as it is to obey Him.
(Jerry Bridges)

*Y*es, faith is active; there are steps we can take to express and nurture our faith. But is it possible to go through all the motions—read Scripture, serve others, faithfully attend church services—and not have a drop of authentic, internal faith? Possibly, though probably not. There are simply some seasons when we "feel" our faith more than others.

But it's still a good idea to audit our own hearts. What is our sincerity level today? Have we let our hearts and minds wander? Why do we do what we do? Is it out of duty or faith? Remember that God prizes our service; but more than that, He wants to be known and loved.

Lord, thank You for revealing Yourself to me. Rekindle my love for You and my passion to do Your will. Amen.

Belief As Commitment

*I believe that you are the Christ, the Son of God, who was to
come into the world.* (John 11:27)

*When we are engaged in His work we are very close to Christ. We are
expending our anxiety and affections on the same objects on which
His heart is set.* (James Stalker)

A Classic Devotion from Oswald Chambers

*M*artha believed in the power available to Jesus Christ; she
believed that if He had been there He could have healed
her brother. . . . But Jesus continued to attract and draw her in until
her belief became an intimate possession. It then slowly emerged
into a personal inheritance—"Yes, Lord, I believe that You are the
Christ" (John 11:27).

Is the Lord dealing with you in the same way? . . . Are you facing an area of doubt in your life? Have you come, like Martha, to a
crossroads of overwhelming circumstances where your theology is
about to become a very personal belief? This happens only when a
personal problem brings the awareness of our personal need.

To believe is to commit. In intimate personal belief I commit
myself spiritually to Jesus Christ and make a determination to be
dominated by Him alone.[51]

Lord, I commit myself to You and pray that You would
meet me here in my need. Amen.

A Royal Priesthood

Therefore he is able to save completely those who come to God through him, because he always lives to intercede for them. Such a high priest meets our need—one who is holy, blameless, pure, set apart from sinners, exalted above the heavens. (Hebrews 7:25–26)

The priest is not made. He must be born a priest; must inherit his office. I refer to the new birth—the birth of water and the Spirit. Thus all Christians must become priests, children of God and co-heirs with Christ the Most High Priest. (Martin Luther)

*I*n all religions and all ages, a priest is an intermediary who ushers common people into the presence of divinity. This has usually involved special rituals, including, for some faiths, a sacrifice that would remove sin or any other barriers separating man from God. In the person of Jesus, something amazing happens. The "divine"—the one to be worshipped—becomes His own priest, His own sacrifice, and the One who brings us directly into the presence of God. The writer of Hebrews says we should "approach the throne of grace with confidence" (4:16). No one need usher us before God.

We need not go through any intermediary for salvation, and in the same way, we can go directly to God's Word to receive the encouragement and challenge He has for us.

Lord, help me to honor the privilege of interacting with
You through Your Word today. Amen.

Prayers for a Nation

"If my people, who are called by my name, will humble themselves and pray and seek my face and turn from their wicked ways, then will I hear from heaven and will forgive their sin and will heal their land." (2 Chronicles 7:14)

Our prayers lay the track down on which God's power can come. Like a mighty locomotive, his power is irresistible, but it cannot reach us without rails. (Watchman Nee)

*M*ost reading these words are from the United States, but even if you are from another country, you will appreciate prayers of leaders for the spiritual life of a nation.

- George Washington: "Bless the people of this land, be a father to the fatherless, a comforter to the comfortless, a deliverer to the captives, and a physician to the sick."
- Thomas Jefferson: "Almighty God . . . we humbly beseech Thee that we may always prove ourselves a people mindful of Thy favor and glad to do Thy will."
- Abraham Lincoln: "With malice toward none, with charity for all, with firmness in the right as God gives us to see the right, let us finish the work we are in . . . to do all which [we] may achieve and cherish a just and a lasting peace among ourselves and with all nations."

God, I pray for Your hand on our nation today. Amen.

A Prayerful Heart

Undisturbed

"Peace I leave with you; my peace I give you." (John 14:27)

Peace rules the day when Christ rules the mind. (author unknown)

A Classic Devotion from Oswald Chambers

*A*re you painfully disturbed just now, distracted by the waves and billows of God's providential permission, and having, as it were, turned over the boulders of your belief, are you still finding no well of peace or joy or comfort; is all barren? Then look up and receive the undisturbedness of the Lord Jesus. If you allow anything to hide the face of Jesus Christ from you, you are either disturbed or you have a false security.

Are you looking unto Jesus now, in the immediate matter that is pressing and receiving from Him peace? If so, He will be a gracious benediction of peace in and through you. But if you try to worry it out, you obliterate Him and deserve all you get. We get disturbed because we have not been considering Him. When one confers with Jesus Christ the perplexity goes, because He has no perplexity, and our only concern is to abide in Him. Lay it all out before Him, and in the face of difficulty, bereavement and sorrow, hear Him say, "Let not your heart be troubled."[52]

Lord, I know that You offer perfect peace. Help me bring
my entire mind to You today. Amen.

A Prayer for Our Children

Come, my children, listen to me; I will teach you the fear of the LORD.
(Psalm 34:11)

The greatest gift we can give to others is our prayers.
(author unknown)

A Classic Devotion from Jeremy Taylor

O almighty and most merciful Father, who hast promised children as a reward to the righteous, and hast given them to me as a testimony of thy mercy, and an engagement of my duty, be pleased to be a Father unto them, and give them healthful bodies, understanding souls, and sanctified spirits, that they may be thy servants and thy children all their days. Let a great mercy and providence lead them through the dangers and temptations and ignorances of their youth, that they may never run into folly and the evils of an unbridled appetite. So order the accidents of their lives, that by good education, careful tutors, holy example, innocent company, prudent counsel, and thy restraining grace, their duty to thee may be secured in the midst of a crooked and untoward generation. Amen.[53]

God, thank You for my children. Teach me to pray for them
and care for them as You care for me. Amen.

Unrecognized Blessings

*Let them give thanks to the L*ORD *for his unfailing love
and his wonderful deeds for men,
for he satisfies the thirsty
and fills the hungry with good things.*
(Psalm 107:8–9)

*How many times do we miss God's blessings because they are not
packaged as we expected?* (author unknown)

A poverty-stricken elderly woman in Europe complained that her wealthy son in America was cruel and ungrateful. "Does he never send you any money?" a friend asked. "Never a penny," she replied. "He sends me pictures quite often, but I do not need pictures; I need money." The friend said, "Do you have any of these pictures?" "Oh, yes, I have them all. They are here in the old Bible." When she pulled them out, her friend gasped. The "pictures" were fresh, crisp fifty- and hundred-dollar bills, a huge and generous gift at the turn of the nineteenth century.

In order to enjoy our blessings, we first have to realize what we have. We might be sulking in squalor while we are surrounded by abundance. Are you missing any blessings in your life? Have you allowed misplaced values to rob you of the abundance God has given you?

Lord, open my eyes to see the gifts You have given me. Amen.

I Choose Joy

Be joyful always. (1 Thessalonians 5:16)

I choose joy. I will invite my God to be the God of circumstance. I will refuse the temptation to be cynical, the tool of the lazy thinker. I will refuse to see people as anything less than human beings, created by God. I will refuse to see any problem as anything less than an opportunity to see God. (Max Lucado)

What will your attitude be today? Positive or negative? Dissatisfied or grateful? Optimistic or cynical? Unhappy or joyful?

All good gifts come from God, including joy. But God still invites us to participate in receiving His gifts and blessings through our own free will. We can't save ourselves, but we must say yes to salvation. We can't walk worthy of His calling on our own, but we can say yes to His strength through simple obedience. And we can't force ourselves to be joyful. But we can say yes to God's kind and delightful offering by saying yes through our attitudes.

Have you chosen joy for your life? For today?

Heavenly Father, I say yes to You and
Your gift of joy today. Amen.

The Ripples of Disobedience

A prudent man gives thought to his steps. (Proverbs 14:15)

The cost of obedience is nothing compared to the cost of disobedience. (author unknown)

When we are disobedient to God's will and ways, we create a negative impact not only for ourselves but often for those around us. Ever since the sin of Adam and Eve in the garden of Eden, the consequences of disobedience have been staggering. Cain's disobedience led to Abel's murder. David's infidelity led to the death of a trusted comrade and ultimately the splitting of a kingdom. Judas' betrayal abetted Jesus' arrest.

There's a crucial life-and-death lesson in these Bible stories for all of us. Even if some people seem to get away with wrongdoing—maybe even prosper in it—there is a price to pay for disobedience, and we can't necessarily protect those around us. If there is a temptation in your life right now that has become even more alluring because you've started to think that acting on it wouldn't hurt anyone else, ask God to check your spirit and provide you with the wisdom and perspective that will help you flee from the very idea of it. Some actions can't be taken back, nor can their consequences be contained or controlled.

God, I don't want my sin to affect the lives of others—or my own life. Teach me to bring my whole heart to You in obedience. Amen.

A Deep River

Thanks be to God for his indescribable gift! (2 Corinthians 9:15)

Grace is always given to those ready to give thanks for it.
(Thomas à Kempis)

A Classic Devotion from C. H. Spurgeon

*E*very attribute of God should become a fresh ray in the sunlight of our gladness. That he is wise should make us glad, knowing as we do our own foolishness. That he is mighty should cause us to rejoice who tremble at our weakness. That he is everlasting, should always be a theme of joy when we know that we wither as the grass. That he is unchanging, should perpetually yield us a song, since we change every hour. That he is full of grace, that he is overflowing with it, and that this grace in covenant he has given to us; that it is ours to cleanse us, ours to keep us, ours to sanctify us, ours to perfect us, ours to bring us to glory— all this should tend to make us glad in him. This gladness in God is as a deep river; we have only as yet touched its brink, we know a little of its clear, sweet, heavenly streams, but onward the depth is greater, and the current more impetuous in its joy.[54]

> Lord, I know that You are good. Help me to experience
> Your goodness more deeply each day of my life. Amen.

Hope Changes Lives

Through him you believe in God, who raised him from the dead and glorified him, and so your faith and hope are in God. (1 Peter 1:21)

What oxygen is to the lungs, such is hope to the meaning of life.
(Emil Brunner)

A self-made millionaire, Eugene Land, forever changed the lives of a sixth-grade class in East Harlem through a simple act of hope. Mr. Land had been asked to speak to a class of fifty-nine sixth graders. Scrapping his prepared notes, he decided to speak to them from his heart.

"Stay in school," he admonished, "and I'll help pay the college tuition for every one of you." Now that's a speech! And it had an impact for years to come. In a time and place when few students graduated from high school, nearly 90 percent of that class went on to attend and graduate from college!

Hope is powerful. When we cultivate hope and share it with others, we create a brighter future for them and us. Hope truly changes lives.

Father, help me to give away what has been given to
me in abundance: hope. Amen.

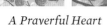

The Written Word of God

No prophecy of Scripture is a matter of one's own interpretation, for no prophecy was ever made by an act of human will, but men moved by the Holy Spirit spoke from God. (2 Peter 1:20–21 NASB)

God's word in the Bible can have power only because it corresponds to God's word in the universe. It is the present Voice which makes the written Word all-powerful. (A. W. Tozer)

Some Bible teachers have suggested that we should read the Bible each time as if we have never read from its pages before. Easier said than done. Passages from Scripture are entrenched in our culture and have been infused with certain imagery and emotions, an effect compounded if you grew up in church. But the point is, behind the words of the Bible beats the heart of God, and we should strive to encounter His message and meaning in a fresh way every time we open our Bibles.

Maybe a good first step is to slow down. Emphasize small chunks of Scripture rather than long passages. Go over the words more than once, even out loud if you'd like. And let their meaning penetrate your heart. The important thing is that if you've not established the regular practice of reading God's Word, get started! As you read, realize that God is speaking directly to you.

God, thank You for Your inspired Word. Give me grace and understanding to allow it deep into my life. Amen.

Until the End

*Let us not become weary in doing good, for at the proper time we will
reap a harvest if we do not give up.* (Galatians 6:9)

*Always respond to every impulse to pray. The impulse to pray may
come when you are reading or when you are battling with a text. I
would make an absolute law of this—always obey such an impulse.*
(Martyn Lloyd-Jones)

While very ill, John Knox, the founder of the Presbyterian
Church in Scotland, called to his wife and said, "Read me
that Scripture where I first cast my anchor." After he listened to
the beautiful prayer of Jesus recorded in John 17, he seemed to forget his weakness. He began to pray, interceding earnestly for his
fellow men. He prayed for the ungodly who had thus far rejected
the gospel. He pleaded on behalf of people who had been recently
converted. And he requested protection for the Lord's servants,
many of whom were facing persecution. As Knox prayed, his spirit
went home to be with the Lord. The man of whom Queen Mary
had said, "I fear his prayers more than I do the armies of my enemies," ministered through prayer until the moment of his death.

There are many needs around us—our neighbors, families,
friends, and coworkers could all use a touch from God in some
area or another. We have the privilege of bringing those needs to
God in prayer. And we are blessed when we do so.

Lord, open my heart so that I can see the needs around me
and bring them to You. Amen.

Faith and Trust

May your whole spirit, soul and body be kept blameless at the
coming of our Lord Jesus Christ. The one who calls you is faithful
and he will do it. (1 Thessalonians 5:23–24)

God is God. Because He is God, He is worthy of my trust and
obedience. I will find rest nowhere but in His holy will, a will that
is unspeakably beyond my largest notions of what He is up to.
(Elisabeth Elliot)

*W*e operate by faith every day. When we sit on a chair, we trust that it will hold us; when we get behind the wheel of our car, we put faith in the brakes to work; we accelerate after a green light, believing cross traffic will stop for reds; we drink bottled water because we believe it has been purified and is safe. Without thinking or questioning, we act as if the objects and many of the circumstances in our lives will come through for us, will be safe for us, because they almost always have been.

Putting trust in an invisible God is different and can be a scarier proposition. We can't physically see Him the way we see a chair or a car or the clarity of water or the smiles on neighbors' faces. But when we seek to know Him, we can know His character. And we find that He will always come through for us. With that thought firmly in our minds, we can trust Him.

Lord, help me to know You and overcome any doubts.
I want to trust You more than anything. Amen.

Where Joy Won't Be Found

*Why spend money on what is not bread, and your labor on
what does not satisfy? (Isaiah 55:2)*

Joy is the most infallible sign of the presence of God. (Leon Bloy)

Men have pursued joy in every avenue imaginable; some have successfully found it, while others have not. But we can know for sure that joy cannot be found in these places.

- Not in unbelief: Voltaire remains one of the greatest cynics and skeptics in literature. He wrote, "I wish I had never been born."
- Not in pleasure: Lord Byron lived a life of pleasure if anyone did. He wrote, "The worm, the canker, and grief are mine alone."
- Not in money: Millionaire Jay Gould had plenty of that. On his deathbed, he said, "I suppose I am the most miserable man on earth."
- Not in position and fame: Lord Beaconsfield enjoyed more than his share of both. Yet he wrote, "Youth is a mistake; manhood a struggle; old age a regret."
- Not in military glory: Alexander the Great conquered the known world in his day. Having done so, he wept in his tent and said, "There are no more worlds to conquer."

Lord, I know that the real joy in life is in Christ alone. Thank You for sending Your Son that I might know joy in Him. Amen.

Righteous Disobedience

Judge for yourselves whether it is right in God's sight to obey
you rather than God. For we cannot help speaking about what
we have seen and heard. (Acts 4:19–20)

Trust in God's promises comes to light in obedience to his
commands. (Scott Hafemann)

*T*he apostle Paul reminds us that if we obey our government's
laws, we will save ourselves a lot of trouble in life (Romans
13:1–7). But from a biblical perspective, it also appears there is a
time when disobedience to a governing body is the proper Christian
response. When religious and civil rulers ordered John and Peter
to stop preaching the gospel of Jesus Christ, their response was:
"We must obey God rather than men!" (Acts 5:29). Even today, all
over the world, more Christians are killed for their faith each year
than in the first two thousand years combined.

Our freedom to express our faith sometimes seems under
assault, but we still enjoy legal protection of worship and—for
now, at least—don't have to defy our government to call ourselves
Christians. But one thing all of us can do is reflect on our loyalty to
God over our loyalty to earthly powers. And all of us can pray for
Christian brothers and sisters all over the world whose faith has
made them outlaws.

Lord, I know that I am a citizen of Your kingdom and owe You,
first and foremost, my obedience. Please give me wisdom and
discernment to follow You as I live in the world. Amen.

The Master Potter at Work

I went down to the potter's house, and I saw him working at the wheel. But the pot he was shaping from the clay was marred in his hands; so the potter formed it into another pot, shaping it as seemed best to him. (Jeremiah 18:3–4)

The Spirit brings order out of chaos and beauty out of ugliness. He can transform a sin-blistered man into a paragon of virtue. The Spirit changes people. The Author of life is also the Transformer of life. (R. C. Sproul)

*T*he potter must remake his vessels when there is a flaw in the clay that will cause it to crack later or when the color smears and he cannot get it to blend perfectly. He knows his craft and he knows when to take it down from his wheel and start all over, to remake it into a fine vessel that will appeal to customers and serve the one who buys it.

In the same way, God knows us intimately—He did create us, after all—and He knows how to shape us into who He created us to be. He uses different ways, often tests and trials, to make us more like Jesus. The process is lengthy and often painful, but we will be amazed by God's handiwork in the long run if we simply submit to His loving hand.

Lord, I believe that You can make me who You want me to be. Please use the events in my life to teach me to follow You more closely. Amen.

Pursue Unity

Aim for perfection, listen to my appeal, be of one mind, live in peace.
And the God of love and peace will be with you. (2 Corinthians 13:11)

All the gifts of prayer, and of preaching; all the zeal, the ardor,
the love, the self-denial in the church, are produced by the same
Spirit. There should be, therefore, unity. The church is united in the
agency by which it is saved; it should be united in the feelings which
influence its members. (Albert Barnes)

Churches, companies, families, charities, and other groups of people have split apart over the simplest and deepest disagreements. Something as crazy as the color of new carpet in the sanctuary has led some people to leave a church fellowship. To a church situated in the diverse and contentious city of ancient Corinth, Paul writes with instructions to the believers to be of one mind and live in peace. If they will pursue unity, he preaches, they will experience God's peace.

We too live in a diverse and discordant culture. Civility has become the exception, not the rule. Rudeness is not only tolerated, but it is sometimes applauded. This condition permeates politics, news, and entertainment, and it encroaches into every area of community, including church and family.

Are you a peacemaker? Do your words and actions pursue a path of peace? If not, today is a new day to get started.

Heavenly Father, give me the wisdom and poise to
build unity in my world. Amen.

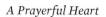

The Wish List

The prayer of the upright pleases him. (Proverbs 15:8)

Prayer is request. The essence of request, as distinct from compulsion, is that it may or may not be granted. And if an infinitely wise Being listens to the requests of finite and foolish creatures, of course He will sometimes grant and sometimes refuse them. (C. S. Lewis)

Scripture is full of assurances that God will hear and answer our prayers. Of course, there's a danger in taking this wonderful truth and turning God into a personal valet, ready to meet our every whim and fancy. In our praying, we have a responsibility to seek God's will. Our wish is not His command.

Perhaps the best way to avoid turning your prayer time into reciting a wish list is to remember that prayer is a real relationship. It's not magic. God has invited us into a relationship with Him and provided us the means to reach Him, through His Son. When we ask Him for good gifts—something He encourages us to do—we should remember that we're talking to someone who loves us, wants what's best for us, and knows what we really need.

Most important, when we go to God in prayer, we are communing with the One who seeks a relationship of love with us.

Lord, help me to pray not as an exercise of my will but
as a surrender to Yours. Amen.

A Gift of Gratitude

Give thanks to the God of heaven.
His love endures forever.
(Psalm 136:26)

Blessings hemmed with praise will not unravel. (author unknown)

*M*other Teresa told the story of finding four starving people on a Calcutta street. She told the other nuns with her to take care of three of them while she attended to a woman who looked to be in the worst condition. They got them back to their clinic and Mother Teresa put the woman in bed and attended to her needs. The woman took hold of Mother Teresa's hand, smiled, and said only two words, "Thank you," before passing into eternity. Mother Teresa was deeply moved and blessed.

In the most tender and delicate moments of our lives, gratitude is often the most precious gift we can give. It affirms; it heals; it forgives. It's important to remember, though, that we can give that gift anytime. There might be some people in our lives who desperately need it sooner rather than later.

Lord, I pray that You would help me show kindness and
thankfulness to someone close to me today. Amen.

From the Beginning of Time

"For God so loved the world that he gave his one and only Son, that whoever believes in him shall not perish but have eternal life." (John 3:16)

The work of Christ on the cross did not influence God to love us, did not increase that love by one degree, and did not open any fount of grace or mercy in His heart. He had loved us from eternity, and needed nothing to stimulate that love. The cross is not responsible for God's love; rather it was His love which conceived the cross as the one method by which we could be saved. (A. W. Tozer)

others love their children before they are even born. Why else would they have names picked out? Rooms brightly painted? Clothes neatly folded and books lined on the shelves to read? Rarely does a mother need to be told to love her newborn infant. Even during the terrible twos and the tumultuous teens, mothers steadfastly love their children.

God has loved us—has loved you—from the foundation of the world. You could never be a mere accident or unexpected surprise to Him. He loved you in your mother's womb and He loves you today.

Heavenly Father, I stand in awe of Your love for me. Thank You for Your never-ending love. Amen.

The Choice to Be Happy

*We proclaim to you what we have seen and heard, so that you
also may have fellowship with us. And our fellowship is with
the Father and with his Son, Jesus Christ. We write this to
make our joy complete.* (1 John 1:3–4)

*We all desire to be happy. That is something that is innate in human
nature; nobody wants to be miserable, though I am aware of the fact
that there are people who seem to enjoy being miserable and some who
seem to find their happiness in being unhappy!* (Martyn Lloyd-Jones)

*D*o we have a choice when it comes to joy? The apostle James
said, "Consider it pure joy, my brothers, whenever you face
trials of many kinds" (James 1:2). Paul said, "Rejoice in the Lord
always. I will say it again: Rejoice!" (Philippians 4:4). Jesus said
to His disciples, "Do not let your hearts be troubled and do not be
afraid" (John 14:27).

Is joy a choice? The biblical answer is clearly yes. But throughout Scripture there is a strong recognition that it is not always an
easy choice. Life can be tough. We get hurt. There are disappointments. Sometimes circumstances seem to conspire against us. And
yet as an act of worship, as a matter of prayer, as a declaration of
faith, as an act of love for Jesus, we can choose joy. Just the fact that
God has given us a choice to experience joy is a reason to rejoice.

Heavenly Father, I choose to walk in the joy You have so
graciously given to me. Thank You! Amen.

Fasting

After fasting forty days and forty nights, he was hungry. (Matthew 4:2)

*Christian fasting, at its root, is the hunger of a
homesickness for God.* (John Piper)

*P*rayer should be as natural as breathing in and out, a seamless part of our everyday lives. But many of us also find that pulling away for a time of focused prayer is incredibly beneficial. Reading a short devotion and then having a brief time of prayer is part of morning preparation for many Christians, and some go on retreats to spend an entire weekend in prayer.

There is another special practice that has been used with prayer through the centuries. The discipline of fasting is modeled for us by Jesus Christ Himself (Matthew 4:1–11). Fasting is the choice to give up something—usually food—in order to focus all our attentions and energies on communing with God. Many have sought prayer and fasting when an urgent need arises. For Jesus, facing the beginning of His ministry, a forty-day fast provided a way to face every temptation that Satan would throw His way in the years to come.

Is there an urgent need in your life? In your family? Your church? Your business? Consider a time of prayer and fasting to lay your heart bare before God and find His will and answers for you.

Lord Jesus, teach me to fast in a way that brings
me closer to You. Amen.

Different Vantage Points

He who dwells in the shelter of the Most High
will rest in the shadow of the Almighty.
(Psalm 91:1)

If you want to hear God's voice clearly and you are uncertain, then
remain in His presence until He changes that uncertainty. Often, much
can happen during this waiting for the Lord. Sometimes, He changes
pride into humility, doubt into faith and peace. (Corrie ten Boom)

*A*fter a long flight from the South Pacific, a family picked up their car and began a long drive from California to the East Coast, delighted to see America after several years away. As they neared Tombstone, Arizona, a huge storm reached the height of its intensity; thunder and lightning boomed and flashed ferociously. They were in awe and wanted to get closer to see the majestic beauty as lightning seemed to dance across the sky and around the buildings. It was a different kind of natural display than what they saw in the South Pacific, a display only Creator God could perform, with lightning and thunder in perfect unison.

From one vantage point, a storm poses danger and warrants fear. From another vantage point, storms provide us with a beautiful display that entertains and excites the senses. The secret is to see God in the storm.

Father, give me patience and wisdom so that I
might see Your hand at work in my world, creating
something beautiful. Amen.

The Paths of Wisdom

Blessed is the man who finds wisdom,
the man who gains understanding,
for she is more profitable than silver
and yields better returns than gold.
(Proverbs 3:13–14)

Knowledge is horizontal. Wisdom is vertical; it comes
down from above. (Billy Graham)

*I*f we were asked how wise we are, most of us wouldn't know exactly how to answer. We talk a lot about intelligence, but not very much about wisdom, so we don't always know what wisdom looks like. Solomon gives one sign that helps us recognize wisdom in our own life and the lives of others when he writes of wisdom: "Her ways are pleasant ways, and all her paths are peace" (Proverbs 3:17).

Nobody's life is always and only pleasant. No one walks exclusively on paths of peace. Not even our Lord, Jesus Christ, experienced such a life, and He was the wisest man who ever lived.

But there can still be great insight gained by asking ourselves the question "Do my decisions, attitudes, words, and lifestyle create peace or discord?" How we answer might suggest something about our current state of wisdom—and how we may become wiser with God's help.

Lord, give me the gift of wisdom that I may walk
in paths of peace. Amen.

Listen for His Voice

*After the earthquake came a fire, but the L*ORD *was not in the fire.*
And after the fire came a gentle whisper. (1 Kings 19:12)

Why is it important that you are with God and God alone on the
mountain top? It's important because it's the place in which you can
listen to the voice of the One who calls you the beloved. To pray is to
let that voice speak to the center of your being, to your guts, and let
that voice resound in your whole being. (Henri Nouwen)

*D*o you know someone who is a chronic interrupter? Someone who you know isn't really listening to you or others but thinking of what to say next? Has that someone ever been you? How about in your prayer life? Do you ever present your needs and thanksgiving and then just pause to listen?

Does God still speak directly today? Many of us will never know because we don't stop, quiet our hearts, and listen. When was the last time you truly prayed without speaking a word? Is today that day for you?

Lord, I quiet my heart and mind before You and listen.
Thank You for speaking to me. Amen.

The Prodigal Son

"Let's have a feast and celebrate. For this son of mine was dead and is alive again; he was lost and is found." (Luke 15:23–24)

Perhaps we should try to write down the blessings of one day. We might begin; we could never end; there are not pens or paper enough in all the world. (George A. Buttrick)

*R*emember the story of the prodigal son? Most retellings of the parable focus closely on the wayward son. But there's another son in the parable: the resentful and grumpy older brother. As the party rang in the distance, he sulked because even though he had never asked his father for anything, he now had to watch him lavish gifts on his ungrateful brother.

Have you ever wondered why God chose to bless someone else, someone who didn't appear to deserve it? If so, the father's words to his son might be meaningful for you as well: "You have always been with me, and all that is mine is yours. But we had to celebrate and rejoice, for this brother of yours was dead and has begun to live, and was lost and has been found" (Luke 15:31–32 NASB).

Like the father in the parable, God richly blesses us every day. When He throws a party for someone else, we should celebrate too, knowing what a good God we have.

Thank You, God, for the blessing of being Your child.
I choose today to be happy for the blessings I see in
the lives of others. Amen.

Love for God

Your love, O LORD, reaches to the heavens,
your faithfulness to the skies.
(Psalm 36:5)

Though our feelings come and go, God's love for us does not.
(C. S. Lewis)

The young woman sobbed as she told her small group of friends of the divorce she had gone through years before. Remarried and in love with a wonderful man, she had never been treated better in her life. But she could not get over feelings of abandonment from her first marriage and lived in constant fear that once again someone she loved deeply would leave her.

Healing didn't take place all at once but it began in a profound way when one of the women said to her:

I can't promise you that your husband will be faithful to you and never leave you. I can't even promise you that I'll always be here for you. Humans are not always true. But God is One who will never leave you alone. If you can't trust your husband right now, don't worry about that, and start learning to trust God more. Everything else will fall into place.

Thank You, Lord, for Your faithful love, the anchor of my life. May my entire day be a song of gratitude for Your lovingkindness. Amen.

Too Easily Pleased

"For where your treasure is, there your heart will be also." (Matthew 6:21)

Where your pleasure is, there is your treasure; Where your treasure is, there is your heart; Where your heart is, there is your happiness. (Saint Augustine)

Could it be that so many in our modern culture are unhappy because they have mistaken fleeting pleasures for a deep, abiding joy, and in so doing, have treasured unworthy ends? C. S. Lewis probed this thought in his book *The Weight of Glory*:

> Indeed, if we consider the unblushing promises of reward and the staggering nature of the rewards promised in the Gospels, it would seem that our Lord finds our desires not too strong, but too weak. We are half-hearted creatures, fooling around with drink and sex and ambition when infinite joy is offered us, like an ignorant child who wants to go on making mud pies in the slum because he cannot imagine what is meant by the offer of a holiday at the sea. We are far too easily pleased.

All of us need a spiritual checkup from time to time to make sure our hearts and our desires are in line with God's will for our lives. Where do you find your pleasure? What do you consider your treasure? Have you given your heart to something of infinite worth?

O God, my pleasure is in You. I give You my heart.
I treasure my relationship with You! Amen.

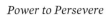

Always Giving Thanks

*Speak to one another with psalms, hymns and spiritual songs. Sing
and make music in your heart to the Lord, always giving thanks to
God the Father for everything, in the name of our Lord Jesus Christ.*
(Ephesians 5:19–20)

Gratitude is the mother of all the virtues. (G. K. Chesterton)

A Classic Devotion from Albert Barnes

*W*e can always find something to be thankful for, and there
may be reasons why we ought to be thankful for even those
dispensations which appear dark and frowning. A man owes a debt
of obligation to him for anything which will recall him from his
wanderings, and which will prepare him for heaven. Are there
any dealings of God towards men which do not contemplate such
an end? Is a man ever made to drink the cup of affliction when
no drop of mercy is intermingled? Is he ever visited with calamity
which does not in some way contemplate his own temporal or
eternal good? Could we see all, we should see that we are never
placed in circumstances in which there is not much for which we
should thank God. And when, in his dealings, a cloud seems to cover
his face, let us remember the good things without number which
we have received, and especially remember that we are in the
world of redeeming love, and we shall find enough for which to be
thankful.[55]

God, You have given me so many gifts. Thank You. Amen.

Sacramental Service

Now I rejoice in what was suffered for you, and I fill up in my flesh what is still lacking in regard to Christ's afflictions, for the sake of his body, which is the church. (Colossians 1:24)

You and I are human post offices. We are daily giving out messages of some sort to the world. They do not come from us, but through us; we do not create, we convey. (Vance Havner)

A Classic Devotion from Oswald Chambers

The Christian worker has to be a sacramental "go-between," to be so identified with his Lord and the reality of His Redemption that He can continually bring His creating life through him. It is not the strength of one man's personality being superimposed on another, but the real presence of Christ coming through the elements of the worker's life. When we preach the historic facts of the life and death of Our Lord as they are conveyed in the New Testament, our words are made sacramental; God uses them on the ground of His Redemption to create in those who listen that which is not created otherwise.

We have to see that we are in such living sympathy with God that as we proclaim His truth He can create in souls the things which He alone can do.[56]

Lord, I ask for Your presence in me so that everyone I
meet has a chance to see You. Amen.

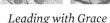 
Bold Peace

*Make every effort to keep the unity of the Spirit through
the bond of peace.* (Ephesians 4:3)

*Courage is almost a contradiction in terms. It means a strong desire
to live taking the form of readiness to die.* (G. K. Chesterton)

*B*eing a peacemaker doesn't make a person a doormat or a
pushover; it doesn't mean the person has no backbone or is
weak; it doesn't even mean that person will never fight.

Men and women of peace, in fact, have a special strength.
They are self-confident and don't create strife with their need to
prove their superiority to others. They are self-sufficient and don't
start battles by grasping and grabbing. That means they are able to
be generous. They have a strong sense of self-worth and don't feel
slighted at every turn of life. They are self-disciplined and don't
make messes for others to clean up.

No, creating peace is not for the weak or lazy. It is a bold
endeavor of those who are strong in spirit. Are you ready to take
the peace challenge?

Dear God, give me the strength that brings peace
to my world. Amen.

The Word and Prayer

"If you remain in me and my words remain in you, ask whatever you wish, and it will be given you." (John 15:7)

There is always something to help you in your Bible, if only you go on reading till you come to the word God specially has for you. (Amy Carmichael)

A Classic Devotion from Andrew Murray

*T*he vital connection between the Word and prayer is one of the simplest and earliest lessons of the Christian life. Before prayer, God's Word strengthens me by giving my faith its justification and its petition. And after prayer, God's Word prepares me by revealing what the Father wants me to ask. In prayer, God's Word brings me the answer, for in it the Spirit allows me to hear the Father's voice.

Prayer is not monologue, but dialogue. Its most essential part is God's voice in response to mine. Listening to God's voice is the secret of the assurance that He will listen to mine. When God reveals Himself in His words, He does indeed give Himself—His love and His life, His will and His power—to those who receive these words, in a reality passing comprehension. In every promise, He gives us the power to grasp and possess Himself. In every command, He allows us to share His will, His holiness, and His perfection. God's Word gives us God Himself.[57]

God, teach me to hear Your voice through Your Word. Amen.

Praying Hands

He has made everything beautiful in its time. (Ecclesiastes 3:11)

In God's faithfulness lies eternal security. (Corrie ten Boom)

*T*wo friends, Albrecht and Franz, both very poor, but both showing great promise as artists, made a deal. They would draw lots; the winner would continue in art school, while the other would work to support both of them. Once the one finished school and began to make money as an artist, he would in turn support the other in his education and work.

Albrecht won the drawing, finished his training, and went on to have a wildly successful career as an artist. Tragically, however, it was no longer possible for Franz to be an artist—his fingers were stiff and twisted from the manual labor. A true friend, Franz did not succumb to bitterness, but was thrilled for Albrecht's success.

One day Albrecht found his friend kneeling, his misshapen hands intertwined in prayer. Struck by sudden inspiration, he grabbed his sketch pad and began work on what was to become his greatest masterpiece.

Five hundred years later, none of Albrecht Durer's works are more famous and loved than *The Praying Hands* he sketched that day.

God can make a work of art out of any circumstances.

Father God, teach me to remain faithful to You and keep
my eyes open for miracles. Amen.

Walking in Peace

*Therefore, having been justified by faith, we have peace with God
through our Lord Jesus Christ.* (Romans 5:1 NKJV)

*A spiritual secret is to learn contentment with the things God
doesn't explain to us.* (Amy Carmichael)

We are blessed to have two types of peace: the peace of God and peace with God. When Christ shed His blood at Calvary, He paid the price for our peace and reconciliation with God. But in addition to no longer being separated from our Creator, when we walk with Christ in faith, we can experience the peace of God no matter what is swirling around us.

It's an incredible privilege being in His presence continuously and knowing that God never forsakes us. We cannot see Him, but we can still know with certainty that He is near as we enjoy His fellowship through prayer and Bible meditation.

God's peace is available to all who will receive Him and allow Him to be an intimate part of their lives. He wants to teach us how to walk in perfect peace. He longs to spend time with us and to be all we need in every situation. He can handle all our cares and pressures. Have you drawn near to God? Have you leaned on Him with all your needs and concerns? Are you ready to enjoy His peace?

Lord, thank You for the peace of knowing You. Give me
grace to walk more closely with You today and enjoy Your
peace more deeply. Amen.

By Faith Alone

The righteous will live by faith. (Romans 1:17)

Faith is a living, bold trust in God's grace, so certain of God's favor that it would risk death a thousand times trusting in it. (Martin Luther)

A Classic Devotion from C. H. Mackintosh

To live by faith is to walk with God: to cling to Him; to lean on Him; to draw from His exhaustless springs; to find all our resources in Him; and to have Him as a perfect covering for our eyes and a satisfying object for our hearts—to know Him as our only resource in all difficulties, and in our trials.

Such is the life of faith. Let us see that we understand it. It must be a reality or nothing at all. It will not do to talk about the life of faith; we must live it; and in order to live it we must know God practically—know Him intimately, in the deep secret of our own souls. It is utterly vain and delusive to profess to be living by faith and looking to the Lord, while in reality our hearts are looking to some creature resource. How often do people speak and write about their dependence upon God to meet certain wants, and by the very fact of their making it known to a fellow-mortal they are, in principle, departing from the life of faith![58]

Lord, I want to live a life of faith in You. Teach me to focus
my heart and mind on following You. Amen.

Seek Understanding

All Scripture is God-breathed and is useful for teaching, rebuking, correcting and training in righteousness, so that the man of God may be thoroughly equipped for every good work. (2 Timothy 3:16–17)

When you are reading a book in a dark room, and come to a difficult part, you take it to a window to get more light. So take your Bibles to Christ. (Robert Murray M'Cheyne)

*M*uch of the Bible is easy to understand. Some parts are difficult. Don't let them throw you off. It's normal to think about and really want to understand harder passages. Here are a few references available:

1. Bible dictionaries: Some words and their uses are not part of our modern vocabulary, so knowing their original meaning helps.
2. Bible handbooks: Some passages are written about and to a very different culture. Learning about those cultures helps.
3. Bible commentaries: These verse-by-verse reference books explain nuances and difficult passages.
4. God's Word: Other passages with similar themes may help clarify a hard passage.

As you read and study, don't forget to pray for understanding and be patient with yourself. Your study is not in vain.

Dear Lord, give me wisdom to hear and heed Your Word. Amen.

The Lion and the Lamb

The wolf and the lamb will feed together,
and the lion will eat straw like the ox. . . .
They will neither harm nor destroy
on all my holy mountain.
(Isaiah 65:25)

Christ alone can bring lasting peace—peace with God—peace among
men and nations—and peace within our hearts. (Billy Graham)

Maybe you remember the story of Koko, the female gorilla that raised several kittens as her own, a rare example of an animal—not a human—caring for babies of a different species. As amazing as that story seems, the Bible describes an era to come when lions and lambs will lie down together.

But that's just a highlight of the glorious future when God redeems the earth: there will be peace so perfect that it defies everything we currently know and believe could be possible.

Today, as has been the case throughout human history, we experience discord and enmity. But we have the promise of God's Holy Spirit working within us now, and we have the promise of a glorious peace in the future. That is something that should motivate us to be peacemakers—and something for which to praise God.

Thank You, Lord, for Your promises and for Your
redeeming power. I pray that You would transform my
heart and make me a peacemaker. Amen.

When Service Hurts

But even if I am being poured out like a drink offering on the sacrifice and service coming from your faith, I am glad and rejoice with all of you. (Philippians 2:17)

The cost of true greatness is humble, selfless, sacrificial service.
(John MacArthur)

*I*n the New Testament, Paul stands as an icon of sacrificial service. He endured beatings and floggings (2 Corinthians 11:25), he wept over wayward and hurtful congregations (2:4), and he frequently went without (Philippians 4:12). Yet he affirmed, "I can do everything through him who gives me strength" (v. 13).

God does not give all of us the same gifts, and He does not call us all to the same vocation. But all of us are called to humility. Paul told the Philippian church, "Your attitude should be the same as that of Christ Jesus: Who, being in very nature God, did not consider equality with God something to be grasped, but made himself nothing" (Philippians 2:5–7). It can be painful to serve God and others to the point of sacrifice. But as Paul discovered, God supplies our every need along the way.

Thank You, God, for so many examples in Scripture and in my life of people who serve You faithfully. Create in me a heart that beats to do Your will. Amen.

Praying People

*And pray in the Spirit on all occasions with all kinds of prayers and
requests. With this in mind, be alert and always keep on praying
for all the saints. (Ephesians 6:18)*

*He who has learned to pray has learned the greatest secret of
a holy and happy life. (William Law)*

A Classic Devotion from E. M. Bounds

*T*he people who are so greatly needed in this age of the church
are those who have learned the business of praying—learned
it on their knees, learned it in the need and agony of their own
hearts. Praying people are the one commanding need of this day,
as of all other days, if God is to intervene in the world.

In doing God's work there is no substitute for praying. People
of prayer cannot be replaced with other kinds of people. People of
financial skill, people of education, people of worldly influence—
none of these can possibly substitute for people of prayer.

The people to whom Jesus Christ committed the fortunes and
destiny of His church were people of prayer. To no other kind of
people has God ever committed Himself.[59]

Lord, I don't know what You have in store for me, but
teach me to prepare myself for what's next through prayer
and communion with You. Amen.

Praying for Others

*Therefore confess your sins to each other and pray for each other
so that you may be healed. The prayer of a righteous man is
powerful and effective.* (James 5:16)

*I have benefited by my praying for others; for by making an errand to God
for them, I have gotten something for myself.* (Samuel Rutherford)

*T*he old religious saying is true: we cannot outgive God. Whatever we do for Him comes back in much greater measure. One way to experience a deep fellowship with God—the greatest gift of all—is to pray for others. In the next few moments, turn your heart toward God and pray for someone you know who might be . . .

- experiencing job or career difficulties
- struggling with a health issue
- dealing with marital difficulties
- attempting a new venture
- wandering in his or her spiritual life

In fact, *you* might be facing some tough needs right now. But there are also plenty of needs in the lives of those around you, and you can't pray for them without being blessed yourself.

Father, thank You that as I pray for others, my own problems
fade into the background and I am blessed. Amen.

Why Worry?

"But seek first his kingdom and his righteousness, and all these things will be given to you as well." (Matthew 6:33)

It is of no use to say to men, "Let not your heart be troubled," unless you finish the verse and say, "Believe in God, believe also in Christ."
(Alexander Maclaren)

In Matthew 6 Jesus told a parable expressing that the lilies of the field and the birds of the air are not concerned about where their food or clothing come from. They are clothed in beauty and eat plenty, even though they do not sow or reap; they have everything they need to live as flowers and birds.

We need to trust God so much that acquiring the daily necessities of life does not feel like a burden to us. If God is great enough to create all that we can see, as well as the vastness of what we cannot see, then He is surely able to provide, as He promised, all that we need to sustain us in life. Now, if you are stewing because you don't have as much as your neighbor, but you have a full stomach, that is another matter to deal with on another day.

But be assured, God will provide you with everything you need. So why worry?

Lord, help me to trust You with the cares that sometimes overwhelm me. Thank You for Your provision for me. Amen.

The Protection of Obedience

*The wise are cautious and avoid danger; fools plunge ahead with
reckless confidence.* (Proverbs 14:16 NLT)

Danger and delight grow on one stalk. (Scottish proverb)

A family visited with friends in a tropical country. In the
midst of a seemingly peaceful moment, the kids playing and the adults conversing casually, the father who called this
exotic island his home suddenly stood up and shouted to his son,
"Hit the ground!" The son did so immediately, crouching under
the large tree nearby. The visiting family was shocked at the
father's tone and the son's instant obedience. Then they learned
that the father saw a poisonous snake hanging from the tree that
was close to striking him. The father's quick reaction and the boy's
quick obedience saved him.

The child obviously sensed the urgency in his father's voice
and facial expression. But he also had an implicit trust in his dad's
judgment and instructions. We ought always to have the same
trust in our heavenly Father's commandments. They are always
for our good and protection.

Lord God, help me to know Your commandments and obey
them without question. Amen.

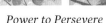

Thankfulness in Tough Times

Though there are no sheep in the pen
and no cattle in the stalls,
yet I will rejoice in the LORD,
I will be joyful in God my Savior.
The Sovereign LORD is my strength.
(Habakkuk 3:17–19)

Gratitude as a discipline involves a conscious choice. . . . It is
amazing how many occasions present themselves in which I can
choose gratitude instead of a complaint. (Henri Nouwen)

*H*abakkuk 3 describes an economic nightmare: the vines are not bearing fruit, the fields are not producing food, livestock is not thriving. When the right (or wrong) conditions conspire, we find ourselves scrambling to get by, staving off desperation, and dreading the future.

Yet even in the midst of crisis, Habakkuk exulted in God. Why? Because God gives us hinds' feet on high places—He enables us to trod rough terrain as nimbly as a deer.

Unhappy with today and fearful about tomorrow? Stop for a minute, take a deep breath, and consciously express praise and thanks to God. He is at work even if you can't see it.

God, even when I'm scared and frustrated, I want to praise
You. Strengthen my heart and give me joy in You. Amen.

Spiritual Understanding

*The man without the Spirit does not accept the things that come
from the Spirit of God, for they are foolishness to him, and he cannot
understand them, because they are spiritually discerned.*
(1 Corinthians 2:14)

*The point of having an open mind, like having an open mouth, is to
close it on something solid.* (G. K. Chesterton)

A Classic Devotion from A. B. Simpson

This is the special work of the Holy Ghost, to give to us a new spiritual vision and organ of apprehension; so that the soul directly perceives divine things and realities. Perhaps the first effect of this divine illumination is that the things of God become intensely real, and stand out with vividness and distinctness, like figures cut in relief on the wall. The person of Christ, the light of His countenance, the distinct sweetness of His Spirit, the "peace that passeth all understanding," the joy of the Lord, the heavenly world, all become to the heart more actual and intensely vivid than the things we see with our outward eyes, and touch with our human hands; so that we can say of Christ with the apostle, "That which we have seen with our eyes, which we have looked upon, and our hands have handled of the Word of Life."[60]

Lord, I pray that You would enlighten my understanding
and help me see You more clearly. Amen.

Shipwrecked

In the day of my trouble I will call to you,
for you will answer me.
(Psalm 86:7)

It is the trial of our faith that is precious. If we go through the trial,
there is so much wealth laid up in our heavenly bank account to draw
upon when the next test comes. (Oswald Chambers)

*P*aul knew something about storms. A man of the world and accustomed to international travel before and after his conversion, he experienced plenty of rough waters and on one occasion was shipwrecked (Acts 27:39–44).

On that occasion, Paul and his shipmates had a very specific message from God: obey and you will be saved. Every single person made it to shore alive—even though the ship itself was torn apart.

When the waters we are sailing on grow turbulent, it's easy to get our eyes off what matters and try some desperate moves. In financial storms, some have stolen and swindled; in relationship storms, some have been unfaithful; in storms at work, some have falsified reports and cheated on margins. The only sure way to get safely to shore is through simple obedience to God's will for our lives.

Lord, give me even greater resolve to do what is right
when storms rage around me. Amen.

You Can Make a Difference

"Father, I thank you that you have heard me. I knew that you always hear me, but I said this for the benefit of the people standing here, that they may believe that you sent me." (John 11:41–42)

I have seen many men work without praying, though I have never seen any good come out of it; but I have never seen a man pray without working. (James Hudson Taylor)

A Classic Devotion from D. L. Moody

Those who have left the deepest impression on this sin-cursed earth have been men and women of prayer. You will find that prayer has been the mighty power that has moved not only God, but man also.

We read that Elijah brought fire down on Mount Carmel (1 Kings 18:17–39). The prophets of Baal cried long and loud, but no answer came. The God of Elijah heard and answered his prayer. Let us remember that the God of Elijah still lives. As we go to the throne of grace, let us always remember that God answers prayer.

All through the Scriptures you will find that when believing prayer went up to God, the answer came down.[61]

Lord, I can't do anything apart from You. I ask You to work through me to make a difference in the world. Amen.

Love Sees No Color

There is neither Jew nor Greek, slave nor free, male nor female, for you are all one in Christ Jesus. (Galatians 3:28)

Hatred paralyzes life; love releases it. Hatred confuses life; love harmonizes it. Hatred darkens life; love illuminates it. (Martin Luther King Jr.)

It has been said that Sunday morning is the most racially segregated time of the week in America. Whether true or not, and even as far as we've come as a nation in turning from racism, all of us as individuals still have room to grow in our love for those who are superficially different from us. God makes no distinction among colors, races, or nationalities. God loves all types of people, and He has given everyone on earth the opportunity to experience salvation and follow Him. When Christ looks at someone, He sees the heart, not color or nationality.

Jesus commanded us to love as He loves. He said that our love for each other will serve as proof that we are His disciples. The only way to love as Christ loves is to love without barriers. It might take a little extra effort to get to know people of other backgrounds and love them with God's love, but the rewards are rich.

Lord, help me to love everyone with Your love, and give me courage to build bridges in my sphere of influence. Amen.

Peace and Encouragement

We Can Trust God

How great is your goodness,
which you have stored up for those who fear you,
which you bestow in the sight of men
on those who take refuge in you.
(Psalm 31:19)

God has wisely kept us in the dark concerning future events and
reserved for himself the knowledge of them, that he may train us
up in a dependence upon himself and a continued readiness for
every event. (Matthew Henry)

A Classic Devotion from Samuel Rutherford

*D*uties are ours, events are the Lord's. When our faith goeth to meddle with events, and to hold a court (if I may so speak) upon God's providence, and beginneth to say, "How wilt thou do this and that?" we lose ground. We have nothing to do there. It is our part to let the Almighty exercise his own office, and steer his own helm. There is nothing left for us, but to see how we may be approved of him, and how we roll the weight of our weak souls in well-doing upon him, who is God omnipotent: and when what we thus essay miscarrieth, it will neither be our sin nor our cross.[62]

> Lord, I know that there are so many things I can't
> control—but You can. Help me to do Your will and
> entrust myself to Your care. Amen.

Obeying and Praying

Dear friends, if our hearts do not condemn us, we have confidence before God and receive from him anything we ask, because we obey his commands and do what pleases him. (1 John 3:21–22)

All true knowledge of God is born out of obedience. (John Calvin)

A Classic Devotion from R. A. Torrey

The one who expects God to do as he asks Him must on his part do whatever God bids him. If we give a listening ear to all God's commands to us, He will give a listening ear to all our petitions to Him. If, on the other hand, we turn a deaf ear to His precepts, He will be likely to turn a deaf ear to our prayers. Here we find the secret of much unanswered prayer. We are not listening to God's Word, and therefore He is not listening to our petitions.

If we would have power in prayer, we must be earnest students of His Word to find out what His will regarding us is, and then having found it, do it. One unconfessed act of disobedience on our part will shut the ear of God against many petitions.[63]

Father, help me to love You so deeply that I will always obey You. Thank You for hearing my prayers. Amen.

Good Soil

*Let the word of Christ dwell in you richly as you teach and admonish
one another with all wisdom, and as you sing psalms, hymns and
spiritual songs with gratitude in your hearts to God.* (Colossians 3:16)

*The unthankful heart discovers no mercies; but let the thankful heart
sweep through the day and, as the magnet finds the iron, so it will find,
in every hour, some heavenly blessings!* (Henry Ward Beecher)

A colloquial story is told of a man who found the barn where
Satan stores the seeds he sows in the human heart: envy,
greed, anger, hatred, lust, and so on. The man noticed that Satan
had more seeds of discouragement than any other kind, and he
learned that those seeds were hardy and fruitful and could be
made to grow almost anywhere. But when Satan was questioned,
he reluctantly admitted that there was one place in which he
could not get them to grow. "Where is that?" asked the man. Satan
replied, "In the heart of a thankful man."

When we choose a thankful attitude, our spirits resist the
cynicism, discouragement, and pessimism that weigh life down.
We're better able to thrive and survive no matter what life throws
at us. And our love for God blooms.

God, I pray for a thankful heart. Please nurture in
me a spirit of gratitude. Amen.

The Joy of Knowing Jesus

"I have told you this so that my joy may be in you and that your joy may be complete." (John 15:11)

According to Jesus, it is God's will that His children be filled with the joy of life. (Catherine Marshall)

A Classic Devotion from Andrew Murray

*A*biding fully in Christ is a life of exquisite and overflowing happiness. As Christ gets more complete possession of the soul, it enters into the joy of its Lord. His own joy, the joy of heaven, becomes its own, and that in full measure, and as an ever-abiding portion.

We all know the value of joy. It alone is the proof that what we have really satisfies the heart. Just this makes gladness such a mighty element in the Christian character: there is no proof of the reality of God's love and the blessing He bestows, which men so soon feel the force of, as when the joy of God overcomes all the trials of life. And for the Christian's own welfare, joy is no less indispensable: the joy of the Lord is his strength; confidence, and courage, and patience find their inspiration in joy. With a heart full of joy no work can weary, and no burden can depress; God Himself is strength and song.[64]

Lord Jesus, I want to be more connected to You and to know Your joy more deeply. Amen.

A Renewed Strength

*But those who hope in the L*ORD
will renew their strength.
They will soar on wings like eagles;
they will run and not grow weary,
they will walk and not be faint.
(Isaiah 40:31)

When God is our strength, it is strength indeed; when our strength is
our own, it is only weakness. (Saint Augustine)

*I*n a world that can wear us down mentally, physically, and spiritually, how do we renew our strength? What do we do in the face of too many projects, too many temptations, too many conflicts, and too many other soul- and energy-sapping dynamics at work in life?

The prophet Isaiah ministered to a nation on the verge of collapse. His antidote to spiritual fatigue was simple: hope in the Lord.

Others might help you. Great. But don't put your hope in them. You might be able to muster some more determination to get the job done. Wonderful. But don't even place your hope in yourself. The only place to turn for a renewed spirit is to the One who has given you every good and perfect gift.

Place your hope in the Lord, and let Him give you a supernatural strength.

Heavenly Father, You truly are the source of my hope for today, tomorrow, and all the days ahead. Thank You. Amen.

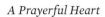

Direct Communication

How sweet are your words to my taste,
sweeter than honey to my mouth!
(Psalm 119:103)

The Bible is a letter from God with our personal address on it.
(Søren Kierkegaard)

A Classic Devotion from A. W. Pink

*I*f it were announced upon reliable authority that on a certain date in the near future an angel from heaven would visit New York and would deliver a sermon upon the invisible world, the future destiny of man, or the secret of deliverance from the power of sin, what an audience he would command! There is no building in that city large enough to accommodate the crowd which would throng to hear him. If upon the next day, the newspapers were to give a verbatim report of his discourse, how eagerly it would be read! And yet, we have between the covers of the Bible not merely an angelic communication but a Divine revelation. How great then is our wickedness if we undervalue and despise it! And yet we do.[65]

Lord, thank You that You communicate with us through
Your Word. I want to know Your will, Lord. Amen.

The Gift of Giving

Each man should give what he has decided in his heart to give, not reluctantly or under compulsion, for God loves a cheerful giver.
(2 Corinthians 9:7)

Nothing is really ours until we share it. (C. S. Lewis)

One of the true tests of our character is what we do with our money. Of course, God calls us to give a portion of our income to Him through ministry (Numbers 18:28) and also to give special sacrificial offerings to meet special needs as we feel directed in our hearts (Numbers 15:3). Paul does say that some people have a special gift of giving (Romans 12:8), but he also points out that God loves a cheerful giver (2 Corinthians 9:7).

When we are generous with our money above and beyond expectations, we experience a number of benefits: We are more aware that all good gifts come from God; we learn to trust and serve Him with a pure heart; and we receive the joy of helping someone in need. Besides all that, there is a strange paradox that the more we give, the more we seem to have.

As you practice giving generously, God will teach you the wonderful truth that whatever we grasp and hoard dries up and suffocates; but whatever we give freely and generously takes off and soars.

God, I want to be generous with my money and time. Help me to serve You by serving others. Amen.

To Be Made Holy

Blessed is the man you discipline, O Lord,
the man you teach from your law.
(Psalm 94:12)

The vinedresser is never nearer the branches than when he
is pruning them. (David Jeremiah)

A Classic Devotion from Andrew Murray

*E*very child of God must at one time or another enter the school of trial. What the Scriptures teach us is confirmed by experience. They teach us further, that we are to count it a joy when God takes us into this school. It is a part of our heavenly blessedness to be educated and sanctified by the Father through chastisement.

Holiness is the highest glory of the Father, and also of the child. He "chastens us for our profit that we may be partakers of His Holiness." In trial the Christian would often have only comfort. Or he seeks to be quiet and contented under the special chastisement. This is indeed the beginning; but the Father desires something else, something higher. He would make him holy, holy, for his whole life.[66]

Thank You for the challenges You allow in my life to make
me stronger and draw me closer to You. Amen.

Obedience Brings Blessing

*Be careful to obey all these regulations I am giving you, so that it
may always go well with you and your children after you, because
you will be doing what is good and right in the eyes of the LORD
your God.* (Deuteronomy 12:28)

*God is more anxious to bestow his blessings on us than we
are to receive them.* (Saint Augustine)

A Classic Devotion from C. H. Spurgeon

*T*hough salvation is not by the works of the law, yet the blessings which are promised to obedience are not denied to the faithful servants of God. The curses our Lord took away when He was made a curse for us, but no clause of blessing has been abrogated.

We are to note and listen to the revealed will of the Lord, giving our attention not to portions of it but to "all these words." There must be no picking and choosing but an impartial respect to all that God has commanded. This is the road of blessedness for the Father and for His children. The Lord's blessing is upon His chosen to the third and fourth generation. If they walk uprightly before Him, He will make all men know that they are a seed which the Lord has blessed.[67]

God, thank You for the blessings that flow when I obey You. I
pray for a heart that longs to follow Your rules for living. Amen.

Keep Going

*Let us draw near to God with a sincere heart in full assurance
of faith, having our hearts sprinkled to cleanse us from a guilty
conscience and having our bodies washed with pure water.*
(Hebrews 10:22)

*A true faith in Jesus Christ will not suffer us to be idle. No, it is an
active, lively, restless principle; it fills the heart, so that it cannot be
easy till it is doing something for Jesus Christ.* (George Whitefield)

During a long race, it's easy to get discouraged. But what most runners know is that being familiar with the course helps to keep up momentum and motivation. When you know what to expect, you're able to pace yourself and not become discouraged when the road seems endless.

God doesn't map out for us the exact course of our lives. But there are some things we can know without a shadow of a doubt. We know troubles will come. We know that God will never abandon us. We know that He has good plans for us. And we know that He will ultimately overcome evil in the world. That knowledge and faith help us persevere when the going gets tough and the race gets long.

God, give me greater confidence in You so that I might
persevere in the race of life. Amen.

A Sudden Change

But the fruit of the Spirit is love, joy, peace, patience, kindness, goodness, faithfulness, gentleness and self-control. Against such things there is no law. (Galatians 5:22–23)

Joy is the echo of God's life in us. (Joseph Marmion)

A Classic Devotion from Thomas Watson

Spiritual joy is a sweet and delightful passion, arising from the apprehension and feeling of some good, whereby the soul is supported under present troubles, and fenced against future fear. Joy is not a fancy, or conceit; but is rational, and arises from the feeling of some good, as the sense of God's love and favour. Joy is so real a thing that it makes a sudden change in a person; and turns mourning into melody. As in the spring-time, when the sun comes to our horizon, it makes a sudden alteration in the face of the universe: the birds sing, the flowers appear, the fig-tree puts forth her green figs; every thing seems to rejoice and put off its mourning, as being revived with the sweet influence of the sun; so when the Sun of Righteousness arises on the soul, it makes a sudden alteration, and the soul is infinitely rejoiced with the golden beams of God's love.[68]

Father, may Your comforts delight my soul
with Your great joy. Amen.

A Hopeless Hope

Against all hope, Abraham in hope believed and so became the father of many nations, just as it had been said to him, "So shall your offspring be." (Romans 4:18)

Hope against hope, and ask till ye receive. (James Montgomery)

Abraham is known as the father of our faith. That title didn't come easily! First of all, he left his home in a sophisticated and affluent part of the world because he heard God calling him to a new land. Throughout his story in Genesis, the one constant is that he picked up his tent stakes and moved on.

But that was just the beginning of his challenges. When he got to the land, it was filled with warring tribes. Even harder to deal with, he and his wife seemingly could not have children. How do you become the father of a nation when you have no land and no child? But Abraham never gave up, and at an old age he received his reward.

Will your faith persevere when you see no immediate results to feed your hope?

Lord, thank You for speaking to me and giving me a vision of my future. Keep my faith and sense of hope strong! Amen.

A Prayerful Heart

The Heart Behind the Words

"Whoever humbles himself like this child is the greatest in the kingdom of heaven." (Matthew 18:4)

When you can't put your prayers into words, God hears your heart.
(author unknown)

"God is grape. God is goo," intoned the little boy before meal-time. Over and over, his mom would stop him and explain the proper way to say the words in the blessing "God is great. God is good." But sure enough, before the next meal she would hear the boy's usual prayer, "God is grape. God is goo."

After a while, it finally dawned on this mom that God was probably amused. He may have even called the angels over to hear her son as he prayed. More than likely, God wasn't as concerned about him pronouncing the words correctly as He was that her son stopped long enough to thank God for the food He had provided.

When we pray, we don't have to impress God. In fact, we can't impress God. All that matters is that we come to Him with child-like wonder and thanksgiving. Even if our words aren't impressive, the heart behind them moves God's heart.

Lord, thank You for the gift of coming to You in prayer, and thank You that You delight in my feeble attempts. Amen.

Spiritual Gifts

"His master replied, 'Well done, good and faithful servant! You have been faithful with a few things; I will put you in charge of many things. Come and share your master's happiness!'" (Matthew 25:23)

In the great orchestra we call life, you have an instrument and a song, and you owe it to God to play them both sublimely. (Max Lucado)

Albert Schweitzer, winner of the Nobel Peace Prize in 1952, was a biblical scholar (often a controversial one), a medical doctor and missionary, and a celebrated musician. Few people achieve his success in even one arena, let alone three. In the eyes of God, however, Schweitzer was not greater than anyone else who uses their talents to their utmost in the service of others.

Jesus' parable of the talents gives us some perspective. The master gave his servants a number of talents, "each according to his ability" (Matthew 25:15). The ones who multiplied their talents were rewarded, but the servant who simply buried his talent faced punishment. It's a sobering thought: we will be judged on how well we use our abilities. Even if we have fewer than someone else, we must always put what we have to use.

The gifts and abilities God gives us are to be used for God's kingdom, in service to Him and others. Each time we serve in this way, we increase the potential of our gifts.

Lord, help me to know what my gifts are, and show me
how to use them for You. Amen.

I Love a Rainy Day

"I have set my rainbow in the clouds, and it will be the sign of the covenant between me and the earth." (Genesis 9:13)

Today you will encounter God's creation. When you see the beauty around you, let each detail remind you to lift your head in praise.
(Max Lucado)

When you have an outdoor wedding or a big family-reunion picnic planned, a rainy day feels like a disaster. But most of the time, there are lots of reasons to love rainy days!

- No yard work, and you don't have to wash the car.
- They make for a great time to stay inside and read a book.
- Newly planted flowers need the water.
- They make us appreciate bright, sunny days even more.
- We might get to see a rainbow—God's own sign that He will never destroy the earth by water again.

Rainy days may or may not be your favorite, but like all other days, they offer something positive. And since all days are God's days, a blessing can always be found in a storm cloud!

Father, thank You for both the rain and the sunshine in my life. I know that I need both experiences. And thank You that Your presence and blessings are found no matter the weather. Amen.

Count Your Blessings

Since my youth, O God, you have taught me, and to this day I declare your marvelous deeds. (Psalm 71:17)

No duty is more urgent than that of returning thanks. (Saint Ambrose)

How many ways have you been blessed by God? Relationally? Materially? Spiritually? Physically? His blessings are all around us, but we too easily get distracted. Consider an activity where you write in your journal or on a sheet of paper all the different ways God has blessed you. No only can you divide it by category, but you can also do this for different stages of your life: childhood blessings, teen blessings, young adult blessings, and so on until you hit the present. If this sounds too simplistic, remember that many people have started a gratitude list with skepticism, only to be delightfully surprised by how much the list brightened their outlook.

King David said, "I will meditate on all your works and consider all your mighty deeds" (Psalm 77:12). Another psalm echoes, "Come and listen, all you who fear God; let me tell you what he has done for me" (66:16). Whatever God has done for you, stop to remember His blessings in detail. And say a word of thanks.

> Lord, when I look back, I can see that You have been with me all my life. Thank You for Your goodness to me. Amen.

Make a Plan

All his laws are before me;
I have not turned away from his decrees.
(Psalm 18:22)

For some years now I have read through the Bible twice every year.
If you picture the Bible to be a mighty tree and every word a little
branch, I have shaken every one of these branches because I wanted
to know what it was and what it meant. (Martin Luther)

*E*very Bible reader has a favorite verse or book, one he or she returns to often for comfort and wisdom. But as wonderful as those familiar favorites can be, there are countless other precious gems in Scripture waiting to be discovered. The only way to find them is to read what we've never read before. That's why a Bible reading plan can be such a valuable tool for spiritual growth.

Your Bible may have a reading plan near the front that will direct you to finish the whole Bible in one year. If not, there are plenty of other ways to read a wider range of Scripture than you ever have before. Do an Internet search for reading plans; some sites offer plans you can even check off as you go along. Consider Bible software or even a program for your smart phone that can provide you with a passage of Scripture every day. Select an unfamiliar book of the Bible each month and read through it with a friend. Whatever method or plan you use, ask God to help you grow in love for His Word.

God, thank You for speaking to me through the Bible. Help
me to grow more and more familiar with it. Amen.

Be Thankful

Let the peace of Christ rule in your hearts, since as members of one body you were called to peace. And be thankful. (Colossians 3:15)

We should spend as much time in thanking God for His benefits as we do asking Him for them. (Saint Vincent de Paul)

Which comes first—the gift or the spirit of thanksgiving? Common wisdom says that we get the gift first, then we say thank you for receiving it. While that is true, some gifts will never be recognized or received without a spirit of thanksgiving.

How many people sabotage the blessings in their lives because of a crummy attitude? They are dissatisfied and disappointed—and let the world know it—despite a plethora of gifts from God and others all around them.

All of us can be thankful for the many things God has done for us. But there may be deeper levels of spirituality, even more of His nature and goodness, that we can experience through the attitude of gratitude. Have you said thank you to God today?

Lord, thank You for the gifts and blessings You have
lavished in my life. Amen.

Clothed in Humility

*He guides the humble in what is right
and teaches them his way.*
(Psalm 25:9)

*For those who would learn God's ways, humility is the first thing,
humility is the second, humility is the third.* (Saint Augustine)

In the classic children's story of the emperor's new clothes, the emperor was visited by two swindlers who promised that if he provided them with gold thread, they would produce for him the finest clothes in the world. But not just any clothes; magical clothes. Only those who were smart and fit for their position could see the clothes they made, they promised. That really appealed to his pride.

You know the rest of the story. The emperor paraded through the streets naked, unwilling to admit that he couldn't see the clothes he was wearing (or not wearing). A simple child pointed out that he was wearing nothing, and the emperor was humiliated in front of the whole town. And so were those who pretended to see his clothes.

You will never accidentally leave the house in the buff believing you're wearing fine clothes, and hopefully you will never fall victim to a shady swindler. But all of us are vulnerable to the sin of pride. It makes smart people do dumb things.

Wisdom comes from a proper respect for God and a humble walk before Him.

Lord, I ask You for wisdom and a humble heart. Amen.

Personal Interaction

Trust in him at all times, O people;
pour out your hearts to him,
for God is our refuge.
(Psalm 62:8)

In prayer it is better to have a heart without words than words
without a heart. (John Bunyan)

An anonymous author recounted the story of a traveler in China who visited a temple on a feast day, joining many pilgrims in gathering around a sacred shrine. He noticed that many of them were pulling out strips of paper, rolling them in mud, and tossing them at the idol. When he asked what they were doing, he was told that the pieces of paper were written prayers. They believed that if the mud-wrapped paper stuck to the idol, it would serve as a promise that the prayer would be answered. If it fell off, it meant the prayer had been rejected.

There's no easy way to know how God will respond to our prayers. But would we really want there to be? We grow through prayer and communing with God through His Word and connections with fellow believers. If we interacted with God through anything but personal means, would that experience be as rich and engaging?

God is listening. And if we pay attention, we will hear Him speak back, even if our prayers aren't immediately answered.

God, thank You for interacting with us so personally. Help me to more fully engage in a relationship of prayer. Amen.

Gifts to Give

A generous man will himself be blessed. (Proverbs 22:9)

You cannot outgive God. (Billy Graham)

Go ahead and try. You can't do it. It's impossible to give and not get something in return. Oh, there will be times you extend love and not have it reciprocated; you might give sacrificially from limited funds and still be short on cash; it is possible to help others get their lives in order only to be left completely alone in a moment of need. None of those things are likely, but they are possible.

But you still can't come up empty-handed. It's not possible. Because God, your heavenly Father, sees your gifts of love and is pleased. Even if no one else thanks you, know that He will reward your kindness.

Maybe you won't receive a return on your investment of service in this lifetime. You probably will, but maybe you won't. Be assured, though, that the very best rewards are eternal.

Dear God, thank You that You return my acts of kindness
to me in greater measure than I could ever give. Amen.

In the Day of Trouble

For in the day of trouble
he will keep me safe in his dwelling;
he will hide me in the shelter of his tabernacle
and set me high upon a rock.
(Psalm 27:5)

Let nothing disturb you, let nothing frighten you: everything passes
away except God; God alone is sufficient. (Saint Theresa)

*T*he shepherd boy who wrote and played music that touched the hearts of many had grown into a mighty warrior. He was Saul's beloved champion in battle—and yet the disturbed king burned with jealousy and rage at David's exploits.

He needed and wanted David close, but uncontrollable fits would overcome Saul and he would strike out to slay him. David's life was not safe. He lived in a state of vigilant fear, wondering what mood the king would be in at a particular moment.

But even in these unreliable circumstances, David believed God's hand of mercy and protection was on his life—that God would "hide me" or "set me high upon a rock." Few of us live in such an insecure state as David did. But we have troubles of our own. How is your faith?

Lord, You do protect and provide for me in all
circumstances of life. Thank You for Your hand of mercy.
Amen.

Our First Love

"I remember the devotion of your youth." (Jeremiah 2:2)

God thirsts to be thirsted after. (Saint Augustine)

A Classic Devotion from Oswald Chambers

*A*m I as spontaneously kind to God as I used to be, or am I only expecting God to be kind to me? Am I full of the little things that cheer His heart over me, or am I whimpering because things are going hardly with me? There is no joy in the soul that has forgotten what God prizes. It is a great thing to think that Jesus Christ has need of me—"Give Me to drink." How much kindness have I shown Him this past week? Have I been kind to His reputation in my life?

God is saying to His people—You are not in love with Me now, but I remember the time when you were—"I remember . . . the love of thine espousals." Am I as full of the extravagance of love to Jesus Christ as I was in the beginning, when I went out of my way to prove my devotion to Him? Does He find me recalling the time when I did not care for anything but Himself? Am I there now, or have I become wise over loving Him?[69]

Lord, I pray that I would never lose my love for You. Help me remember what first drew me to You, and renew the gratitude I felt when You first saved me. Amen.

Self-Inflicted Storms

Before I was afflicted I went astray,
but now I obey your word.
It was good for me to be afflicted
so that I might learn your decrees.
(Psalm 119:67, 71)

He may sometimes chasten us, it is true, but even this He does with a
smile, the proud, tender smile of a Father who is bursting with pleasure
over an imperfect but promising son who is coming every day to look
more and more like the One whose child he is. (A. W. Tozer)

Not every calamity that comes our way is an accident of nature or a trial God has allowed to help us grow. Some storms are self-inflicted:

- health problems after years of bad eating habits
- broken relationships after infidelity or a pattern of cruelty
- financial woes after overspending for years

Those are storms—and they aren't unfair. Yet God is a God of second chances. He won't eliminate every consequence of dumb behavior, but He will give us new meaning and purpose in life when we return to Him.

Is there someone in your life who needs to hear again that God gives second chances? If it's you, will you receive His mercy today?

Thank You for forgiveness and for never giving
up on me, God! Amen.

Be of Good Cheer

*"I have told you these things, so that in me you may have peace.
In this world you will have trouble. But take heart! I have
overcome the world."* (John 16:33)

*If our hearts have been attuned to God through an abiding faith in
Christ, the result will be joyous optimism and good cheer.*
(Billy Graham)

"Don't worry, be happy" may be too simplistic of a formula for life, but the "be happy" part is definitely a principle from God's Word.

David said, "You have filled my heart with greater joy than when their grain and new wine abound" (Psalm 4:7). Solomon said, "A cheerful heart is good medicine, but a crushed spirit dries up the bones" (Proverbs 17:22). Jesus said, "In the world you will have tribulation; but be of good cheer, I have overcome the world" (John 16:33 NKJV).

Even if you have problems and worries that are gnawing at you today, all the more reason to make a conscious decision to shake off the blues and embrace a cheerful disposition.

Dear God, thank You for the gift of joy. I choose
happiness in You today. Amen.

The Soul of a Nation

I urge, then, first of all, that requests, prayers, intercession and thanksgiving be made for everyone—for kings and all those in authority, that we may live peaceful and quiet lives in all godliness and holiness. (1 Timothy 2:1–2)

For my own part, I sincerely esteem [the Constitution] a system which without the finger of God, never could have been suggested and agreed upon by such a diversity of interests. (Alexander Hamilton)

What makes a country great? No question, it is tied to its spiritual quality.

- Samuel Adams: "[Impress] the minds of men with the importance of educating their little boys and girls, inculcating in the minds of youth the fear and love of the Deity."
- Patrick Henry: "It cannot be emphasized too clearly and too often that this nation was founded, not by religionists, but by Christians; not on religion, but on the gospel of Jesus Christ."
- John Jay: "We've staked the future of all our political institutions upon our capacity to sustain ourselves according to the Ten Commandments of God."

Our earliest leaders committed their work to God. We can't make that same choice for all our fellow citizens, but we can make it for ourselves.

Lord, I want to follow You in everything I do. Amen.

God's Promises

*For by these He has granted to us His precious and magnificent promises,
so that by them you may become partakers of the divine nature, having
escaped the corruption that is in the world by lust.* (2 Peter 1:4 NASB)

*You never know how much you really believe anything until its truth
or falsehood becomes a matter of life and death to you.* (C. S. Lewis)

A Classic Devotion from C. H. Spurgeon

*I*f you would know experimentally the preciousness of the
promises, and enjoy them in your own heart, meditate much
upon them. There are promises which are like grapes in the wine-
press: if you will tread them the juice will flow. Thinking over
the hallowed words will often be the prelude to their fulfillment.
Many a Christian who has thirsted for the promise has found the
favor which it ensured gently distilling into his soul even while he
has been considering the divine record; and he has rejoiced that
ever he was led to lay the promise near his heart. . . .

Speak to thy soul thus, "My soul, it is God, even thy God, God
that cannot lie, who speaks to thee. Therefore, seeing that it is the
word of a God so true, so immutable, so powerful, so wise, I will
and must believe the promise."[70]

Lord, I know that You are faithful. Today I praise You for
Your promises and Your goodness to me. Amen.

Serve Where You Are

He appointed the priests to their duties and encouraged them in the service of the LORD's temple. (2 Chronicles 35:2)

In the Kingdom of God, service is not a stepping-stone to nobility: it is nobility, the only kind of nobility that is recognized. (T. W. Manson)

A Classic Devotion from C. H. Spurgeon

*D*ear friends, do you not think we frequently limit our estimate of serving God to the public exercises of the sanctuary, and forget the strong claims that our Lord has upon our private fidelity and obedience? You say, "I cannot serve God," when you cannot teach in the school or preach in the pulpit, when you are unable to sit on a committee or speak on a platform: as if these were the only forms of service to be taken into account. Do you not think that a mother nursing her baby is serving God? Do you not think that men and women going about their daily toil with patient industry discharging the duties of domestic life are serving God? If you think rightly you will understand that they are. The servant sweeping the room, the mistress preparing the meal, the workman driving a nail, the merchant casting up his ledger, ought to do all in the service of God.[71]

> Lord, I want to do everything I do to the best of my abilities and serve You even in the small things. Amen.

Peace with Myself

We have different gifts, according to the grace given us. (Romans 12:6)

Through my handicaps, I have found my self, my work, my God.
(Helen Keller)

Some people don't need to fight with anyone to be at war. Their battles are with themselves.

Maybe it was a tough upbringing. Maybe it was a traumatic event. Maybe it was a lost opportunity or relationship. Or maybe their battles within are the result of exalted opinions of themselves.

On this earth, few of us will ever be 100 percent satisfied with who we are and be totally at peace within. As we grow older, we should naturally experience that peace to a greater degree. But when self-warring is strong enough to hinder all other relationships, we need to take a good look inside.

Are you at peace with God? Do you believe He made you the way you are for a purpose? Your answers will lead you to how you need to pray!

God, thank You for making me who I am, with the people
You put in my life, and with the plans You have for me.
Amen.

The Eye of the Beholder

I will extol the LORD at all times;
his praise will always be on my lips. (Psalm 34:1)

Pride slays thanksgiving, but a humble mind is the soil out of which
thanks naturally grow. A proud man is seldom a grateful man, for he
never thinks he gets as much as he deserves. (Henry Ward Beecher)

*I*n Depression-era America, a lawyer successfully handled a difficult case for a wealthy friend. Following the happy outcome of the case, the friend went to the lawyer's office, expressed his appreciation of his work, and handed him a handsome Moroccan leather wallet. The lawyer looked at the wallet in astonishment and handed it back with a sharp reminder that a wallet could not possibly compensate him for his services. "My fee for that work," snapped the attorney, "is five hundred dollars."

The client opened the wallet, removed a one-thousand dollar bill, replaced it with a five-hundred dollar bill, and handed it back to the lawyer with a smile.

We can easily be too quick to assess what life gives us and demand more. Greed can squash gratitude. But an attitude of contentment turns everything into a gift.

God, help me to see the best in others and in
what You give me. Amen.

Victory Begins with a Thankful Heart

Grace and peace be yours in abundance through the knowledge of God and of Jesus our Lord. (2 Peter 1:2)

Strength, rest, guidance, grace, help, sympathy, love—all from God to us! What a list of blessings! (E. Stenbock)

A Classic Devotion from D. L. Moody

*W*e ought to be more thankful for what we receive from God. Here we are, getting blessings from God day after day, yet how little praise and thanksgiving there is in the church of God!

It is said that in a time of great despondency among the first settlers in New England, it was proposed in one of their public assemblies to proclaim a fast. An old farmer arose. He spoke of their provoking heaven with their complaints. He reviewed their measures, showed that they had much to be thankful for, and moved that instead of appointing a day of fasting, they should appoint a day of thanksgiving. This was done, and the custom has been continued ever since.

Even if we had nothing else to be thankful for, we would always have ample cause for giving thanks in that Jesus Christ loved us and gave Himself for us (Gal. 2:20).[72]

Lord, thank You for being in my life. I choose today to be grateful to You all day. Amen.

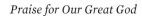

Because He Loves

*If you have any encouragement from being united with Christ, if
any comfort from his love, if any fellowship with the Spirit, if any
tenderness and compassion, then make my joy complete by being
like-minded, having the same love, being one in spirit and purpose.*
(Philippians 2:1–2)

*This is the secret of joy. We shall no longer strive for our own way;
but commit ourselves, easily and simply, to God's way, acquiesce in
His will, and in so doing find our peace.* (Evelyn Underhill)

A Classic Devotion from Alexander Maclaren

We may think of the joy that belongs to the Divine Nature as
coming from the completeness of His being, which is raised
far above all that makes of sorrow. But it is not in Himself alone
that He is glad; but it is because He loves. The exercise of love is
ever blessedness. His joy is in self impartation; His delights are
in the sons of men. His gladness is in His children when they let
Him love them, and do not throw back His love on itself. He is
glad when His face is mirrored in ours, and the rays from Him are
reflected from us.[73]

God, it's amazing to me that You delight in us, Your
children. Help me to understand Your love and
rejoice in You today. Amen.

A Day Set Aside

Now, our God, we give you thanks,
and praise your glorious name.
(1 Chronicles 29:13)

It is therefore recommended to set apart Thursday the eighteenth day
of December next, for solemn thanksgiving and praise, that with one
heart and one voice the good people may express the grateful feelings
of their hearts and consecrate themselves to the service of their divine
benefactor. (Samuel Adams)

*T*he Founding Fathers of the United States of America saw the need for the nation to celebrate the new beginnings of the country, and they instituted the first national day of thanksgiving. Although the Thanksgiving we know—the fourth Thursday of November—wasn't made official by Congress until 1941, many presidents between Washington and Franklin D. Roosevelt understood the value of a national day of gratitude. Canada set its Thanksgiving on the second Monday of every October. Other countries celebrate similarly.

This Thanksgiving, as you gather with family and friends, why not adopt the age-old tradition of asking each guest at your table to name something he or she is thankful for? No matter what country you call home, as you ponder your own list of things to be grateful for individually, don't forget about the blessings your nation has received collectively. All of us have much for which to give thanks.

God, thank You for Your provision for me, my family,
and my country. Amen.

A Thankful Blessing

Give thanks to the LORD, call on his name; make known among the nations what he has done. (1 Chronicles 16:8)

Thankfulness to God is a recognition that God in His goodness and faithfulness has provided for us and cared for us, both physically and spiritually. (Jerry Bridges)

A Thanksgiving Prayer by Scott Wesemann

Lord, so oftentimes, as any other day, when we sit down to our meal and pray we hurry along and make fast the blessing— "Thanks, amen. Now please pass the dressing."

We're slaves to the olfactory overload. We must rush our prayer before the food gets cold. But Lord, I'd like to take a few minutes more to really give thanks for what I'm thankful for.

For my family, my health, a nice soft bed, my friends, my freedom, a roof over my head.

I'm thankful right now to be surrounded by those whose lives touch me more than they'll ever possibly know.

Thankful, Lord, that You've blessed me beyond measure, thankful that in my heart lives life's greatest treasure, that You, dear Jesus, reside in that place, and I'm ever so grateful for Your unending grace.

So please, heavenly Father, bless this food You've provided and bless each and every person invited. Amen!

Lord, this Thanksgiving, help me reflect on
what really matters. Amen.

Happy Thanksgiving

And do not forget to do good and to share with others, for with such sacrifices God is pleased. (Hebrews 13:16)

No matter how little you have, you can always give some of it away.
(Catherine Marshall)

When you go grocery shopping, will you pick up some extra food for a needy family?" Martin asked. "There is a family of eight who needs something to eat for Thanksgiving."

Jean considered her limited funds. Eight people? With the dozen-plus people she would be feeding at her own house that year, she wasn't sure she could afford two Thanksgiving dinners. "I'll do the best I can," she answered. "But on our budget, it is probably an impossible mission."

With her coupons, several buy-one-get-one-free specials, and God's help, Jean bought two carts filled with groceries. Later that day, six gleeful children paraded from the car to their kitchen with enough groceries to feed an army.

Even when we're struggling ourselves, with a little creativity we can often do more than we think we can for someone else. One of the best ways to show our gratitude to God is to help Him help those around us. Who needs your help today?

God, I know that You care about the needs around
me. Show me how I can serve You with gratitude
by serving others. Amen.

For God So Loved You

"For God so loved the world that he gave his one and only Son, that whoever believes in him shall not perish but have eternal life." (John 3:16)

God loves each of us as if there was only one of us. (Saint Augustine)

Very few people question that God is loving. But many of these very same people question whether God truly loves them. They are certain God hears the prayers of others, forgives others, has plans for others, is patient and loving with others—but not with them.

How about you? Do you know that God not only loves the world but that He loves you? Personally. On a first-name basis.

One simple activity that might bring that point home to you in a crystal clear way is to write out John 3:16 but in place of the word *world* insert your own name. For God so loved Lynne . . . Amy . . . Jessica . . . Greg . . . Nathan . . . Troy . . . Then read the verse out loud several times today—and tomorrow. In fact, you might try that right now.

Our lives change when we experience for ourselves the reality that God loves the world—and every individual in it.

Thank You, heavenly Father, for loving me so much
that if I was the only lost person in the world, You
would still die for me. Amen.

Do We Really Have a Choice?

We were therefore buried with him through baptism into death in order that, just as Christ was raised from the dead through the glory of the Father, we too may live a new life. (Romans 6:4)

When we come to the end of ourselves, we come to the beginning of God. (Billy Graham)

For centuries, people have debated what makes us who we are—are we born the way we are, or do we become this way as a result of the things that happen to us? Though our genes and life experiences have a huge impact on us, aren't you glad that there is a miraculous, powerful God who is able to change even the most stubborn, damaged, sinful heart? Paul goes so far as to say, "Therefore, if anyone is in Christ, he is a new creation; the old has gone, the new has come!" (2 Corinthians 5:17).

With grace, with faith, with the help of godly friends, you can say along with Paul: "Forgetting what is behind and straining toward what is ahead, I press on toward the goal to win the prize for which God has called me heavenward in Christ Jesus" (Philippians 3:13–14). Because of Jesus' forgiving, life-changing power, His ultimate concern with your life is not where you've been, but where you are going.

God, thank You for making me new, day by day. I'm so grateful for Your life-changing power. Amen.

Joy Comes in the Morning

Weeping may remain for a night,
but rejoicing comes in the morning.
(Psalm 30:5)

One thing we may be sure of, however: For the believer all pain has
meaning; all adversity is profitable. (Jerry Bridges)

A Classic Devotion from C. H. Spurgeon

Christian! If thou art in a night of trial, think of the morrow; cheer up thy heart with the thought of the coming of thy Lord. Our trials will then seem light and momentary afflictions. Let us go on boldly; if the night be never so dark, the morning cometh, which is more than they can say who are shut up in the darkness of hell. Do you know what it is thus to live on the future—to live on expectation—to antedate heaven? Happy believer is to have so sure, so comforting a hope. It may be all dark now, but it will soon be light; it may be all trial now, but it will soon be all happiness. What matters it though "weeping may endure for a night," when "joy cometh in the morning?"[74]

Father, thank You in advance for rolling away the clouds
in my life and bringing joy in the morning. Thank You,
also, for the strength You give in the middle of the
darkest night. Amen.

Praise for Our Great God

A Walk in the Woods

Burst into song, you mountains,
you forests and all your trees,
for the LORD has redeemed Jacob,
he displays his glory in Israel.
(Isaiah 44:23)

The creation is quite like a spacious and splendid house, provided
and filled with the most exquisite and the most abundant
furnishings. Everything in it tells us of God. (John Calvin)

God brings joy to our lives in various ways: a kind word from a friend, an accomplishment at work, the gentle whisper of His Spirit. But throughout the ages, God has brought joy to us through the wonder of His creation. Feeling down? Maybe all you need is a walk in the woods.

Consider the reaction of Carl Boberg when he looked at the world God made: "When I look down / From lofty mountain grandeur / And hear the brook / And feel the gentle breeze; / Then sings my soul, / My Saviour God, to Thee, / How great Thou art!"

Take time to notice and celebrate God's greatness and gifts, and you'll suddenly find many reasons to be joyful.

Thank You, God, for the beauty of creation. Help me to see
You in the world around me today. Amen.

Family Time

And over all these virtues put on love, which binds them all together in perfect unity. (Colossians 3:14)

The blessing of an earthly family gives only a hazy picture of the blessing in God's heavenly family. (Janette Oke)

*F*amilies that sweat together, stick together. Okay, that may not be a pleasant thought, but the point is crystal clear. Healthy family interaction enriches each family member's emotional and spiritual health. The holiday season is a time for family interaction. Board games. Backyard football. Touring the city to see Christmas lights. Delivering turkey dinners to needy families. Christmas Eve candlelight service. A fun seasonal movie night. Opening gifts together. Meals with everyone at the table. Reading the Christmas story (Luke 2) out loud on Christmas morning.

If this hasn't been the experience of your family, select one activity from the list above and do all you can to make it happen. If this is how your family interacts during the holidays, thank God for the blessing of time together. If you are living on your own and away from family right now, create holiday traditions with a group of friends—or become an "adopted" member of a family at your church or in your neighborhood. Ask God to make this a season of togetherness for you and those you love.

God, thank You for the people in my life. Be close to us, and draw us near to You and near to each other. Amen.

Meaningful Prayer

I call on you, O God, for you will answer me;
give ear to me and hear my prayer.
(Psalm 17:6)

Prayer keeps us in constant communion with God, which is the goal
of our entire believing lives. (Beth Moore)

A Classic Devotion from R. A. Torrey

Stop a moment and think. Is it not often the case, when men stand up to pray in public, or kneel down to pray in private, that they are thinking far more of what they are asking for than they are of the great God who made heaven and earth, and who has all power? Is it not often the case that in our prayers our thoughts are wandering off everywhere? We take the name of God on our lips, but there is no real conscious approach to God in our hearts.

If there is to be any power in our prayer, if our prayer is to get anything, the first thing to be sure of when we pray is that we really have come into the presence of God, and are really speaking to Him. Oh, let those two words, "to God," "to God," "to God," sink deep into your heart; and from this time on never pray, never utter one syllable of prayer, until you are sure that you have come into the presence of God and are really talking to Him.[75]

Father God, it is a privilege to come into Your presence.
Give me a reverence for You as I sit down to pray. Amen.

Faith Shows Love

The only thing that counts is faith expressing itself through love.
(Galatians 5:6)

*Love is an attribute of God. To love others is evidence of
a genuine faith.* (Kay Arthur)

A Classic Devotion from Martin Luther

*H*e who does not firmly believe in God's grace assuredly will not extend kindness to his neighbor, but will be tardy and indifferent in aiding him. In proportion to the strength of his faith will be his willingness and industry in helping his neighbor. Thus faith incites love, and love increases faith.

All Christian doctrines and works, all Christian living, is briefly, clearly and completely comprehended in these two principles, faith and love. They place man as a medium between God and his neighbor, to receive from above and distribute below. Thus the Christian becomes a vessel, or rather a channel, through which the fountain of divine blessings continuously flows to other individuals.[76]

God, please fill me with Your love and increase
my faith in You. Amen.

The Healer of a Broken Heart

He heals the brokenhearted
and binds up their wounds.
(Psalm 147:3)

In this crazy world, there's an enormous distinction between good
times and bad, between sorrow and joy. But in the eyes of God,
they're never separated. Where there is pain, there is healing. Where
there is mourning, there is dancing. Where there is poverty, there is
the kingdom. (Henri Nouwen)

A Classic Devotion from C. H. Spurgeon

*T*here are many sorts of broken hearts, and Christ is good at healing them all. The patients of the great Physician are those whose hearts are broken through sorrow. . . . Hearts are broken in ten thousand ways, for this is a heart-breaking world; and Christ is good at healing all manner of heart-breaks.

I would encourage every person here, even though his heartbreak may not be of a spiritual kind, to make an application to him who healed the broken in heart. Come hither, ye that are burdened, all ye that labor and are heavy laden; come hither, all ye that sorrow, be your sorrow what it may; come hither, all ye whose hearts are broken, be the heart-break what it may, for he healeth the broken in heart.[77]

God, I know that You can heal my broken heart. Help me
experience Your healing touch today. Amen.

Worry and Faith

I pray that out of his glorious riches he may strengthen you with power through his Spirit in your inner being, so that Christ may dwell in your hearts through faith. (Ephesians 3:16–17)

I am inwardly fashioned for faith, not for fear. Fear is not my native land; faith is. I am so made that worry and anxiety are sand in the machinery of life; faith is the oil. (E. Stanley Jones)

Fear and faith are diametrically opposed. When we live in fear, it erodes our faith in God. When worries creep in and dominate our thinking, we start to feel far from God.

How can we overcome the force of worry and choose faith instead? One simple discipline that will help is choosing to let problems and worries drive you to God instead of away from Him. Instead of mulling incessantly over the mortgage payment, pray and thank God for His provision. When someone you love is sick, meditate on verses that celebrate God as a healer. If work pressures are constantly gnawing at you, commit your work to God and begin each day with prayer.

The only way to grow spiritually is to bring more and more of ourselves to our relationship with God. Don't suppress or deny your fears. Let them lead you to God.

Lord, sometimes I get so anxious. I pray that You would heal me and help me keep my mind on You. Amen.

Just Another Night

For to me, to live is Christ and to die is gain. (Philippians 1:21)

No matter what may be the test, God will take care of you. (C. D. Martin)

*O*n the night before Nicholas Ridley's execution in 1555, just hours before he was to become a martyr for his faith, his brother offered to remain with him in the prison chamber to help comfort him. But Nicholas declined the offer and replied that he intended to go to bed and sleep the same as he would on any other night of his life. Even his accusers were amazed at his peace and calm.

Ridley was undoubtedly well versed on the life of Paul. The man who took Christianity to the world wrote a letter to the Philippian church that became known as the "epistle of joy," even though it was written from a prison cell as he was en route to Rome to face his death.

Our lives may not be threatened for the faith we hold dear, but we are still promised a supernatural peace when we lay down our heads at night, resting in the everlasting arms of God.

Father, Your gifts of grace amaze me. Help me to steep myself so deeply in the knowledge of Your promises and goodness that nothing disturbs my peace. Amen.

How to Be Happy

*Though you have not seen him, you love him; and even though
you do not see him now, you believe in him and are filled with an
inexpressible and glorious joy.* (1 Peter 1:8)

*Happy is the person who not only sings, but feels God's eye is on the
sparrow, and knows He watches over me.* (C. C. Colton)

A Classic Devotion from R. A. Torrey

*T*he text tells us that the way to obtain this "inexpressible and glorious joy," the way to be inexpressibly happy at all times and under all circumstances, is just by believing on the unseen Christ Jesus. What does it mean to believe on Jesus Christ? There is no mystery at all about that. It simply means to put confidence in Jesus Christ to be what He claims to be and what He offers Himself to be to us, to put confidence in Him as the One who died in our place; to put confidence in Him as the One who was raised from the dead and who now has "all power in heaven and on earth," and therefore is able to keep us day by day, and give us victory over sin; and to put confidence in Him as our absolute Lord and Master, and therefore to surrender our thoughts and wills and lives entirely to His control; and worship and adore Him. It is wonderful the joy that comes to him who thus believes on Jesus Christ. But one must really believe on Jesus Christ to have this joy.[78]

Lord, I know that trusting You completely will bring me
fullness of joy. Teach me to rely on You. Amen.

Ready for a Surprise

*Because Joseph her husband was a righteous man and did not want
to expose her to public disgrace, he had in mind to divorce her quietly.*
(Matthew 1:19)

*Have your heart right with Christ, and He will visit you often, and
so turn weekdays into Sundays, meals into sacraments, homes into
temples, and earth into heaven.* (C. H. Spurgeon)

Christmas is full of surprises each year. But perhaps no one faced a greater surprise than Joseph did in the months before that first Christmas. What was his surprise? The news that his betrothed, whom he had never slept with, was pregnant. How did he handle it? With a cautious, respectful decision to cancel the wedding with as little embarrassment and shame to Mary as possible. But then Joseph received another surprise. An angel visited him and gave him the news of a miracle. Joseph's response was immediate, simple, selfless obedience.

What prepared Joseph to handle these surprises with such grace? We are told that Joseph was a righteous man. *Righteousness*, in the Old Testament world of Joseph, was defined as being innocent and doing right. For Matthew, the most Jewish of the gospel writers, *righteousness* meant being ethical and doing the will of God. What's the best preparation for any surprise that comes your way in life? Righteousness.

Heavenly Father, give me a righteousness that will allow
me to do Your will in every area of my life. Amen.

Hearing God's Voice

*Very early in the morning, while it was still dark, Jesus got up,
left the house and went off to a solitary place, where he prayed.*
(Mark 1:35)

Most of man's trouble comes from his inability to be still.
(Blaise Pascal)

*M*usic. Television. Traffic and other background noises. The ticking of a clock. Is there ever a moment of quiet and silence for the modern soul? How about you? How do you do without sound? Are you distracted when there are no distractions?

Perhaps we never hear God's voice because we always have some other sound turned on. How would you feel if you were trying to say something to someone with earbuds in their ears connected to a tiny music player? How easy is it to have a conversation when the other person keeps texting or picking up other calls?

Jesus Christ Himself pulled away from crowds for some alone time with His Father. How much more important is that for us?

Lord, help me to shut off the noise of everyday life so I
can hear Your voice. Amen.

Charity

Suppose a brother or sister is without clothes and daily food. If one
of you says to him, "Go, I wish you well; keep warm and well fed,"
but does nothing about his physical needs, what good is it? In the
same way, faith by itself, if it is not accompanied by action, is dead.
(James 2:15–17)

Without charity external work is of no value, but anything done
in charity, be it ever so small and trivial, is entirely fruitful
inasmuch as God weighs the love with which a man acts rather
than the deed itself. (Thomas à Kempis)

Is it possible to do good things for the wrong reasons? Absolutely. Does that mean these good deeds are worthless and achieve no good ends? Not necessarily. Your good deeds, done for the wrong reasons, may very well bless others tremendously. However, the benefit to you and your soul is negated.

Faith without actions is a dead faith, but conversely, actions without love are rarely as effective in making a lasting difference in the world, and are spiritually dead for the one who is doing them.

We experience peace and joy when there is agreement between our internal beliefs and external actions. Is it time for you to ask God to kindle within you a love for others? Is it time to express your love and faith in tangible acts?

Heavenly Father, change me from the inside so I change
the world through my service. Amen.

A Real Home

God sets the lonely in families. (Psalm 68:6)

A home is a house with a heart inside. (author unknown)

She was a single mother with a five-year-old son and a ton of bills. Just to stay afloat, she rented a musty, cramped camper at a local RV park. She was embarrassed and discouraged by her surroundings. She cringed one day as she overheard someone ask her little boy if he wished they had a real home. But her grimace was replaced with a tear and a smile when she heard him give this reply: "We do have a real home. We just don't have a house to put it in."

Maybe you're not happy where you are. But no matter how bad things look, don't get so focused on where you want to go that you miss the good things you have right now. God has a good plan for your future—but He has also sprinkled gifts and blessings in the life you have now.

Make sure your eyes—and heart—are open to see them.

Dear Father, thank You for bringing me into Your family and thank You for those intangible blessings that make life wonderful. Amen.

The Holy of Holies

I will listen to what God the Lord *will say;*
he promises peace to his people, his saints.
(Psalm 85:8)

It is not thy hold on Christ that saves thee; it is Christ. (C. H. Spurgeon)

A Classic Devotion from A. W. Tozer

*T*he interior journey of the soul from the wilds of sin into the enjoyed presence of God is beautifully illustrated in the Old Testament tabernacle.... [A] veil separated [people] from the Holy of Holies where above the mercy seat dwelt the very God Himself in awful and glorious manifestation. While the tabernacle stood, only the high priest could enter there, and that but once a year, with blood which he offered for his sins and the sins of the people. It was this last veil which was rent when our Lord gave up the ghost on Calvary, ... [which] opened the way for every worshiper in the world to come by the new and living way straight into the divine Presence.

Ransomed men need no longer pause in fear to enter the Holy of Holies. God wills that we should push on into His presence and live our whole life there.[79]

God, thank You for sending Your Son so that I might
live in Your presence. Amen.

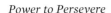

The Door of Hope

Never be lacking in zeal, but keep your spiritual fervor, serving the Lord. Be joyful in hope, patient in affliction, faithful in prayer. (Romans 12:11–12)

God is the only one who can make the valley of trouble a door of hope. (Catherine Marshall)

*T*hink about it. If you had everything you wanted, if there were no challenges in your life, if you didn't have any questions about why things are the way they are, and if you didn't feel there was something for you to accomplish that is bigger than your abilities; what would you have to hope for? Nothing, of course. You would already have everything.

We know that's not the way the world works—but sometimes we act and feel as though that's exactly what we believe. We seem surprised by problems and challenges.

Our fallen world accounts for so many of the trials we face. But beyond that, God wants us to live in reliance on Him. For that reason, He doesn't grant our every wish and give us everything our heart desires exactly when we want it. He wants us to grow in the ways that really matter—patience, kindness, self-control, and other fruits of the spirit (see Galatians 5:22–23 for a list).

Don't have everything you want right now? Well, that gives you something to hope for!

Lord, as I work and wait for various blessings in my life,
help me to grow in character and maturity. Amen.

A Testimony to Joy

Who can proclaim the mighty acts of the LORD
or fully declare his praise?
(Psalm 106:2)

How many people have you made homesick for God?
(Oswald Chambers)

*O*n the news reports that followed the infamous Hurricane Katrina, viewers sadly shook their heads or just looked on in horror as they saw images of the New Orleans streets underwater, waterlogged homes, and stranded survivors. But even amid all the shock and horror at the destruction, some interviewees gave testimony of God's protection and provision during the storm. They praised Him with gratitude for the whole nation to hear. Other tragedies have generated similar displays of amazing joy.

One of the reasons we are to rejoice in God is so that others will know of His goodness. Yes, it's good for our own soul, but it also blesses others. Our testimony of God's joy—even in the midst of difficulties—can be a life-changing witness to those around us. And in the process, we stir and reinforce our own faith.

Lord, help me to shout for joy as I seek to share Your
goodness with others. Amen.

The Wise Still Seek

Where is the one who has been born king of the Jews? We saw his
star in the east and have come to worship him. (Matthew 2:2)

Lord Jesus, master of both the light and the darkness, send your Holy
Spirit upon our preparations for Christmas. We are your people,
walking in darkness, yet seeking the light. To you we say, "Come
Lord Jesus!" (Henri Nouwen)

What does the world seek in life? Many seek riches. Others chase fame. Still others race after success. Some pursue pleasure.

Who were these magi of the East? We don't know a lot about them, not even how many there were, but we do know that they were men of goodwill who wanted to discover spiritual truth. The cost of their journey and the gifts they carried would have been staggering, so they weren't in this for personal gain. Their first concern wasn't their own safety or they would have let Herod know the location of the child on their return home. If it was comfort they sought, they would have never begun the journey in the first place.

No, these men had sincere hearts. They knew there was something greater than they already knew and they were willing to pay the cost to discover it. In the same way, if we are wise, we still seek to know God in His fullness today. And that trip begins with a visit to a manger.

Father, help me to know You and Your ways and Your
truth as never before. Amen.

Teach Us to Pray

Lord, teach us to pray, just as John taught his disciples. (Luke 11:1)

Prayer is not so much an act as it is an attitude—an attitude of dependency, dependency upon God. (Arthur W. Pink)

*O*ne day when Jesus had just finished praying, one of His disciples came to Him with a request. He wanted Jesus to teach them how to pray. At that moment, Jesus gave His disciples the Lord's Prayer, the model for Christian prayer throughout the centuries. He went on to teach them more about prayer, saying, "Ask and it will be given to you; seek and you will find; knock and the door will be opened to you. For everyone who asks receives; he who seeks finds; and to him who knocks, the door will be opened" (Luke 11:9–10).

There is no one better than Jesus Christ to teach us how to relate to and interact with God. He offers us teaching about how to pray, and in the Gospels He models for us a diligent and dedicated prayer life. If we ask Him to, He can show us how to pray effectively.

Thank You, Jesus, for being such a good Teacher. Teach
me to live closely with You. Amen.

On the Front Lines

Be ready to do whatever is good. (Titus 3:1)

The man or woman who is compelled by Jesus' love and empowered
by His Spirit does the will of God from the heart. (F. F. Bruce)

The life of first responders—EMTs, firefighters, police offi-
cers, and others—is undeniably stressful and challenging
when emergencies strike. They go through extensive and continual training to be ready for such moments. And they must always
be ready for whatever comes their way, whether it's the grisly
scene of an accident or the duty of informing a stranger that their
loved one won't be coming home tonight. Some days, nothing big
happens. Other days, something huge happens.

God calls us to be ever vigilant, always ready to explain our
hope in God to someone who doesn't believe in Him, always alert
to spiritual attacks, quick with love and kindness to those in need.
We never know when someone around us might need God to work
through us.

Are you ready to spring into action?

Lord, help me be alert to Your plans, ready to
do Your will. Amen.

Not Just Another Day

And there were shepherds living out in the fields nearby, keeping watch over their flocks at night. An angel of the Lord appeared to them, and the glory of the Lord shone around them, and they were terrified. (Luke 2:8–9)

Their night watch had been interrupted by an explosion of light from heaven and a symphony of angels. God goes to those who have time to hear him—and so on this cloudless night he went to simple shepherds. (Max Lucado)

Can you think of anything more boring than watching sheep eat and sleep? Well, it might be pleasant on a vacation in Scotland, but that will only last so long. It wouldn't be interesting hour after hour, day after day, night after night, and week after week. Oh, undoubtedly there were moments of excitement for a shepherd when keeping a wolf or lion away from his flock, but the job undoubtedly was filled with drudgery.

Do you ever wake up knowing that this day will be the same as all others? Isn't that probably what the shepherds felt that first Christmas Eve more than two thousand years ago? Do you ever feel as though nothing ever changes? Even Christmas and the holidays are the same every year? We've all gotten into a rut and felt that way. But what if this year a new star shines in the night sky and the evening is filled with angels?

It happened to some simple shepherds. It could happen to you.

Lord, keep my sense of wonder alive. Help me to see what great thing You are doing in my world and life. Amen.

The Second Birth

Therefore, if anyone is in Christ, he is a new creation; the old has gone, the new has come! All this is from God, who reconciled us to himself through Christ and gave us the ministry of reconciliation.
(2 Corinthians 5:17–18)

Will-power does not change men. Time does not change men. Christ does. (Henry Drummond)

*T*hink about it: you can be made new! Even if you have failed in business. Even if you have experienced broken relationships. Even if you turned your back on God and did exactly what you wanted to do even though you knew those things were wrong.

Everyone living has experienced a natural birth. But just as Jesus promised Nicodemus in a late-night meeting (John 3), we can also be reborn, born into the kingdom of God, becoming His children by spiritual rebirth. What a gift!

With this new status as children of God, we receive a new purpose, a new mission in life. In Matthew 28:19–20, Jesus tells His disciples—and us—to take the good news of forgiveness and new beginnings throughout the world: to our own family and friends, to our next-door neighbors, to our coworkers, and every other person we know and meet. We become ambassadors for Christ's message of new life, sharing this message of hope with a world that desperately needs it!

Lord, thank You for saving me and for giving me the opportunity to share Your love with others. Amen.

The Milk of Life

*Like newborn babies, long for the pure milk of the word, so that by it
you may grow in respect to salvation.* (1 Peter 2:2 NASB)

*The precepts of the LORD are right, rejoicing the heart;
The commandment of the LORD is pure, enlightening the eyes.*
(King David, Psalm 19:8 ESV)

*W*hen new parents-to-be begin learning all they need to know about raising a baby, the subject of feeding usually takes up plenty of their time. Those early feedings are so important. The baby needs the nourishment that only Mommy can give within the first few days of birth; the milk provides antibodies that will contribute vitally to the overall well-being of the baby.

Just as newborn babies need their mothers' milk, new Christians need the rich milk of the Word of God to prepare them for life as God's child. Studying the Bible, learning from Christ in prayer, and receiving mentorship from stronger, more seasoned Christians are all vital to help a newfound faith grow strong and resilient.

But the Word of God is vital no matter when you became a Christian. It's what establishes those early steps, and also what keeps you going in the middle.

Lord, I pray that Your Word would nurture my spirit and
give me faith and confidence in You, come what may.
Amen.

A Heart Filled with Worship

From now on all generations will call me blessed, for the Mighty One has done great things for me—holy is his name. (Luke 1:48–49)

This is Christmas: not the tinsel, not the giving and receiving, not even the carols, but the humble heart that receives anew the wondrous gift, the Christ. (Frank McKibben)

*A*ll mothers feel a sense of joy at the moment of birth. The day has been arduous and often painful, but the miracle of birth fills the hearts of all witnesses, including medical professionals who have "been there and done that" hundreds of times, first-time fathers who sometimes are a bit weak in the knees, and grandparents and siblings who are outside the room anxiously awaiting word.

Shepherds. Magi. Joseph. Maybe an innkeeper's wife or servant. All were filled with wonder and delight at the birth of Jesus. But no one experienced the birth like the Baby's mother. Mary, weary from a journey on the back of a donkey and the delivery in a primitive stable, listening to the shepherds' testimony about the angels' song and the significance of this child, "treasured up all these things and pondered them in her heart" (Luke 2:19).

When a baby is born, all those close to the family celebrate. When Jesus was born, something happened that gives the whole world reason to celebrate and worship.

Father God, my heart is filled with worship and adoration
to You for the gift of salvation that You gave to me
through the birth of Jesus Christ. Amen.

Keep It Simple, Keep It Secret

"When you pray, do not be like the hypocrites, for they love to pray standing in the synagogues and on the street corners to be seen by men. I tell you the truth, they have received their reward in full."
(Matthew 6:5)

We should speak to God from our own hearts and talk to Him as a child talks to His father. (C. H. Spurgeon)

In the Sermon on the Mount, Jesus advises His listeners not to pray for show, and not to pray with endless repetition. He tells us to keep it simple, and to pray in secret, not flaunting our spirituality before other people. Prayer is meant to be communion with God. When we pray for show, our hearts and minds are on what others think, not what God thinks. And when we pray with many words, we get caught up in the action of prayer and forget to direct our thoughts to God.

There are many simple prayers that can be said quietly and quickly, but deeply express our need for God: "Lord, help." "Lord, have mercy." "Your will be done." All it takes to pray meaningfully is to bring our whole hearts to God. And that can be done in very few words.

Lord, I need You. Teach me to bring my
needs before You. Amen.

A Prayer for Christmas Morning

*I pray that you, being rooted and established in love, may have
power, together with all the saints, to grasp how wide and long and
high and deep is the love of Christ.* (Ephesians 3:17–18)

*God grant you the light in Christmas, which is faith; the warmth
of Christmas, which is love; the radiance of Christmas, which is
purity; the righteousness of Christmas, which is justice; the belief
in Christmas, which is truth; the all of Christmas, which is Christ.*
(Wilda English)

A Classic Devotion from Henry Van Dyke

The day of joy returns, Father in Heaven, and crowns another year with peace and good will. Help us rightly to remember the birth of Jesus, that we may share in the song of the angels, the gladness of the shepherds, and the worship of the wisemen. Close the doors of hate and open the doors of love all over the world. Let kindness come with every gift and good desires with every greeting. Deliver us from evil, by the blessing that Christ brings, and teach us to be merry with clean hearts. May the Christmas morning make us happy to be thy children, and the Christmas evening bring us to our bed with grateful thoughts, forgiving and forgiven, for Jesus' sake.

Amen.[80]

Lord, this Christmas, please let Your kingdom come in me
and make me more like You. Amen.

I Packed Your Parachute

And whatever you do, whether in word or deed, do it all in the name
of the Lord Jesus, giving thanks to God the Father through him.
(Colossians 3:17)

God has created me to do him some definite service; he has
committed some work to me which he has not committed to another.
I have my mission. I never may know it in this life, but I shall be told
it in the next. (John Henry Newman)

Charles Plumb was a U.S. Navy jet pilot in Vietnam. After seventy-five combat missions, his plane was shot down, and Plumb parachuted into enemy territory, becoming a POW. He survived his ordeal, however, and eventually returned home. While eating in a restaurant one day, he was approached by a scruffy-looking man who said, "You're Plumb! You flew jet fighters in Vietnam and were shot down!"

"How did you know that?" asked Plumb.

"I packed your parachute," the man replied. "I guess it worked!"

Plumb couldn't sleep that night, thinking about the unknown man who'd saved his life. From that day on, he determined to always take notice of—and say thank you to—those who "pack his parachute" each day.

Make the most of each day by thanking those who "pack your parachute" and by making an effort to do the same for someone else.

Father, thank You for all the little things people do for me, and help me to be an encouragement to someone else today. Amen.

A Baby Changes Everything

Glory to God in the highest,
and on earth peace to men on whom his favor rests.
(Luke 2:14)

Love came down on Christmas Day so many years ago and brought
the greatest happiness the world would ever know. Peace came
down on Christmas Day to fill the hearts of men with all the
sweet tranquility each Christmas brings again. Joy came down on
Christmas Day as angels came to earth heralding the miracle of our
Messiah's birth. (author unknown)

A mentally disturbed king. A powerful conqueror. A tumultuous engagement. A new marriage. A pregnancy that generated whispers and rumors. An arduous journey. The wrong setting to deliver a child.

But a baby is born, and this baby changes everything. Angels sing. Shepherds and wise men worship. A mother's prayer of praise is heard throughout generations.

No matter what circumstances surround you this Christmas, never forget. A baby changes everything.

I praise You, heavenly Father, for the gift of a baby. Amen.

His Birth and Our New Birth

The virgin will be with child and will give birth to a son, and will call him Immanuel. (Isaiah 7:14)

When Christ entered our world, he didn't come to brighten our Decembers, but to transform our lives. (Rich Miller)

A Classic Devotion from Oswald Chambers

His Birth in History. "Therefore also that holy thing which shall be born of thee shall be called the Son of God" (Luke 1:35). Jesus Christ was born into this world, not from it. He did not evolve out of history; He came into history from the outside. Our Lord's birth was an advent.

His Birth in Me. "Of whom I travail in birth again until Christ be formed in you" (Gal. 4:19). Just as Our Lord came into human history from outside, so He must come into me from outside. Have I allowed my personal human life to become a "Bethlehem" for the Son of God? I cannot enter into the realm of the Kingdom of God unless I am born from above by a birth totally unlike natural birth. The characteristic of the new birth is that I yield myself so completely to God that Christ is formed in me. Immediately Christ is formed in me, His nature begins to work through me.

God manifest in the flesh—that is what is made profoundly possible for you and me by the Redemption.[81]

Lord, thank You for coming to earth. Please be born in my heart this Christmas. Amen.

God with Us

She will give birth to a son, and you are to give him the name Jesus,
because he will save his people from their sins. (Matthew 1:21)

If we could condense all the truths of Christmas into only three
words, these would be the words: "God with us." We tend to focus our
attention at Christmas on the infancy of Christ. The greater truth of
the holiday is His deity. More astonishing than a baby in the manger
is the truth that this promised baby is the omnipotent Creator of the
heavens and the earth! (John MacArthur)

The hundred-mile journey to Bethlehem might have taken as many as eight or ten days by donkey and foot. The road ahead was full of rocks and steep hills, not to mention the danger of thieves. When Mary and Joseph reached their destination, Mary gave birth to the baby they named Jesus.

Sometimes life gets hard. We can't see exactly where we're going; we face formidable obstacles. But just as the star shone down over Bethlehem that night, a beacon of hope shines over our own lives—all because of the baby in the manger. With the birth of Jesus came the promise that God is with us, for us, willing to do whatever it takes to save us.

So no matter what happens around us, we have the comfort of the angels proclaiming, "Peace on earth and good will toward men."

Lord, thank You for the abundant hope You offer in Jesus.
Help me never lose faith in Your goodness. Amen.

The Joy of God's Presence

Light is shed upon the righteous
and joy on the upright in heart.
Rejoice in the LORD, you who are righteous,
and praise his holy name.
(Psalm 97:11–12)

The more we enjoy of God, the more we are ravished with delight.
(Thomas Watson)

There's a popular legend told in the Middle East of a wise and good king who loved his people. He often dressed as a working man or a beggar and visited the homes of the poor. None of them suspected that he was their ruler. On one occasion, he visited a very poor man, ate the same poor-quality food the man ate, and spoke kind, comforting words to him. Later he visited the poor man again. This time, he decided to reveal his true identity and told him, "I am your king." He thought the man would surely ask for a gift or favor. But instead, the man said, "You left your palace to visit me. You ate my food and sat with me in this dreary place. You were kind to me. To others you have given your rich gifts. But to me you have given yourself!"

God has done everything good and kind and generous to have fellowship with us, even becoming a human. When we recognize His presence, we experience gladness of heart. We have a King who is with us always.

Lord God, thank You for coming into my life. Amen.

Focus on Christ

There is but one God, the Father, from whom all things came and for whom we live; and there is but one Lord, Jesus Christ, through whom all things came and through whom we live. (1 Corinthians 8:6)

Christ is the desire of nations, the joy of angels, the delight of the Father. What solace then must that soul be filled with, that has the possession of Him to all eternity! (John Bunyan)

*D*ecember is a month that draws our attention back to Christ. We are reminded that Christ's birth brought salvation to the world and to each one of us (John 3:16–17). This is a good thing. When we keep our eyes on Christ, we are able to handle any challenge, any disappointment, any heartache. Jesus said of Himself, "I, when I am lifted up from the earth, will draw all men to myself" (12:32).

Because the scenery and images are so different, we usually think of Christmas and Easter as two very separate events. After all, one observance is about a birth and the other about a death. But in the divine picture of life, the birth of Jesus is woven together with the death and resurrection. All are acts of grace from God.

No matter what life holds for you right now, there is still only one true Source for experiencing the life God has planned for us: Jesus Christ. Focus on Him today.

Lord Jesus, I am so glad I know You. In the coming new year, help me focus on You. Amen.

A Prayerful Heart

Another Year

*"See, the former things have taken place, and new things I declare;
before they spring into being I announce them to you."* (Isaiah 42:9)

*We will open the book. Its pages are blank. We are going to put
words on them ourselves. The book is called Opportunity and its first
chapter is New Year's Day.* (Edith Lovejoy Pierce)

*A*nother year has come and gone. How will this one go down in the books for you? Did you meet new friends? Did you start or finish any new projects? Did you take a class or learn anything new? Did you read any books? Did you bless those around you? Your family? Your neighbors? Did you serve at your church? Did you share your faith? Did you pray more or less? Did you draw closer to God?

Years come and go. Are we growing and making a difference in the time God has given us?

Consider writing down a highlight of your year before you even begin thinking about goals for next year. Do this thoughtfully and prayerfully. Ask God to convict you in areas that need to change. Let Him affirm you in areas where He is pleased with your life. Let this account of your year challenge and encourage you to live your best life yet in the days ahead.

God, as I sit down to take stock of the year, I want to thank
You for Your blessings and ask for Your guidance. Help me
to make this year count for You. Amen.

Room in the Inn

She wrapped him in cloths and placed him in a manger, because there was no room for them in the inn. (Luke 2:7)

In the same manner in which we clean and prepare our homes in the anticipation of welcomed guests and family members this Christmas season, let us also prepare our hearts in anticipation of the Lord's coming. (Katherine Walden)

How many blessings and miracles have we missed because we didn't have room in our hearts and homes to receive them? Too often we fill our lives to overflowing with activities and entertainment—much of it good, but much of it unimportant and distracting—so that we couldn't hear God's voice even if He spoke audibly to us.

Bethlehem was not a large town, but there were numerous inns and many homes. Any one of them could have welcomed the birth of the Christ child. But only one innkeeper, the one who first said he had no room, found a warm, dry place for the baby Jesus to be born.

Out of room in your life? No more time, money, energy, and other resources to make a difference? To welcome Jesus? Look around your home. Search your heart. Is there a warm, dry space for Jesus to visit you?

Gracious God, thank You for sending Christ to my home and my heart. I welcome Him now. Amen.

True Confidence

"Have I not commanded you? Be strong and courageous. Do not be terrified; do not be discouraged, for the Lord your God will be with you wherever you go." (Joshua 1:9)

You don't have to be great to start, but you have to start to be great.
(Zig Ziglar)

*C*onfidence is . . .

- diving off the high dive.
- introducing yourself to someone new in a social gathering.
- attending a workshop or seminar not because it's required at work but "just because."
- visiting patients in a hospital or prisoners in a jail even though you've never met them before.
- looking at someone who has told you about a difficulty he or she is experiencing and asking them, "Can I pray for you right now?"

Confidence means taking bold steps. And each of us can do just that, even if we don't consider ourselves to be very confident. Why? Because God is with us wherever we go.

Lord, help me to do the best job I can for You. Amen.

The God of the Living

"He is not the God of the dead, but of the living, for to him all are alive." (Luke 20:38)

I cannot make a new me or a new you, but Christ can make you new and me new, as well, if we decide for Him. (Frank Harrington)

Skeptics hounded Jesus with questions and objections to His teachings and ministry. Some undoubtedly had honest questions to discuss; others were simply trying to catch Him in error and undermine Him.

A Sadducee, a teacher who didn't believe in the afterlife, tried to make Jesus look foolish by asking which man a woman would be married to in heaven if her first husband died and she had taken a second husband (Luke 20:27–39).

Jesus simply hijacked the question and made the bold proclamation that all that really matters is whether you—that Sadducee, the other listeners, and each of us reading His words today—have been made new and have personally experienced the power of the resurrection.

That doesn't happen through having devotions or being a good person. It's a miracle we must ask for and receive as a gift from God.

Have you been made alive?

Father, I pray that You would make me alive through the power of Christ's resurrection. Amen.

Sources

1. A. W. Tozer, *The Pursuit of God* (New York: SoHo Books, 2011).
2. R. A. Torrey, *The Power of Prayer and Prayer of Power* (New York: Cosimo, 2009).
3. Albert B. Simpson, *The Holy Spirit: Power from on High* (New York: The Christian Alliance Publishing Company, 1895).
4. T. M. Anderson, *Prayer Availeth Much* (Grand Rapids: Christian Classics Ethereal Library, n.d.).
5. Andrew Murray, *With Christ in the School of Prayer* (New York: Fleming H. Revell, 1885).
6. Dietrich Bonhoeffer, *Life Together* (New York: Harper & Row, 1954).
7. Charles H. Spurgeon, *Morning and Evening* (New Kensington, PA: Whitaker House, 2001).
8. E. M. Bounds, *The Weapon of Prayer* (New Kensington, PA: Whitaker House, 1996).
9. John Wesley, *Sermons on Several Occasions* (New York: Ezekiel Cooper and John Wilson, 1806).
10. Charles H. Spurgeon, *Morning and Evening* (New Kensington, PA: Whitaker House, 2001).
11. Ibid.
12. Oswald Chambers, *My Utmost for His Highest* (Grand Rapids: Discovery House Publishers, 2008).
13. Robert Murray M'Cheyne, Sermon VII, "The Free Obedience of Christ," http://www.the-highway.com/MCheyne7.html.
14. Alexander Maclaren, *Expositions of Holy Scripture: Psalms* (Charleston: BiblioBazaar, 2007).
15. Richard Baxter, *The Practical Works of Richard Baxter* (London: George Virtue, 1838).
16. A. W. Tozer, "Rut, Rot or Revival," http://www.dimensionsoftruth.org/aw-tozer/a-christians-greatest-enemy/.

17. J. C. Ryle, *Holiness: Its Nature, Hindrances, Difficulties, and Roots* (Chicago: The Moody Bible Institute, 2010).

18. John Henry Jowett, *Brooks by the Traveler's Way* (Whitefish, MT: Kessinger Publishing, 2010).

19. G. P. Pardington, *The Still Small Voice* (Charleston: BiblioBazaar, 2009).

20. William Booth, *Visions* (London: The Salvation Army Book Department, 1906).

21. Oswald Chambers, *My Utmost for His Highest* (Grand Rapids: Discovery House Publishers, 2008).

22. Albert B. Simpson, *The Holy Spirit: Power from on High* (New York: The Christian Alliance Publishing Company, 1895).

23. F. B. Meyer, *Great Verses Through the Bible* (Grand Rapids: Zondervan Publishing House, 1982).

24. Adam Clarke, *Clarke's Christian Theology* (Nicholasville, KY: Schmul Publishing Company, 1990).

25. Charles H. Spurgeon, *Morning and Evening* (New Kensington, PA: Whitaker House, 2001).

26. Ibid.

27. John Bunyan, *The Complete Works of John Bunyan* (Philadelphia: Bradley, Garretson & Company, 1873).

28. Oswald Chambers, *My Utmost for His Highest* (Grand Rapids: Discovery House Publishers, 2008).

29. Charles G. Trumbull, *Messages for the Morning Watch: Devotional Studies in Genesis* (Charleston: BiblioLife, 2011).

30. E. M. Bounds, *The Weapon of Prayer* (New Kensington, PA: Whitaker House, 1996).

31. Charles H. Spurgeon, *Morning and Evening* (New Kensington, PA: Whitaker House, 2001).

32. Andrew Murray, *The Ministry of Intercession: A Plea for More Prayer* (Charleston: BiblioBazaar, 2009).

33. Martin Luther, "An Introduction to St. Paul's Letter to the Romans from Dr. Martin Luther's Vermischte Deutsche Schriften,"

Johann K. Irmischer, ed., http://www.iclnet.org/pub/resources/text/wittenberg/luther/luther-faith.txt.

34. Charles Grandison Finney, *Sermons on Gospel Themes* (Whitefish, MT: Kessinger Publishing, 2007).

35. Mrs. Charles E. Cowman, *Streams in the Desert* (Grand Rapids: Zondervan Publishing House, 1974).

36. Thomas Boston, "Useful Directions for Reading and Searching the Scriptures," *Fire and Ice: Puritan and Reformed Writings*, www.puritansermons.com.

37. Dietrich Bonhoeffer, *The Cost of Discipleship* (New York: Touchstone, 1995).

38. Andrew Murray, *Absolute Surrender* (Montoursville, PA: Lamp Post, 2009).

39. Dwight L. Moody, *Moody's Latest Sermons* (Chicago: The Bible Institute Colportage Association, 1900).

40. Ibid.

41. Alexander Smellie, *On the Hour of Silence* (Whitefish, MT: Kessinger Publishing, 2010).

42. Oswald Chambers, *My Utmost for His Highest* (Grand Rapids: Discovery House Publishers, 2008).

43. Psalm 119:105–114 NIV.

44. Thomas à Kempis, *The Imitation of Christ* (Mineola, New York: Dover Publications, 2003).

45. Charles H. Spurgeon, *Morning and Evening* (New Kensington, PA: Whitaker House, 2001).

46. George Müller, *A Narrative of Some of the Lord's Dealings* (Charleston: BiblioBazaar, 2008).

47. Saint Augustine, "Let Us Sing to the Lord." Sermon found at http://catholicradiodramas.com/saints/a-augustine/augustine/let-us-sing-to-the-lord/.

48. Oswald Chambers, *My Utmost for His Highest* (Grand Rapids: Discovery House Publishers, 2008).

49. Alexander Maclaren, *Expositions of Holy Scripture: Psalms* (Charleston: BiblioBazaar, 2007).

50. Brother Lawrence, *The Practice of the Presence of God, and The Spiritual Maxims* (New York: Cosimo, 2006).

51. Oswald Chambers, *My Utmost for His Highest* (Grand Rapids: Discovery House Publishers, 2008).

52. Ibid.

53. Jeremy Taylor, *The Whole Sermons of Jeremy Taylor* (Edinburgh: A. & C. Black, 1841).

54. Charles H. Spurgeon, *Morning and Evening* (New Kensington, PA: Whitaker House, 2001).

55. Albert Barnes, *Notes, Explanatory and Practical, on the Epistles of Paul to the Thessalonians, to Timothy, to Titus, and to Philemon* (New York: Harper & Brothers, 1850).

56. Oswald Chambers, *My Utmost for His Highest* (Grand Rapids: Discovery House Publishers, 2008).

57. Andrew Murray, *With Christ in the School of Prayer* (New York: Fleming H. Revell, 1885).

58. C. H. Mackintosh, "Things New and Old." Devotion found at http://livingstonesmagazine.homestead.com/HallofFaithMackintoshJan05.html.

59. E. M. Bounds, *The Weapon of Prayer* (New Kensington, PA: Whitaker House, 1996).

60. Albert B. Simpson, *Walking in the Spirit* (New York: The Christian Alliance Publishing Company, 1889).

61. Dwight L. Moody, *Prevailing Prayer: What Hinders It?* (Chicago: Fleming H. Revell, 1884).

62. Samuel Rutherford, *Letters of Samuel Rutherford* (New York: Robert Carter & Brothers, 1863).

63. R. A. Torrey, *How to Pray* (New Kensington, PA: Whitaker House, 1983).

64. Andrew Murray, *Abide in Christ* (New Kensington, PA: Whitaker House, 1979).

65. Arthur W. Pink, *The Divine Inspiration of the Bible* (Lafayette, IN: Sovereign Grace Publishers, 2003).

66. Andrew Murray, *The New Life: Words of God for Young Disciples of Christ* (New York: A. D. F. Randolph & Company, 1891).

67. Charles H. Spurgeon, *Morning and Evening* (New Kensington, PA: Whitaker House, 2001).

68. Thomas Watson, *A Body of Divinity* (London: Banner of Truth, 1957).

69. Oswald Chambers, *My Utmost for His Highest*, (Grand Rapids: Discovery House Publishers, 2008).

70. Charles H. Spurgeon, *Morning and Evening* (New Kensington, PA: Whitaker House, 2001).

71. Ibid.

72. Dwight L. Moody, *Prevailing Prayer: What Hinders It?* (Chicago: Fleming H. Revell, 1884).

73. Alexander Maclaren, *Expositions of Holy Scripture: Psalms* (Charleston: BiblioBazaar, 2007).

74. Charles H. Spurgeon, *Morning and Evening* (New Kensington, PA: Whitaker House, 2001).

75. R. A. Torrey, *The Power of Prayer and Prayer of Power* (New York: Cosimo, 2009).

76. Martin Luther, *Luther's Christmas Sermons* (Minneapolis: The Luther Press, 1908).

77. Charles H. Spurgeon, *Morning and Evening* (New Kensington, PA: Whitaker House, 2001).

78. R. A. Torrey, "How to Be Inexpressibly Happy." Devotion found at http://ratorrey.webs.com/How%20to%20be%20Inexpressibly%20 Happy.htm.

79. A. W. Tozer, *The Pursuit of God* (New York: SoHo Books, 2011).

80. Henry Van Dyke, "A Prayer for Christmas Morning," *A Treasury of Christmas Stories.*

81. Oswald Chambers, *My Utmost for His Highest* (Grand Rapids: Discovery House Publishers, 2008).

Notes

Notes

Notes

Notes

Notes

Notes

Notes